THE CAMBRIDGE BIBLE COMMENTARY

NEW ENGLISH BIBLE

GENERAL EDITORS

P. R. ACKROYD, A. R. C. LEANEY

J. W. PACKER

NUMBERS

NUMBERS

COMMENTARY BY

JOHN STURDY

Dean and Fellow of Gonville and Caius College, Cambridge

CAMBRIDGE UNIVERSITY PRESS

CAMBRIDGE

LONDON · NEW YORK · MELBOURNE

Published by the Syndics of the Cambridge University Press
The Pitt Building, Trumpington Street, Cambridge CB2 1RP
Bentley House, 200 Euston Road, London NW1 2DB
32 East 57th Street, New York, NY 10022, USA
296 Beaconsfield Parade, Middle Park, Melbourne 3206, Australia

First published 1976

Printed in Great Britain
at the
University Printing House, Cambridge
(Euan Phillips, University Printer)

Library of Congress cataloguing in publication data
Bible.   O.T.   Numbers.   English.   New English.   1976.
Numbers.
(The Cambridge Bible Commentary, New English Bible)
Bibliography: p.
Includes index.
1. Bible.   O.T.   Numbers – Commentaries.
I. Sturdy, John. II. Title. III. Series.
BS1263.S78   222′.14′077   75-39373
ISBN 0 521 08632 9 hard covers
ISBN 0 521 09776 2 paperback

GENERAL EDITORS' PREFACE

The aim of this series is to provide the text of the New English Bible closely linked to a commentary in which the results of modern scholarship are made available to the general reader. Teachers and young people have been especially kept in mind. The commentators have been asked to assume no specialized theological knowledge, and no knowledge of Greek and Hebrew. Bare references to other literature and multiple references to other parts of the Bible have been avoided. Actual quotations have been given as often as possible.

The completion of the New Testament part of the series in 1967 provides a basis upon which the production of the much larger Old Testament and Apocrypha series can be undertaken. The welcome accorded to the series has been an encouragement to the editors to follow the same general pattern, and an attempt has been made to take account of criticisms which have been offered. One necessary change is the inclusion of the translators' footnotes since in the Old Testament these are more extensive, and essential for the understanding of the text.

Within the severe limits imposed by the size and scope of the series, each commentator will attempt to set out the main findings of recent biblical scholarship and to describe the historical background to the text. The main theological issues will also be critically discussed.

Much attention has been given to the form of the volumes. The aim is to produce books each of which will be read consecutively from first to last page. The introductory material leads naturally into the text, which itself leads into the alternating sections of the commentary.

The series is accompanied by three volumes of a more general character. *Understanding the Old Testament* sets out to provide the larger historical and archaeological background, to say something about the life and thought of the people of the Old Testament, and to answer the question 'Why should we study the Old Testament?'. *The Making of the Old Testament* is concerned with the formation of the books of the Old Testament and Apocrypha in the context of the ancient near eastern world, and with the ways in which these books have come down to us in the life of the Jewish and Christian communities. *Old Testament Illustrations* contains maps, diagrams and photographs with an explanatory text. These three volumes are designed to provide material helpful to the understanding of the individual books and their commentaries, but they are also prepared so as to be of use quite independently.

P. R. A.
A. R. C. L.
J. W. P.

CONTENTS

LIST OF MAPS

THE FOOTNOTES TO THE
N.E.B. TEXT

The footnotes to the N.E.B. text are designed to help the reader either to understand particular points of detail – the meaning of a name, the presence of a play upon words – or to give information about the actual text. Where the Hebrew text appears to be erroneous, or there is doubt about its precise meaning, it may be necessary to turn to manuscripts which offer a different wording, or to ancient translations of the text which may suggest a better reading, or to offer a new explanation based upon conjecture. In such cases, the footnotes supply very briefly an indication of the evidence, and whether the solution proposed is one that is regarded as possible or as probable. Various abbreviations are used in the footnotes.

(1) Some abbreviations are simply of terms used in explaining a point: *ch(s).*, chapter(s); *cp.*, compare; *lit.*, literally; *mng.*, meaning; *MS(S).*, manuscript(s), i.e. Hebrew manuscript(s), unless otherwise stated; *om.*, omit(s); *or*, indicating an alternative interpretation; *poss.*, possible; *prob.*, probable; *rdg.*, reading; *Vs(s).*, Version(s).

(2) Other abbreviations indicate sources of information from which better interpretations or readings may be obtained.

Aq. Aquila, a Greek translator of the Old Testament (perhaps about A.D. 130) characterized by great literalness.

Aram. Aramaic – may refer to the text in this language (used in parts of Ezra and Daniel), or to the meaning of an Aramaic word. Aramaic belongs to the same language family as Hebrew, and is known from about 1000 B.C. over a wide area of the Middle East, including Palestine.

Heb. Hebrew – may refer to the Hebrew text or may indicate the literal meaning of the Hebrew word.

Josephus Flavius Josephus (A.D. 37/8 – about 100), author of the *Jewish Antiquities*, a survey of the whole history of his people, directed partly at least to a non-Jewish audience, and of various other works, notably one on the *Jewish War* (that of A.D. 66–73) and a defence of Judaism (*Against Apion*).

Luc. Sept. Lucian's recension of the Septuagint, an important edition made in Antioch in Syria about the end of the third century A.D.

Pesh. Peshitta or Peshitto, the Syriac version of the Old Testament. Syriac is the name given chiefly to a form of Eastern Aramaic used by the Christian community. The translation varies in quality, and is at many points influenced by the Septuagint or the Targums.

Sam. Samaritan Pentateuch – the form of the first five books of the Old Testament as used by the Samaritan community. It is written in Hebrew in a special form of the Old Hebrew script, and preserves an important form of the text, somewhat influenced by Samaritan ideas.

Scroll(s) Scroll(s), commonly called the Dead Sea Scrolls, found at or near Qumran from 1947 onwards. These important manuscripts shed light on the state of the Hebrew text as it was developing in the last centuries B.C. and the first century A.D.

Sept. Septuagint (meaning 'seventy'; often abbreviated as the Roman numeral LXX), the name given to the main Greek version of the Old Testament. According to tradition, the Pentateuch was translated in Egypt in the third century B.C. by 70 (or 72) translators, six from each tribe, but the precise nature of its origin and development is not fully known. It was intended to provide Greek-speaking Jews with a convenient translation. Subsequently it came to be much revered by the Christian community.

Symm. Symmachus, another Greek translator of the Old Testament (beginning of the third century A.D.), who tried to combine literalness with good style. Both Lucian and Jerome viewed his version with favour.

Targ. Targum, a name given to various Aramaic versions of the Old Testament, produced over a long period and eventually standardized, for the use of Aramaic-speaking Jews.

Theod. Theodotion, the author of a revision of the Septuagint (probably second century A.D.), very dependent on the Hebrew text.

Vulg. Vulgate, the most important Latin version of the Old Testament, produced by Jerome about A.D. 400, and the text most used throughout the Middle Ages in western Christianity.

[. . .] In the text itself square brackets are used to indicate probably late additions to the Hebrew text.

(Fuller discussion of a number of these points may be found in *The Making of the Old Testament* in this series.)

NUMBERS

* * * * * * * * * * * * * *

THE CONTENTS OF THE BOOK

The story of Numbers begins with a picture of the people of Israel gathered together in the Wilderness of Sinai, in the Sinai peninsula, having not long before fled from Egypt under the leadership of Moses and his brother Aaron, and receiving there commands from their God. It ends forty years later, with the people still led by Moses, Aaron having recently died, close to the promised land of Canaan (the land later called Israel), on its eastern side. So the book starts and finishes at rather odd points. Furthermore its contents are not, as we might expect, a continuous story of what happened to the Israelites in this period, but particular stories of the beginning and end of the period, centring on the theme of grumbling and rebellion on the part of the people, answered with both punishment and forgiveness on the part of God. These stories are interspersed with a large number of laws and regulations given by God, and with two censuses of the people. It is in fact from these censuses, minor features though they are of the whole book, that it gets its name, Numbers, which it was first given in the Greek translation of the original Hebrew. The Hebrew name was 'in the wilderness', taken (as was usual) not very imaginatively from the first verse of the book; but it gives in fact a rather better description of what it is about. The book is not much of a unity. This is because it is one part of a longer work, which has been rather arbitrarily divided up into books.

THE LONGER WORK OF WHICH NUMBERS IS A PART

Numbers comes to us as the fourth of a group of five books, the first five books in the Bible. These are often known by the technical term the Pentateuch, or 'group of five', and in Judaism as the Law (Torah). This is one of the three great divisions of the Hebrew Bible (which is the Christian Old Testament). It was separated off as a group of 'holy books' earlier than the rest, some time between the fifth and the third centuries B.C. Numbers follows on well enough from the previous book, Leviticus, but does not lead into the next book, Deuteronomy, which reads like an intrusion in its present position. We have in fact to leap ahead to the last chapter of Deuteronomy to find the continuation of Numbers. So there has been a complicated development of the material. What is taken by most scholars to have happened is as follows.

The Pentateuch is the end-product of a development lasting over 600 years, in which the Israelites formulated and elaborated the story of their past. Deuteronomy, though not the last part to be written, is the last part to be added to the collection Genesis–Numbers, and to tie it in with this collection the story of the death of Moses (Deut. 34), which had originally come at the end of Genesis–Numbers, was transferred to the end of Deuteronomy, to form a rounded whole. The history of Genesis–Numbers is complicated. There are two main blocks of material in it, one early and one late.

The late material comes from a writer, or a group of writers of similar interests, probably from about 500–400 B.C.; that is, after the great turning-point in the history of the nation, the exile to Babylon in 586 B.C., which was accompanied by the end of the monarchy and of political independence. This writer, whose name is unknown, we call the Priestly Writer, or P for short. The name is given because his interests suggest strongly that he was a priest. He wrote a book which was designed to supplement rather than replace the earlier material then known; and after a time this was naturally enough united with the older material in one continuous story. Since the Priestly Writer had the clearer form, and was governed by a lucid and comprehensive chronological framework, his work was subsequently used as the basis of the story, into which the older material was placed as appropriate, some of it being lost. For much longer, however, the work of the Priestly Writer continued to be added to by later writers of the same school of thought, so that it holds together the thought of different writers, who are nevertheless in sympathy with one another.

The older material in Numbers comes from a good 500 years earlier. Very probably it reached a fixed form as a book in about the reign of David or of Solomon, which was a time of a great literary flowering in Israel (about 1000 to 930 B.C.). It rested on traditions going back a good deal earlier, which were passed down by word of mouth. In this process of oral tradition they were rounded off and re-shaped to form stories that told well, and will often have reached a fixed form already before they were written down. The actual writing was done by a great writer and collector of traditions, who was concerned to build up a picture of the history of his nation which should also contain a theological lesson for his own day, a writer known today as the Yahwist, or J.

HOW MANY OLDER SOURCES?

This early material has traditionally been divided between two early sources, which have been called J and E. J uses Yahweh as the name of God from the beginning of Genesis, while E uses the word for God, *'elōhīm*, in Genesis, not introducing his name until Exodus. J comes from the southern kingdom (Judah), E from the north (Ephraim). The two differ slightly, it is claimed, in the choice of Hebrew words, and in the way they tell stories. They overlap substantially, however, in their content, and it has recently come to be seen that an essential further part of this theory is the view that both are built on a common outline of traditions formed in the period of the united monarchy, under David and Solomon, which passed into the keeping of both north and south when they split, developing different literary forms in the process.

3

Much the greater part of the older material is attributed to J; E, it is thought, survives only in smaller sections, which were incorporated into the fabric of J after the northern kingdom had fallen in 722 B.C.

It is not however necessary to assign passages between J and E in this commentary. On the traditional view E used *'elōhīm* distinctively only up to Exod. 3: 15, when the name Yahweh is revealed to Moses, and thereafter the allocation of older passages between the two sources is highly uncertain. A detailed recent study of the older narratives in Num. 10–21 concluded that there was no trace of E in this section. There is furthermore a group of scholars who do not believe there was a separate source E at all, and think in terms of a single line of older tradition formed under David or Solomon, and passed down in the southern kingdom, which came to incorporate various individual traditions not assimilated to the older material, so giving rise to the inconsistencies on which the two-source theory leans for evidence. This is the view taken by the writer of this commentary. But in the light of the uncertainties in allocating material to E in Numbers among those who believe in an E source, it is in any case simply more sensible to write in terms of 'the older material' without attempting such an uncertain division of the text.

THE HISTORICAL VALUE OF NUMBERS

The period of the wandering in the wilderness is usually dated to about 1250 B.C. So there is a long interval before J writes down the traditions about this period 300 years later, and a much greater interval still before P writes his version of them perhaps 800 years after the event. It could not be expected that any traditions of value would survive to be incorporated into P which J had not taken up; and at many places P's version is clearly dependent on that of J, and the detail it has which was not in J is unhistorical.

It is harder to say how much historical value is to be given to the account in J. The biblical account of the exodus from Egypt and the entry into Palestine has seriously oversimplified a complicated picture. Not all the Israelites of later times in Palestine, even perhaps not many of them, had ancestors who had come out of Egypt; and those who came out of Egypt may well have done so in several small groups, rather than in one large group. One of these, perhaps a few hundreds in number, was led by Moses, a man whose name itself reveals him to be of Egyptian upbringing, if not descent. It is not however certain whether he led the group directly into Palestine, or as the tradition claims went on a journey to Sinai, standing somewhere in the Sinai peninsula, and there underwent an experience which he and the Israelites interpreted as a revelation by God of himself. The tradition goes on to tell how this was followed by a lengthy period of wandering in the wilderness, a time of repeated rebellion against God and of punishment for rebellion by failure to enter into Canaan as they had hoped. But the reliability of this part of the tradition is open to serious question. There are some signs that J originally had a tradition of moves to enter Palestine from the south, which in fact succeeded, as well as other traditions of an entry of the tribe of Benjamin from the east across the Jordan by way of Jericho. He has harmonized these with one another by making the tradition of entry from the south a story of a defeat; and then has to introduce into the tradition a lapse of time to allow the Israelites to move from south to east. He explains the defeat at Hormah as due to rebellion against God by the people. Only God's mercy gives them a second chance, and that comes after the death of all who wrongly murmured against God. If this interpretation is right, traditions of entry from both south and east for different groups underlie the story we find in Numbers, while the themes of the rebellion and the forty years in the wilderness are not based on historical recollection, but are theological reflection by J.

But whatever value we put on the evidence of Numbers for

the period of the wilderness wanderings, both J and P provide important material for understanding the period at which they write in the stories they tell. In J the stress laid on the rebellion of the people and on God's forgiveness and guidance may well reflect the religious situation of his day. When David was expanding his empire he simply incorporated into Israel all the Canaanites, and we hear no more of them after his time. But this did not alter their fundamental religious loyalties, and Solomon and his successors governed a people containing a very substantial number who superficially conformed to the worship of Yahweh, but remained basically faithful to the Canaanite set of gods, to El, Baal and Asherah. It is this situation which underlies J's special concern with themes of rebellion, punishment and forgiveness. On the other hand the sense of achievement in the empire of David and Solomon, a pride in what Yahweh has made of Israel, comes out clearly in the oracles of Balaam, especially the final one, which looks forward to the building up of David's empire as the fulfilment of God's purposes for his own people.

In the work of the P writer too, although in a rather different way, we can see the interests of the writer's own date reflected. The nation is now much more introverted, and does not move on the stage of international history. So we find reflections in his work of arguments about whether the Korahites are to retain their position as one of the great guilds of temple-singers, and of discussion of the age at which the Levites should begin their service, which we can see in Numbers being lowered from thirty to twenty-five. But most characteristic of P is his picture of the nation as the great multitude united under God's leadership and following his law and will to the letter under its inspired leaders Moses and Aaron; and it is the degree of idealism in this picture which by contrast underlines for us the insignificant status and unsatisfactory religious devotion of the Judah of the Priestly Writer's day.

6

NUMBERS AS A THEOLOGICAL WORK

What is really most important in any book of the Old Testament is the theological ideas, ideas about God and his relationship to the men he has created, which are to be seen in it. But these are not always easy to find. Numbers for instance is part of a larger whole, Genesis–Numbers, artificially separated off, and contains within itself the ideas of two quite separate schools of thought divided by 500 years or so in time (as far apart as Chaucer and Jane Austen). We cannot read straight through Numbers, jotting down ideas that we find, but need to attend separately to the ideas of J and those of P, both of which are parts of a larger whole.

J is the first writer in Israel to create a great historical epic of the origins of the nation, spanning time from the first days of creation and fall, through the promises to Israel's early ancestors the patriarchs, on to the exodus from Egypt, and through the times of trial in the wilderness to the entry into the promised land. There was something strikingly new in portraying a people's religious relationship to its God in terms of its history, of a continuous story that is told. The idea may have grown out of the feasts in the calendar, at which great events of the past were commemorated and realized anew in retelling, as was done for the exodus at the Passover, for creation very probably at Tabernacles, and for Sinai at the feast of Weeks. But these separate commemorations are now drawn together into a continuous story. Two constant theological ideas run through it, tied closely together: God's love for man, his concern to protect him and redeem him, if necessary through punishment, on the one hand, man's recurrent sinfulness and rebellion on the other. J looks to God's mercy as triumphing in the end. These themes do in fact come out most clearly in the wilderness stories in Numbers; so that far from being rather marginal in importance, this tradition contains within itself some of the most central

7

concerns of J. It is because the writer is concerned with disobedience and rebellion as a religious problem of his own day that he sees it ranking so large in the period of the wilderness. This is part of a more general tendency to place in this period, as the archetypal period in the development of Israel, the origin of events and institutions found later. The calves idolatrously set up by King Jeroboam are in Exodus attributed to an act of idolatry by Aaron himself in setting up a Golden Calf; the origin of Nehushtan, a cult object in the form of a serpent in the temple in Jerusalem, is attributed to Moses; some hold that the very covenant made with Moses at Sinai is a projection into the wilderness period of a tradition of covenant that has its real roots in Israel itself. So the period in the wilderness is a time of the greatest significance for J, in which the outlines of the later behaviour of Israel and of the response of its God are already being marked out.

The Priestly Writer, in the period after the exile, retells the story told by J, at times presupposing it, at times reshaping it to indicate his own concerns. While the picture of disobedience and promise of redemption remains central, there is a new development of the greatest importance. For P the worship of the temple, the cult by which men are reconciled to God and atonement made, is of vital significance. It matters so much because he thinks of God himself as being in some sense present in the temple with his people, awesome and unapproachable, but dwelling with them. It is a sort of sacramental presence, for God is not contained within the temple: he remains in the heavens. But his 'glory', a visible realization of his nature, is in the temple. Again the writer is reflecting the beliefs of his own day, and projects them back into the wilderness in his picture of an ideal Israel moving in ordered ranks, with God's presence in the Tent, forerunner of the temple, unapproachable in their midst. A feeling of great awe and fear of God comes over in the work of P. This stress on God's presence and on the reconciling work of the cult also reflects the problem P faces in his own day, the indifference of many in Israel to the due forms of worship which matter so much to him.

Substantial additions are made in Numbers to the work of P, in a fundamentally similar style, but with a slant of their own. It is here that we find the censuses (the 'Numbers' from which the book gets its name), the detailed enumerations of the proper offerings at different feasts, the pattern of strange rituals like that of the ordeal or of the 'Red Cow'. These are in fact the parts of Numbers which modern readers find the most tedious, and the hardest to sympathize with. One might compare the kind of mind that now finds its satisfaction in the constant making of lists, or the collecting of engine or bus numbers. The reader who does not share this mentality might at least attempt by an act of sympathetic imagination to feel in this sort of writing too a quite genuine, if oddly expressed, passion for due reverence to God himself.

Lastly a later editor has put together the books of J and P, and in the process adjusted them to one another. This process is known technically as redaction, and so he is usually called the Redactor (or R). He uses P as his framework, for he feels no doubt about its authenticity, and so when the two overlap it is J material that is lost. The Redactor has no theological position of his own to impose on the material, but he implies that both accounts have a high standing in his day, so that it is his aim to fuse the two and preserve as much as he can of each. By this composition he makes a definitive version of the picture given us by J and P of God's people moving forward under his guidance in the wilderness, sinning and rebelling, and yet constantly reclaimed by God's chastisement and love, and reconciled with him to be the people he has chosen.

✳   ✳   ✳   ✳   ✳   ✳   ✳   ✳   ✳   ✳   ✳   ✳   ✳

Israel in the wilderness of Sinai

✳ The first nine chapter of Numbers are for most readers a rather forbidding start to the book. They come from the pen of P (the Priestly Writer; see pp. 2f.) writing after the exile, and they cover topics of great interest to him, an interest which in many cases modern readers find it hard to share. They show Israel still in camp beside Mount Sinai, after God has revealed his covenant to them through Moses (Exod. 19–34). They recount a census of the tribes (ch. 1), their arrangement in camp (ch. 2), a census of the Levites and an account of their duties (chs. 3–4), followed by a series of regulations of very mixed character including the form of trial by ordeal (ch. 5), rules about Nazirites (ch. 6), the offerings of the chiefs (ch. 7), and more material about the Levites (ch. 8). It will be realized as we go along that little if anything in these chapters is a true recollection of life in the wilderness. They are an idealizing reconstruction of it. Their interest must lie in what they tell us about the burning concerns of the Priestly school in the reconstruction of the life of Judah in their own day; and although these concerns are sometimes centred on matters that seem very remote from us, their importance consists in helping us to understand in detail the form of Jewish religion from which both Christianity and modern Jewish faith have come.

It is widely agreed that these chapters contain not only the work of P himself, but supplements added in by his school over a period probably of centuries. We shall not attempt to disentangle the possible layers, since there is very little agreement on this yet, but shall point out some instances where discrepancies between different parts of chs. 1–9 suggest different authors. ✳

INSTRUCTIONS FOR A CENSUS

O N THE FIRST DAY of the second month in the second 1
year after the Israelites came out of Egypt, the LORD
spoke to Moses at the Tent of the Presence in the wilderness of Sinai in these words: 'Number the whole com- 2
munity of Israel by families in the father's line, recording
the name of every male person aged twenty years and 3
upwards fit for military service. You and Aaron are to
make a detailed list of them by their tribal hosts, and you 4
shall have to assist you one head of family from each
tribe. These are their names: 5

of Reuben, Elizur son of Shedeur;
of Simeon, Shelumiel son of Zurishaddai;   6
of Judah, Nahshon son of Amminadab;   7
of Issachar, Nethaneel son of Zuar;   8
of Zebulun, Eliab son of Helon;   9
of Joseph: of Ephraim, Elishama son of Ammihud;   10
          of Manasseh, Gamaliel son of Pedahzur;
of Benjamin, Abidan son of Gideoni;   11
of Dan, Ahiezer son of Ammishaddai;   12
of Asher, Pagiel son of Ocran;   13
of Gad, Eliasaph son of Reuel;*a*   14
of Naphtali, Ahira son of Enan.'   15

These were the conveners of the whole community, 16
chiefs of their fathers' tribes and heads of Israelite clans.
So Moses and Aaron took these men who had been 17
indicated by name.

[a] *So Sept. (cp. 2: 14); Heb.* Deuel.

II

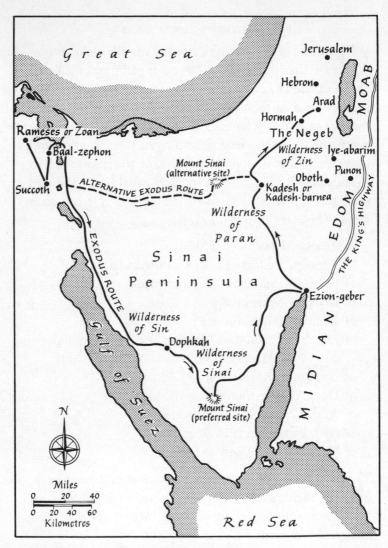

1. Through the wilderness

✷ Moses is instructed to take a census of the fighting men of Israel tribe by tribe, with the help of a leader from each tribe. The purpose is perhaps to represent in this way the totality and the strength of Israel. It is interesting to note that there is no sign here of the displeasure of God with David's taking a census which is reported in 2 Sam. 24. We must assume there is some special factor involved there which the story does not make clear. Obviously the Israelites did not believe that God was generally opposed to the taking of a census.

1. *On the first day of the second month*: a month has elapsed since the Tabernacle was set up (Exod. 40: 17). It is mid-April to mid-May. *at the Tent of the Presence*: P uses this term to refer to the Tabernacle, his artificial picture of a movable sanctuary which he has described in detail in Exod. 25–31, and again in 35–9, and which is based on the sanctuary of the temple in Jerusalem. The term emphasizes that God is thought of as present to the Israelites through the medium of the Tent. *in the wilderness of Sinai*: the desert country near to the mountain. Mount Sinai has been located by a long tradition at Jebel Musa (the Mountain of Moses) at the southern end of the Sinai peninsula, and though attempts have been made to suggest that it lay much further east, in north-west Arabia, or to the north near Kadesh, it is probable that the traditional site is correct.

2. *Number the whole community*: it is the men of military age who are to be counted. This must have been the most common form of census in the ancient world, giving information of direct usefulness, such as a grand total of the people would not have. *by families in the father's line*: or, 'by families, by father's houses'. The natural subdivisions within the twelve tribes are used.

3. *You and Aaron*: Aaron, who is taken to be Moses' brother, and the ancestor of the priestly line, was often added in at a later stage to stories concerning Moses. But by the time of P we cannot be certain if this was still being done, or if his presence was so much taken for granted that he can without

difficulty appear half-way through a story as he does here. In Exod. 4: 14–16 God declares Aaron will be Moses' mouthpiece.

4. *one head of family from each tribe*: since these are not mentioned at all in the course of the story of the census in verses 20–46, and the story could read well without them, it is often assumed that they are a later addition in this story. The heads of family are listed again in chs. 2 and 7 and in 10: 14–27. It is impossible to be sure in which of these they first appeared.

5. *These are their names*: these twenty-four names are often claimed to come from a very early list which has somehow survived into the period after the exile. But although some of them are of a type which was used in early times, such as Amminadab or Ammihud, some are of a pattern which only became popular in the period after the exile, such as Nethaneel (the same name as that of Nathanael of John 1: 45–51), or Gamaliel; and the actual names are found again most often in late books like Chronicles. So it looks as if the list as it stands is post-exilic, not genuine recollection. Whether it is simply invented or is an actual list attributed to an early date we cannot now tell. *of Reuben*: in Israelite tradition Jacob had twelve sons, who were the ancestors of the twelve tribes of Israel. One of them was Levi, and in early lists Levi is included as a tribe. But in later times Levi is the name for a group of priests with no territory, and is excluded from the lists of the twelve tribes. We cannot tell if Levi as a priestly group developed out of the secular tribe, or has a quite different origin. Joseph then has to be divided into two tribes, regarded as being his two sons, Ephraim and Manasseh. The tribes are listed in varying order in different lists. The list here is not quite identical even with that of verses 20–43, but it is close to it and to that in ch. 26. Of older lists Gen. 49 is most similar to these, and has perhaps been drawn on here with slight alterations. It is not clear if it was so important to the author to get the order right.

14. *son of Reuel*: as the footnote indicates, the Hebrew text has Deuel. Reuel occurs in ch. 2, but Deuel in chs. 7 and 10. *r* and *d* in the later Hebrew script are easily confused, and Reuel is in itself a more probable form for a Hebrew name.

16. *clans*: the word literally means thousands; it refers to a fairly large sub-group within the tribe. *

THE CENSUS NUMBERS

They summoned the whole community on the first 18 day of the second month, and they registered their descent by families in the father's line, recording every male person aged twenty years and upwards, as the 19 LORD had told Moses to do. Thus it was that he drew up the detailed lists in the wilderness of Sinai:

The tribal list of Reuben, Israel's eldest son, by families 20 in the father's line, with the name of every male person aged twenty years and upwards fit for service, the num- 21 ber in the list of the tribe of Reuben being forty-six thousand five hundred.

The tribal list of Simeon, by families in the father's 22 line, with the name of every male person aged twenty years and upwards fit for service, the number in the list 23 of the tribe of Simeon being fifty-nine thousand three hundred.

The tribal list of Gad, by families in the father's line, 24 with the names of all men aged twenty years and up- wards fit for service, the number in the list of the tribe 25 of Gad being forty-five thousand six hundred and fifty.

The tribal list of Judah, by families in the father's 26 line, with the names of all men aged twenty years and upwards fit for service, the number in the list of 27 the tribe of Judah being seventy-four thousand six hundred.

28 The tribal list of Issachar, by families in the father's line, with the names of all men aged twenty years and
29 upwards fit for service, the number in the list of the tribe of Issachar being fifty-four thousand four hundred.

30 The tribal list of Zebulun, by families in the father's line, with the names of all men aged twenty years and
31 upwards fit for service, the number in the list of the tribe of Zebulun being fifty-seven thousand four hundred.

32 The tribal lists of Joseph: that of Ephraim, by families in the father's line, with the names of all men aged twenty
33 years and upwards fit for service, the number in the list of the tribe of Ephraim being forty thousand five hund-
34 red; that of Manasseh, by families in the father's line, with the names of all men aged twenty years and upwards
35 fit for service, the number in the list of the tribe of Manas-seh being thirty-two thousand two hundred.

36 The tribal list of Benjamin, by families in the father's line, with the names of all men aged twenty years and
37 upwards fit for service, the number in the list of the tribe of Benjamin being thirty-five thousand four hundred.

38 The tribal list of Dan, by families in the father's line, with the names of all men aged twenty years and upwards
39 fit for service, the number in the list of the tribe of Dan being sixty-two thousand seven hundred.

40 The tribal list of Asher, by families in the father's line, with the names of all men aged twenty years and upwards
41 fit for service, the number in the list of the tribe of Asher being forty-one thousand five hundred.

42 The tribal list of Naphtali, by families in the father's

line, with the names of all men aged twenty years and upwards fit for service, the number in the list of the tribe 43 of Naphtali being fifty-three thousand four hundred.

These were the numbers recorded in the detailed lists 44 by Moses and Aaron and the twelve chiefs of Israel, each representing one tribe and being the head of a family.*a* The total number of Israelites aged twenty years and 45 upwards fit for service, recorded in the lists of fathers' families, was six hundred and three thousand five hundred 46 and fifty.

* In this tribal list by families the tribes are given in the same order as in verses 5–15, except that Gad is moved up to third place. The census is recounted in an unvarying fixed formula. This may at first seem tedious to the modern reader, but we could perhaps as we read it try to recapture the feeling of satisfaction which this recitation would give its original hearers as they gradually approach a complete tally of all Israel.

20. *by families in the father's line*: the formulas used repeat those of verse 2, and indicate that the orders are being strictly carried out.

46. *six hundred and three thousand five hundred and fifty*: both the total, and the numbers given for the individual tribes, are artificial, and reflect Israel's pride in its past, rather than historical memory. A total of 603,550 fighting men must imply a total population with old men, women and children of quite 2 million, and it is inconceivable that the Sinai peninsula could support any number nearly as large (in recent times its population has been of the order of 15,000). Attempts have been made to understand the numbers either by arguing that they are the figures of a census in the time of David, and true for that date; or that the word for thousands earlier meant a

[a] each . . . family: *prob. rdg. (cp. Sam. and Sept.)*; *Heb.* each representing a family.

unit, a 'troop', and that the original figures ran, for instance, Reuben 46 troops, 500 men. This would give us much lower figures, with about 10 men in each troop, but a variation between 5 and 15 in the size of the troops of different tribes. It is hard to believe that really early figures would have been so preserved down the centuries. While these may alternatively be figures from a census of the time of David, they could come from earlier or later, or be simply invented by our author to give the kind of totals he thought correct. It is in any case in the cumulative wholeness that the author is interested, rather than the specific totals.✶

THE DUTIES OF THE LEVITES

47 A list of the Levites by their fathers' families was not made.

48,49 The LORD spoke to Moses and said, 'You shall not record the total number of the Levites or make a detailed
50 list of them among the Israelites. You shall put the Levites in charge of the Tabernacle of the Tokens, with its equipment and everything in it. They shall carry the Tabernacle and all its equipment; they alone shall be its
51 attendants and shall pitch their tents round it. The Levites shall take the Tabernacle down when it is due to move and shall put it up when it halts; any unqualified person
52 who comes near it shall be put to death. All other Israelites shall pitch their tents, each tribal host in its proper
53 camp and under its own standard. But the Levites shall encamp round the Tabernacle of the Tokens, so that divine wrath may not follow the whole community of Israel; the Tabernacle of the Tokens shall be in their keeping.'

The Israelites did exactly as the LORD had told Moses 54
to do.

* Levi is not included in the census. Much more is said of
Levi in chs. 3 and 4, including a census of the tribe's numbers.
Verses 48–54 in part anticipate this, and are perhaps put here
for that purpose at a late date in the development of chs. 1–9.
The identity of the Levites will be discussed in the notes to
ch. 3.

50. *the Tabernacle of the Tokens*: it is the duties of the Levites
in connection with the Tabernacle that are stressed in this
section. The term used here is uncommon in P, and occurs
only here, at 10: 11 and at Exod. 38: 21. The Tokens are the
tablets of the ten commandments, kept in the Ark of the
covenant. The term used stresses the presence of the objects
given by God, rather than his presence, as in the 'Tent of the
Presence', and in this reflects, we may suppose, a late tendency
to avoid the idea of the nearness of God himself.

53. *so that divine wrath may not follow the whole community of
Israel*: the Levites alone may come close to the tent, and so
insulate the rest of Israel from the, as it were, electric and
dangerous presence of God. This idea of the nature of God's
presence, found early for instance in 2 Sam. 6: 6–8 (the story
of Uzzah being struck dead for touching the Ark), is still
alive when P writes, and comes again later in Numbers, as
in 8: 19. *

THE ARRANGEMENT OF THE CAMP

The LORD spoke to Moses and Aaron and said, 'The 2 1,2
Israelites shall encamp each under his own standard by
the emblems of his father's family; they shall pitch their
tents round the Tent of the Presence, facing it.

'In front of it, on the east, the division of Judah shall 3
be stationed under the standard of its camp by tribal

hosts. The chief of Judah shall be Nahshon son of Am-
4 minadab. His host, with its members as detailed, numbers
5 seventy-four thousand six hundred men. Next to Judah
the tribe of Issachar shall be stationed. Its chief shall be
6 Nethaneel son of Zuar; his host, with its members as
detailed, numbers fifty-four thousand four hundred.
7 Then the tribe of Zebulun: its chief shall be Eliab son of
8 Helon; his host, with its members as detailed, numbers
9 fifty-seven thousand four hundred. The number listed
in the camp of Judah, by hosts, is one hundred and eighty-
six thousand four hundred. They shall be the first to
march.

10 'To the south the division of Reuben shall be stationed
under the standard of its camp by tribal hosts. The chief
11 of Reuben shall be Elizur son of Shedeur; his host, with
its members as detailed, numbers forty-six thousand
12 five hundred. Next to him the tribe of Simeon shall be
stationed. Its chief shall be Shelumiel son of Zurishaddai;
13 his host, with its members as detailed, numbers fifty-
14 nine thousand three hundred. Then the tribe of Gad:
15 its chief shall be Eliasaph son of Reuel; his host, with its
members as detailed, numbers forty-five thousand six
16 hundred and fifty. The number listed in the camp of
Reuben, by hosts, is one hundred and fifty-one thousand
four hundred and fifty. They shall be the second to
march.

17 'When the Tent of the Presence moves, the camp of
the Levites shall keep its station in the centre of the other
camps; they shall all move in the order of their encamp-
ing, each man in his proper place under his standard.

18 'To the west the division of Ephraim shall be stationed

under the standard of its camp by tribal hosts. The chief
of Ephraim shall be Elishama son of Ammihud; his host, 19
with its members as detailed, numbers forty thousand
five hundred. Next to him the tribe of Manasseh shall 20
be stationed. Its chief shall be Gamaliel son of Pedahzur; his host, with its members as detailed, numbers 21
thirty-two thousand two hundred. Then the tribe of 22
Benjamin: its chief shall be Abidan son of Gideoni; his 23
host, with its members as detailed, numbers thirty-five
thousand four hundred. The number listed in the camp of 24
Ephraim, by hosts, is one hundred and eight thousand one
hundred. They shall be the third to march.

'To the north the division of Dan shall be stationed 25
under the standard of its camp by tribal hosts. The chief
of Dan shall be Ahiezer son of Ammishaddai; his host, 26
with its members as detailed, numbers sixty-two thousand
seven hundred. Next to him the tribe of Asher shall be 27
stationed. Its chief shall be Pagiel son of Ocran; his host, 28
with its members as detailed, numbers forty-one thousand
five hundred. Then the tribe of Naphtali: its chief shall 29
be Ahira son of Enan: his host, with its members as 30
detailed, numbers fifty-three thousand four hundred.
The number listed in the camp of Dan is a hundred and 31
fifty-seven thousand six hundred. They shall march,
under their standards, last.'

These were the Israelites listed by their fathers' families. 32
The total number in the camp, recorded by tribal hosts,
was six hundred and three thousand five hundred and
fifty.

The Levites were not included in the detailed lists with 33
their fellow-Israelites, for so the LORD had commanded

34 Moses. The Israelites did exactly as the LORD had commanded Moses, pitching and breaking camp standard by standard, each man according to his family in his father's line.

* A pattern of the arrangement of the tribes in the camp and for the march, with the Tent of the Presence in the middle, and the tribes in a square around it, three on each side, is here set out. The tribe of Levi surrounds the Tent of the Presence, and ch. 3 gives details of how they are disposed.

Asher Dan Naphtali

Benjamin		N.		Issachar
Ephraim	W.	Tent of the Presence	E.	Judah
Manasseh		S.		Zebulun

Gad Reuben Simeon

This chapter is perhaps based on traditions of great crowds gathering in tents at a sanctuary for a pilgrim festival, but its purpose is to express a theological ideal of Israel as a whole gathered round the God whose presence was in their midst. This presence of God with his people is one of the continuous themes of the Bible, which sees it first as almost material in quality, and transmuting it until it becomes the picture of the heavenly presence which is painted in Revelation (Rev. 21: 1–4).

2. *under his own standard*: a military banner, or flag. *the emblems of his father's family*: it is not known what these were. *facing it*: or it is possible that the word means 'at a distance'. This is how the Jewish tradition interpreted it, adducing the distance kept from the Ark of 'a thousand yards' in Josh. 3: 4.

3. *the division of Judah*: the arrangement of the tribes is the same as in ch. 1, except that Judah and its two companions are brought up to first position (verses 3–9). The names of the

leaders, and the total numbers in each tribe, are the same as in ch. 1.

17. This verse does not fit in very well with the rhythm of those around it, and it may have been added later to show where the tribe of Levi was, in anticipation of ch. 3.

25. *To the north*: the three tribes here, Dan, Asher and Naphtali, do in fact appear eventually in the northern part of the land, although Dan is described (cp. Judg. 13–16) as originally settled west of Jerusalem, and later as moving to the north (cp. the story in Judg. 17–18).

33. This repeats what has been said already in 1: 47, but adds that it was God's command.

34. Like 1: 54 this verse stresses the exact correlation between command and action. Israel is totally obedient. ✽

THE APPOINTMENT OF THE LEVITES TO SERVE THE PRIESTS

These were the descendants of Aaron and Moses at the 3 time when the LORD spoke to Moses on Mount Sinai. The names of the sons of Aaron were Nadab the eldest, 2 Abihu, Eleazar and Ithamar. These were the names of 3 Aaron's sons, the anointed priests who had been installed in the priestly office. Nadab and Abihu fell dead before 4 the LORD because they had presented illicit fire before the LORD in the wilderness of Sinai. They left no sons; Eleazar and Ithamar continued to perform the priestly office in their father's presence.

The LORD spoke to Moses and said, 'Bring forward 5, 6 the tribe of Levi and appoint them to serve Aaron the priest and to minister to him. They shall be in attendance 7 on him and on the whole community before the Tent of the Presence, undertaking the service of the Tabernacle. They shall be in charge of all the equipment in the Tent 8

of the Presence, and be in attendance on the Israelites,
9 undertaking the service of the Tabernacle. You shall
assign the Levites to Aaron and his sons as especially
10 dedicated to him out of all the Israelites. To Aaron and his
line you shall commit the priestly office and they shall
perform its duties; any unqualified person who intrudes
upon it shall be put to death.'

11, 12   The LORD spoke to Moses and said, 'I take the Levites
for myself out of all the Israelites as a substitute for the
eldest male child of every woman; the Levites shall be
13 mine. For every eldest child, if a boy, became mine
when I destroyed all the eldest sons in Egypt. So I have
consecrated to myself all the first-born in Israel, both man
and beast. They shall be mine. I am the LORD.'

* The next two chapters are concerned with the position
and duties of the Levites. In the period after the exile when
these chapters were written the Levites had a position as
ministers in the Jerusalem temple inferior to the priests
proper, and the ancestry of the Levites is traced to the tribe
of Levi, that of the priests to a subdivision within Levi, of the
descendants of Aaron. The Levites attend the priests, purify
the holy things, are custodians of the Ark, prepare the bread,
sing the praises of God, and have the general care of the
sanctuary (so 1 Chron. 23: 28–32). The origin of the Levites
is a still unsolved problem. Early in the history of Israel there
was a secular tribe called Levi, famed for its violence (Gen.
34: 25–31; 49: 5–7). We do not know whether they lost their
territory, and were transformed into the landless tribe of
sanctuary attendants, or whether after some particularly
violent episode they were wiped out, and a religious order
with the same name came to be regarded as a tribe in their
place. Levites as priests come clearly into view first in Judg. 17,

from which we gather that others could be priests, but Levites were preferred: Micah of Ephraim appointed his own son priest in the shrine he built, but replaced him by a Levite when one appeared. It does not seem that the house of Eli, who had charge of the Ark at the time of Samuel, were Levites. By the time of Deuteronomy (usually placed towards the end of the monarchy, but possibly from the time of the exile) all priests are Levites, but it is not clear whether all Levites are priests, or whether some Levites form a lower order of temple attendants. Certainly in the idealized plan for the future in Ezek. 40–8 (from the early years of the exile if it is substantially by Ezekiel, but of later date, possibly the fifth century B.C., if it is not) the Levites are priests who have charge of the temple, but only the Zadokites (the priests of Jerusalem descended from Zadok, high priest of David) may draw near to the altar (Ezek. 40: 45–6 and 44: 6–19). After the exile, the position of the Levites is clearly controversial. Both in Chronicles and in P there are echoes of particular disputes, and changes in the position of the Levites, and these are also reflected in chs. 3–4 and 16–17 of Numbers.

1. *These were the descendants*: this is a regular phrase of the Priestly source (as in Gen. 5: 1 or 10: 1), and marks a new start in the narrative beginning with a genealogy. We are told who the Aaronites are before we come to the Levites; but there is no close connection between verses 1–4 and what follows, and this is probably a late addition to the chapter. *and Moses*: but the descendants of Moses are not in fact listed, and this seems to be a rather careless addition made because the two names so often occur together.

3. *the anointed priests*: this is probably a sign that these verses are from a late layer in P. Under the monarchy it is the king who is anointed (that is, oil is poured over his head, 1 Sam. 10: 1), apparently to indicate that he is a vassal of God, as earlier kings of Canaan were anointed to indicate that they were vassals of the king of Egypt. After the exile the high priest is anointed (Exod. 29: 7), and this indicates that he is

seen as taking the place of the king. Later still this is extended to all priests, as in this verse; but the custom of anointing priests had gone out of use by the time of the Roman occupation, for reasons which are not known.

4. *Nadab and Abihu*: this refers to an odd story in Lev. 10: 1–7 of two sons of Aaron, Nadab and Abihu, throwing incense on the fire, and so presenting before God 'illicit fire which he had not commanded'. It has been suggested that the fire in the Tabernacle was produced by unusual means in the period after the exile (there is a story in 2 Macc. 1: 18–36 which claims that in the time of Nehemiah naphtha was found in the place of the fire hidden away by the priests just before the exile), and the point may be that the two men introduced ordinary fire into the sacred place. On the other hand the word translated 'illicit' can also mean 'lay' in P (for instance Num. 16: 40 'unqualified'), and it may simply be meant that they should have known that, unlike Aaron's other sons, they were not authorized to approach the fire. The mention of Nadab and Abihu might appear to have little point if *They left no sons*; but it is likely that there were priestly groups named after Nadab and Abihu who were successfully excluded from the temple some time after the exile, and that the tradition here is a reflection of the struggle.

6. *Bring forward the tribe of Levi*: verses 5–10 make a new start to recount the appointment of the Levites to serve the Aaronites. *to serve Aaron the priest*: and, we are to understand, his descendants of the Aaronite priesthood. The Levites' care for the Tabernacle (see note on 1: 1) and its equipment is to be taken as referring to a duty after the exile to care for the equipment of the innermost part of the temple.

10. *any unqualified person*: this appears to include the Levites, and is perhaps specially directed at them. *shall be put to death*: this is a recognition that his life is forfeit to God, rather than the sentence for an offence punishable by law.

12. *I take the Levites*: verses 11–13 are a later addition, which explains the special position of the Levites as due to God

taking them for his own in compensation for the first-born, whom he made his own when he slew the first-born of Egypt (Exod. 12: 29; 13: 2). Levi thus has concentrated in itself the 'holiness', the belonging to God, of all Israel. This is a late and new explanation; the older idea was that it was the first-born of animals that were sacrificed in place of the first-born of Israel (Exod. 13: 13 and 34: 20).

13. *I am the LORD*: this is a formula to round off an oracle which is specially characteristic of the source found in Lev. 17–26, known as the Holiness Code because of its frequent use of the phrase 'You shall be holy because I, the LORD your God, am holy.' But it occurs occasionally elsewhere in P, and so it is not necessarily the case that the writers of the Holiness Code (which cannot be dated with any confidence, but is clearly older than P) are responsible for these verses. ✲

THE ENUMERATION AND ORDER OF THE LEVITES

The LORD spoke to Moses in the wilderness of Sinai and 14 said, 'Make a detailed list of all the Levites by their famil- 15 ies in the father's line, every male from the age of one month and upwards.'

Moses made a detailed list of them in accordance with 16 the command given him by the LORD. Now these were 17 the names of the sons of Levi:

Gershon, Kohath and Merari.

Descendants of Gershon, by families: Libni and Shimei. 18

Descendants of Kohath, by families: Amram, Izhar, 19 Hebron and Uzziel.

Descendants of Merari, by families: Mahli and Mushi. 20

These were the families of Levi, by fathers' families:

Gershon: the family of Libni and the family of Shimei. 21

These were the families of Gershon, and the number of 22

27

males in their list as detailed, from the age of one month
23 and upwards, was seven thousand five hundred. The
24,25 families of Gershon were stationed on the west, behind
the Tabernacle. Their chief was Eliasaph son of Lael, and
in the service of the Tent of the Presence they were in
charge of the Tabernacle and[a] its coverings, of the screen
26 at the entrance to the Tent of the Presence, the hangings
of the court, the screen at the entrance to the court all
round the Tabernacle and the altar, and of all else needed
for its maintenance.

27   Kohath: the family of Amram, the family of Izhar,
the family of Hebron, the family of Uzziel. These were
28 the families of Kohath, and the number of males, from
the age of one month and upwards, was eight thousand
six hundred. They were the guardians of the holy things.
29 The families of Kohath were stationed on the south, at
30 the side of the Tabernacle. Their chief was Elizaphan
31 son of Uzziel; they were in charge of the Ark, the table,
the lamp-stands and the altars, together with the sacred
vessels used in their service, and the screen with every-
32 thing needed for its maintenance. The chief over all the
chiefs of the Levites was Eleazar son of Aaron the priest,
who was appointed overseer of those in charge of the
sanctuary.

33   Merari: the family of Mahli, the family of Mushi.
34 These were the families of Merari, and the number of
males in their list as detailed from the age of one month
35 and upwards was six thousand two hundred. Their chief
was Zuriel son of Abihail; they were stationed on the
36 north, at the side of the Tabernacle. The Merarites were

[a] *So Sept.; Heb. adds* the tent.

in charge of the planks, bars, posts, and sockets of the Tabernacle, together with its vessels and all the equipment needed for its maintenance, the posts, sockets, pegs, 37 and cords of the surrounding court.

In front of the Tabernacle on the east, Moses was 38 stationed, with Aaron and his sons, in front of the Tent of the Presence eastwards. They were in charge of the sanctuary on behalf of the Israelites; any unqualified person who came near would be put to death.

The number of Levites recorded by Moses[a] on the 39 detailed list by families at the command of the LORD was twenty-two thousand males aged one month and upwards.

✳ The main thread is taken up again with a list of the family groups of the Levites in verses 14–20, and then a detailed census of the numbers in these groups and a statement of their duties in verses 21–39. There is a division into three groups, Gershonites, Kohathites and Merarites, traced back to three sons of Levi, and sub-groups within these. The arrangement no doubt reflects the relationships after the exile of the Levites, and variations in our sources (as when Num. 26: 58 has five sons of Levi as ancestors of the Levites) reflect changes and disputes among the Levites down the years in this period.

15. *from the age of one month and upwards*: because the Levites are a substitute for the first-born, who are not redeemed until they are a month old.

17. *Gershon, Kohath and Merari*: these and the following names are only found in sources dating from after the exile. But Gershon may be a variation of the Gershom son of Moses (Exod. 2: 22) who is the father of the ancestor of the

[a] *So some MSS.; others add* and Aaron.

priesthood of Dan (Judg. 18: 30). If so this may be a real tradition of one of the ancestors of the later Levites.

21–39 is a composite section, containing both census details and a placing of the Levites within the order for the camp of ch. 2, as well as the specific charge of each group. It was no doubt built up gradually to this complex arrangement, but we cannot trace its growth in detail.

22. *seven thousand five hundred*: the numbers here and in verses 28 and 34 add up (see the note on verse 28) to a suspiciously neat round number, 22,000. Although much smaller than the numbers in ch. 1, it is still too large to be correct for the wilderness period. The numbers are artificial.

23. The families of Gershon were stationed on the west; apparently, although this is not explicitly stated, the three sub-groups of the Levites, and the group of Aaron and his sons, are fitted in close to the sanctuary, with the three tribes on each side further out (cp. the note on p. 22).

24. *Their chief was Eliasaph son of Lael*: names of the type of *Lael*, formed with a preposition and a noun, appear only in late books. Probably the names here and in verses 30 and 35 refer to actual, but otherwise no longer remembered, Levite heads of families of the period after the exile.

25. *they were in charge of the Tabernacle and its coverings*: since the Tabernacle as described in Exod. 25–31 is an artificial reconstruction, the division of duties here too must be artificial. No doubt it is an adaptation of the actual duties of different families of the Levites in the temple, but we cannot from this passage reconstruct them. It appears from verse 36 that the Merarites carry the actual wooden framework of the Tabernacle, so that it is the external covering of the Tabernacle, hangings of linen and other materials, that are referred to here. The account presupposes the Exodus description of the Tabernacle, and here especially Exod. 26: 1–14. The Tabernacle is made of ten hangings of linen with yarn woven into it as an inner layer, and a further set of hangings of goats' hair lying on top of them. These were protected

by two further layers of tanned rams' skins and porpoise hides.

26. The court encloses the Tabernacle itself, and so also the altar of whole-offering (Exod. 27: 1–8), the main altar (cp. on verse 31 below).

28. *eight thousand six hundred*: this should probably read 'eight thousand three hundred'. The three numbers add up to 22,300, while verse 39 makes the total 22,000, and verses 43 and 46 confirm this. The misreading assumed is one that could easily be made (*shālōsh* read as *shēsh*).

31. *they were in charge of the Ark, the table, the lamp-stands and the altars*: the Kohathites have the sacred contents of the sanctuary as their responsibility, and so are given the most important task. The Ark is a very ancient symbol of God's leadership in Israel (cp. 10: 33), and P regards it as a box of acacia-wood, envisaged as a container, in which were the two tablets containing the ten commandments. The table is also of acacia-wood, and is to receive the offerings other than animals, especially the 'Bread of the Presence', traditionally called 'shewbread' (Exod. 25: 30; see on 4: 7), and other pots and vessels. The lamp-stands are seven-branched; Numbers comes back to them in 8: 1–4. The *altars*, if the text is correct, must refer to the altar of whole-offering (described in Exod. 27: 1–8) and the altar of incense (Exod. 30: 1–10). The incense altar is a later addition to Exod. 25–31, and so indicates a later date within the evolution of P for the composition of these sections about the Tabernacle (unless the text originally read 'altar' and has been changed later). *the screen*: this must refer to the 'Veil of the screen' of Exod. 35: 12, since the door-hangings of the Tabernacle have already been given to the Gershonites.

32. This is a summary verse of some importance, as indicating priestly control over the Levites. It is placed here in the middle perhaps because Eleazar is himself a Kohathite as grandson of Amram. The verse is probably a later insertion, based on 4: 16.

36. *The Merarites were in charge of the planks, bars, posts and sockets*: they have the wooden framework of the Tabernacle, perhaps treated as the least important part of the whole. The terms come from Exod. 26: 15–30 and 27: 9–19, where the description of how they are put together is far from clear.

38. *Moses was stationed, with Aaron and his sons*: this important but disproportionately small group is included in order to have four groups to take each side of the Tabernacle, and this group is given the side regarded as the most important, in relation to the object they protect, for God himself is there present with them.

39. *Moses*: some manuscripts, as the footnote indicates, have 'Moses and Aaron'. Since this verse is based on 1: 44, where both names occur, the fuller form is probably correct here too. ✶

THE SUBSTITUTION OF THE LEVITES FOR THE FIRST-BORN

40 The LORD said to Moses, 'Make a detailed list of all the male first-born in Israel aged one month and upwards,
41 and count the number of persons. You shall reserve the Levites for me – I am the LORD – in substitution for the eldest sons of the Israelites, and in the same way the Levites' cattle in substitution for the first-born cattle of
42 the Israelites.' As the LORD had told him to do, Moses
43 made a list of all the eldest sons of the Israelites, and the total number of first-born males recorded by name in the register, aged one month and upwards, was twenty-two thousand two hundred and seventy-three.

44, 45   The LORD spoke to Moses and said, 'Take the Levites as a substitute for all the eldest sons in Israel and the cattle of the Levites as a substitute for their cattle. The Levites
46 shall be mine. I am the LORD. The eldest sons in Israel

will outnumber the Levites by two hundred and seventy-three. This remainder must be ransomed, and you shall 47 accept five shekels for each of them, taking the sacred shekel and reckoning twenty gerahs to the shekel; you 48 shall give the money with which they are ransomed to Aaron and his sons.'

Moses took the money paid as ransom for those who 49 remained over when the substitution of Levites was complete. The amount received was one thousand three 50 hundred and sixty-five shekels of silver by the sacred standard. In accordance with what the LORD had said, 51 he gave the money to Aaron and his sons, doing what the LORD had told him to do.

* Verses 40–51 are a later addition to P, harking back to verses 11–13, and giving an illustration of how the substitution of Levites for the first-born worked.

41. *in substitution for the first-born cattle of the Israelites*: 18: 17 is probably earlier, and does not allow this. It was perhaps found impractical for all the 'first-born cattle' to be sacrificed, and an alternative of redemption was found. But that the cattle of the Levites have this origin is an odd, and probably only theoretical, idea.

43. *twenty-two thousand two hundred and seventy-three*: the number is arbitrary (and indeed within P's system would produce absurdly large families if there were not more first-born), and is chosen to be a little over the already given number of the Levites, so that it can be shown how the surplus is dealt with in verse 47.

47. *the sacred shekel*: this is only referred to in P, and regularly explained as consisting of 20 gerahs. The shekel is a weight of silver of about 0.41 oz (11.5 grams). It is not meant to be a coin; coinage was only invented in the seventh century B.C. in Lydia, first reached Judah in the sixth century B.C., and

was first coined there in the fourth century B.C. It seems to be implied that the sacred shekel is different from the ordinary shekel. If this is so, we do not know in what way it was different, and the reference may be to a standard weight kept in the sanctuary.

49. *the money paid as ransom*: this is thought of as a weight in silver. ✡

THE DUTIES OF THE LEVITES IN MORE DETAIL

4 1, 2 The LORD spoke to Moses and Aaron and said, 'Among
the Levites, make a count of the descendants of Kohath
3 between the ages of thirty and fifty, by families in the
father's line, comprising everyone who comes to take
duty in the service of the Tent of the Presence.
4 'This is the service to be rendered by the Kohathites
5 in the Tent of the Presence; it is most sacred. When the
camp is due to move, Aaron and his sons shall come and
take down the Veil of the screen and cover the Ark of
6 the Tokens with it; over this they shall put a covering of
porpoise-hide[a] and over that again a violet cloth all of
7 one piece; they shall then put its poles in place. Over the
Table of the Presence they shall spread a violet cloth and
lay on it the dishes, saucers, and flagons, and the bowls for
drink-offerings; the Bread regularly presented shall
8 also lie upon it; then they shall spread over them a scarlet
cloth and over that a covering of porpoise-hide, and put
9 the poles in place. They shall take a violet cloth and cover
the lamp-stand, its lamps, tongs, firepans, and all the
10 containers for the oil used in its service; they shall put it
with all its equipment in a sheet of porpoise-hide slung

[a] *Strictly* hide of sea-cow.

from a pole. Over the gold altar they shall spread a violet 11
cloth, cover it with a porpoise-hide covering, and put its
poles in place. They shall take all the articles used for the 12
service of the sanctuary, put them on a violet cloth, cover
them with a porpoise-hide covering, and sling them
from a pole. They shall clear the altar of the fat and ashes, 13
spread a purple cloth over it, and then lay on it all the 14
equipment used in its service, the firepans, forks, shovels,
tossing-bowls, and all the equipment of the altar, spread
a covering of porpoise-hide over it and put the poles in
place. Once Aaron and his sons have finished covering the 15
sanctuary and all the sacred equipment, when the camp is
due to move, the Kohathites shall come to carry it; they
must not touch it on pain of death. All these things are
the load to be carried by the Kohathites, the things connected with the Tent of the Presence. Eleazar son of 16
Aaron the priest shall have charge of the lamp-oil, the
fragrant incense, the regular grain-offering, and the
anointing oil, with the general oversight of the whole
Tabernacle and its contents, the sanctuary and its equipment.'

The LORD spoke to Moses and Aaron and said, 'You 17, 18
must not let the families of Kohath be extirpated, and lost
to the tribe of Levi. If they are to live and not die when 19
they approach the most holy things, this is what you
must do: Aaron and his sons shall come and set each
man to his appointed task and to his load, and the 20
Kohathites themselves shall not enter to cast even a passing glance[a] on the sanctuary, on pain of death.'

The LORD spoke to Moses and said, 'Number the 21, 22

[a] to cast . . . glance: *lit.* to look as they swallow.

23 Gershonites by families in the father's line. Make a detailed list of all those between the ages of thirty and fifty who come on duty to perform service in the Tent of the Presence.

24 'This is the service to be rendered by the Gershonite families, comprising their general duty and their loads.
25 They shall carry the hangings of the Tabernacle, the Tent of the Presence, its covering, that is the covering of porpoise-hide which is over it, the screen at the entrance
26 to the Tent of the Presence, the hangings of the court, the screen at the entrance to the court surrounding the Tabernacle and the altar, their cords and all the equipment for their service; and they shall perform all the tasks connected with them. These are the acts of service they
27 shall render. All the service of the Gershonites, their loads and their other duties, shall be directed by Aaron and his sons; you shall assign them the loads for which they
28 shall be responsible This is the service assigned to the Gershonite families in connection with the Tent of the Presence; Ithamar son of Aaron shall be in charge of them.

29 'You shall make a detailed list of the Merarites by
30 families in the father's line, all those between the ages of thirty and fifty, who come on duty to perform service in the Tent of the Presence.

31 'These are the loads for which they shall be responsible in virtue of their service in the Tent of the Presence: the planks of the Tabernacle with its bars, posts, and sockets,
32 the posts of the surrounding court with their sockets, pegs, and cords, and all that is needed for the maintenance of them; you shall assign to each man by name the

load for which he is responsible. These are the duties of 33
the Merarite families in virtue of their service in the Tent
of the Presence. Ithamar son of Aaron the priest shall be
in charge of them.'

* In this chapter the Priestly writer has combined a description of the detailed duties of the three sub-groups of Levites,
the Kohathites, Gershonites and Merarites, with a census of
those among them of age to do service. The duties are carried
on from ch. 3, but given in more detail. The great holiness
of God (understood in terms of a quite physical unapproach-
ability) is emphasized in the elaborate rules for the protection
of the Ark, which none but the priests may touch; while
the portable nature of the Ark, in the midst of the people,
tells us that this God, though holy and beyond human reach,
is close to his people all the time, and on the march with them.
Repetition, as so often, underlines the themes.

2. *the descendants of Kohath*: they have now come to the
fore, and although they were in second place in ch. 3, are
now taken first.

3. *between the ages of thirty and fifty*: the lower limit is later
reduced. In 8: 24 it is twenty-five, and in 1 Chron. 23: 24 it
is down to twenty, on the analogy of straightforward military
service (or perhaps because of a shortage of qualified persons).

4. *This is the service*: their service is not in fact given until
verse 15. First the priests must cover up all the furniture and
utensils, so that the Kohathites cannot touch them (verse 15)
or see them (verse 20).

5. The priests pack the contents of the Tent of the Presence
in six loads. The Ark, the most sacred object, is covered by
three layers, and carried by poles. In the second load is the
Table of the Presence. The lamp-stand and its equipment
form the third load, the gold altar for incense the fourth, the
miscellaneous articles the fifth, and the altar for whole-
offerings the sixth. All are carried from poles (in the case of

the lamp-stand and the miscellaneous articles just one pole) so as not to be touched directly, and all are wrapped in a violet cloth (except the sixth load, in scarlet: this may be to indicate that it stood outside the tent, and was of a lower order of holiness), and this in turn by a hide covering. Only the Ark has the cloth outside the hide, so that it will stand out on the march. *the Veil of the screen*: cp. 3: 31.

6. *a covering of porpoise-hide*: this translation (or the 'hide of sea-cow' of the footnote) is suggested on the basis of an Arabic word similar to the Hebrew, which means dolphin. But it is unlikely that such a skin would be considered 'clean' for the purposes here in mind, or that the author would have thought of it as available to the Israelites in the desert. We cannot be sure what animal is referred to, but 'goatskin' at least must be ruled out.

7–14. On the objects in the tent cp. on 3: 31. *the Bread regularly presented* (verse 7), also called the 'Bread of the Presence' or 'shewbread' (Exod. 25: 30), consists of twelve loaves of bread set out in the sanctuary and renewed each week (Lev. 24: 5–9). It was perhaps originally thought of as food for God, but is later probably thought of as an acknowledgement of his continuing generosity to his people.

15. *they must not touch it on pain of death*: the sanctity of the Ark is emphasized again; cp. how Uzzah is struck dead for touching the Ark in 2 Sam. 6: 6–7.

16. Eleazar has general oversight of the Tabernacle, and care for the specific objects listed, which the Kohathites are not to touch. This oversight is a task of the priests in later times too. *the regular grain-offering*: fine flour is offered to God daily in the temple, in an older tradition in the late afternoon (1 Kings 18: 29, 36), later, both morning and evening (Num. 28: 1–8).

17–20. Another warning is given of the danger that derives from the sanctity of the Ark.

21–8. The Gershonites have the duties already outlined in 3: 24–6, of carrying all the hangings and coverings. They are placed under the direction of Ithamar, the younger surviving son of Aaron, and therefore himself a Kohathite (cp. 3: 19 and Exod. 6: 18 and 20).

29–33. The Merarites carry the wooden framework of the Tabernacle, and everything else of wood (as in 3: 36–7), and are again put under the direction of Ithamar. ✳

CENSUS OF THE LEVITES OF AGE FOR SERVICE

Moses and Aaron and the chiefs of the community made 34 a detailed list of the Kohathites by families in the father's line, taking all between the ages of thirty and fifty who 35 came on duty to perform service in the Tent of the Presence. The number recorded by families in the de- 36 tailed lists was two thousand seven hundred and fifty. This was the total number in the detailed lists of the 37 Kohathite families who did duty in the Tent of the Presence; they were recorded by Moses and Aaron as the LORD had told them to do through Moses.

The Gershonites between the ages of thirty and fifty, 38–39 who came on duty for service in the Tent of the Presence, were recorded in detailed lists by families in the father's line. Their number, by families in the father's line, was 40 two thousand six hundred and thirty. This was the total 41 recorded in the lists of the Gershonite families who came on duty in the Tent of the Presence, and were recorded by Moses and Aaron as the LORD had told them to do.

The families of Merari, between the ages of thirty and 42–43 fifty, who came on duty to perform service in the Tent of the Presence, were recorded in detailed lists by families in the father's line. Their number by families was three 44 thousand two hundred. These were recorded in the 45

Merarite families by Moses and Aaron as the LORD had told them to do through Moses.

46 Thus Moses and Aaron and the chiefs of Israel made a detailed list of all the Levites by families in the father's 47 line, between the ages of thirty and fifty years; these were all who came to perform their various duties and carry their loads in the service of the Tent of the Presence. 48 Their number was eight thousand five hundred and 49 eighty. They were recorded one by one by Moses at the command of the LORD, according to their general duty and the loads they carried.[a] For so the LORD had told Moses to do.

✶ The numbers of Levites of age for service are given in order to impress their importance on the reader. The figures have been related to the figures for the total number of Levites in ch. 3, although all are in fact higher than the usual proportion of males of thirty to fifty to total population, which is about one-eighth. They are again the composition of P. ✶

EXCLUSION OF UNCLEAN PERSONS FROM THE CAMP

5 1,2 The LORD spoke to Moses and said: Command the Israelites to expel from the camp everyone who suffers from a malignant skin-disease or a discharge, and everyone 3 ritually unclean from contact with a corpse. You shall put them outside the camp, both male and female, so that they will not defile your camps in which I dwell 4 among you.[b] The Israelites did this: they put them outside the camp. As the LORD had said when he spoke to Moses, so the Israelites did.

[a] *Prob. rdg.; Heb. adds* and his registered ones.
[b] *So Pesh.; Heb.* their camps . . . among them.

✻ Chs. 5 and 6 come between the ordering of the camp and the preparations for departure. They turn from narrative to laws. These are on an apparently miscellaneous collection of subjects, both rules and rituals, but have more unity than at first sight appears, for they all imply that the people as it sets off must be pure and holy. Each section illustrates this in a different way.

These first verses direct that all unclean persons should be excluded from the camp. This applies to those with a skin-disease, and those who have had contact with a corpse. To P both are contagious forms of pollution. At an early stage of human thought, which still survives among many peoples to this day, there is a close connection between ideas of holiness, purity and taboo. That which is holy is 'clean', and is to be kept rigidly away from that which is 'unclean'. P sees the purity of the camp as so important that a standard of purity must be demanded which is otherwise applied only in a sacred war (cp. Deut. 23: 9–14) or to the priesthood (Lev. 22: 4): since God is himself present the camp must not be defiled.

2. *a malignant skin-disease*: the subject is dealt with in full detail in Lev. 13. The term used here was until recently trans-lated 'leprosy', but the detail of Lev. 13 does not fit the characteristic symptoms of true leprosy; in fact the disease now commonly known as leprosy does not appear to have been known in the Near East in biblical times. It is skin-diseases with open or running sores that are referred to, such as are common in tropical climates to this day. *or a discharge*: this refers to infectious discharges from the genital organs, which are dealt with in detail in Lev. 15. *contact with a corpse*: dealt with later, in Num. 19. *outside the camp*: where they are to go, and whether they die or not, are questions P does not raise. The camp must be undefiled. ✻

41

PAYMENT IN COMPENSATION FOR WRONGS

5, 6 The LORD spoke to Moses and said, Say to the Israelites: When anyone, man or woman, wrongs another and thereby breaks faith with the LORD, that person has 7 incurred guilt which demands reparation. He shall confess the sin he has committed, make restitution in full with the addition of one fifth, and give it to the man to 8 whom compensation is due. If there is no next-of-kin to whom compensation can be paid, the compensation payable in that case shall be the LORD's, for the use of the priest, in addition to the ram of expiation with which the priest makes expiation for him.

9 Every contribution made by way of holy-gift which 10 the Israelites bring to the priest shall be the priest's. The priest shall have the holy-gifts which a man gives; whatever is given to him shall be his.

* The presence of God in the camp demands not only ritual but also ethical purity. The law on restitution given in Lev. 6: 1–7 is restated, and then an added provision made for cases where the man wronged is dead and there is no heir. Compensation then goes instead to the priest as God's representative, who must also receive the regular offering he would get anyway.

7. *with the addition of one fifth*: if, for instance, a man has robbed another of a hundred pieces of silver, he must repay a hundred and twenty. This is the compensation laid down in other cases too where recompense is required, such as the redemption of an unclean animal that has been the subject of a vow (Lev. 27: 11–13), or of tithe (Lev. 27: 31).

8. *next-of-kin*: an important position in Israelite law. The next-of-kin is brother, uncle, cousin (both of these on the

father's side) or other kinsman, whichever is the nearest relation; and his duties include buying back an estate which a kinsman has sold through poverty, and buying back the kinsman himself if he has become a slave through poverty (Lev. 25: 25, 47–52), as well as avenging his death if he is murdered (Num. 35). We have a picture in Ruth 3–4 of a next-of-kin passing on his responsibility for Ruth to Boaz, who was next in line after him. *the ram of expiation*: the regular offering.

9. *holy-gift*: this is any gift freely given or vowed to God.

10. This emphasizes that each priest shall himself keep a gift made to him. ✳

TRIAL BY ORDEAL OF A WIFE SUSPECTED OF ADULTERY

The LORD spoke to Moses and said, Speak to the Israel- 11, 12
ites in these words: When a married woman goes astray,
is unfaithful to her husband, and has sexual intercourse 13
with another man, and this happens without the husband's knowledge, and the crime is undetected, because,
though she has been defiled, there is no direct evidence
against her and she was not caught in the act, but when in 14
such a case a fit of jealousy comes over the husband
which causes him to suspect his wife, she being in fact
defiled; or when, on the other hand, a fit of jealousy
comes over a husband which causes him to suspect his
wife, when she is not in fact defiled; then in either case, 15
the husband shall bring his wife to the priest together
with the prescribed offering for her, a tenth of an ephah
of barley meal. He shall not pour oil on it nor put
frankincense on it, because it is a grain-offering for

jealousy, a grain-offering of protestation conveying an
16 imputation of guilt. The priest shall bring her forward
17 and set her before the LORD. He shall take clean*a* water
in an earthenware vessel, and shall take dust from the
18 floor of the Tabernacle and add it to the water. He shall
set the woman before the LORD, uncover her head, and
place the grain-offering of protestation in her hands; it is
a grain-offering for jealousy. The priest shall hold in his
own hand the water of contention which brings out the
19 truth. He shall then put the woman on oath and say to
her, 'If no man has had intercourse with you, if you have
not gone astray and let yourself become defiled while
owing obedience to your husband, then may your
innocence be established by the water of contention which
20 brings out the truth. But if, while owing him obedience,
you have gone astray and let yourself become defiled, if
any man other than your husband has had intercourse
21 with you' (the priest shall here put the woman on oath
with an adjuration, and shall continue), 'may the LORD
make an example of you among your people in adjura-
tions and in swearing of oaths by bringing upon you
22 miscarriage and untimely birth;*b* and this water that
brings out the truth shall enter your body, bringing upon
you miscarriage and untimely birth.' The woman shall
23 respond, 'Amen, Amen.' The priest shall write these
curses on a scroll and wash them off into the water of
24 contention; he shall make the woman drink the water
that brings out the truth, and the water shall enter her

[a] *Or* holy.
[b] *Lit.* by making your thigh to fall and your belly to melt away;
similarly in verses 22 and 27.

body. The priest shall take the grain-offering for jealousy 25
from the woman's hand, present it as a special gift before
the LORD, and offer it at the altar. He shall take a handful 26
from the grain-offering by way of token, and burn it at
the altar; after this he shall make the woman drink the
water. If she has let herself become defiled and has been 27
unfaithful to her husband, then when the priest makes her
drink the water that brings out the truth and the water has
entered her body, she will suffer a miscarriage or untimely
birth, and her name will become an example in adjuration among her kin. But if the woman has not let herself 28
become defiled and is pure, then her innocence is established and she will bear her child.

Such is the law for cases of jealousy, where a woman, 29
owing obedience to her husband, goes astray and lets
herself become defiled, or where a fit of jealousy comes 30
over a man which causes him to suspect his wife. He shall
set her before the LORD, and the priest shall deal with her
as this law prescribes. No guilt will attach to the husband, 31
but the woman shall bear the penalty of her guilt.

* The need for purity in the community naturally includes
purity in family life. For adultery there was an established
penalty of death (Lev. 20: 10; Deut. 22: 22). When a woman
is suspected of adultery by her husband (even if only in a fit
of jealousy) but he cannot prove it, he can make her undergo
an ordeal, consisting of drinking the 'water of contention',
water containing dust from the floor of the Tabernacle. If
she is innocent nothing happens; if she has lied she suffers a
miscarriage. Though this is not stated, the woman must
clearly already be pregnant, and this is no doubt at the root of
the husband's suspicions.

The ordeal used to be a very common part of legal systems, ancient and mediaeval, including our own. It takes many forms, but in all of them the accused puts his innocence to the test by an external procedure, such as being thrown into deep water, or walking through fire: if unhurt he is innocent. The custom is extremely ancient. It does, however misguidedly, attempt to introduce an element of objectivity into justice, and it need not surprise us that Israel shared it. What is perhaps odder is that there are no other cases for which according to the Bible it is regularly used (perhaps Israel had other uses of the ordeal, already dropped by the time this was written). We do however have a similar procedure in Exod. 32: 20, where Moses grinds the forbidden golden calf to powder, sprinkles it on water, and makes the Israelites drink it; and this may be an allusion to an ordeal ritual of the time when this is written. In the present chapter there is already a development from a primitive idea in that the water is not thought to work automatically, but through the action of God (verse 21). There is a one-sidedness in that only the woman is accused, and the man is expressly declared guiltless even if his charge fails; but such a practice corresponds to the way of thought of the time. However, the humanity of the test should be noticed; no one suffers a miscarriage from the purely physical effects of drinking water with dust in; only a guilty conscience could in such circumstances possibly induce one. A guilty woman may sometimes have escaped detection, but at least the ordeal is not such as to lead to the death of the innocent, as was sometimes the case elsewhere.

14. *a fit of jealousy*: literally a 'spirit' of jealousy. In the Old Testament 'spirit' is used of the wind, and also of an overpowering rush of feeling upon a man, as for example when the spirit of the LORD gives strength to Samson (Judg. 14: 6) or comes upon the elders (Num. 11: 25). *which causes him to suspect his wife*: the rights of the husband are extremely extensive; he may for instance revoke a vow his wife has made to God (30: 10–14).

15. *a tenth of an ephah*: this is a small quantity, 7½ pints (3 or 4 litres). The ephah is a dry measure. *barley meal*: a coarse meal not mentioned otherwise in P, nor in connection with sacrifice, where a fine meal is usual. This may then be the survival of a more primitive usage. *He shall not pour oil on it*: oil and frankincense are used in ordinary sacrifice in P (Lev. 2: 1); their absence is a reminder that this is not a joyful occasion but an ordeal.

16. *before the LORD*: so the case is brought under God's cognizance. Similarly we have an instance of oath-taking 'before thy altar' in 1 Kings 8: 31f.

17. *clean water*: the sense in the footnote, 'holy water', is more probably right. It means water kept in the sanctuary. *dust from the floor of the Tabernacle*: it will be sacred by contact, and will increase the sacredness of the drink, and its danger to a woman who is guilty.

18. *uncover her head*: as a sign probably of shame and mourning. *the water of contention which brings out the truth*: a difficult phrase, more often translated 'the waters of bitterness, which bring a curse'. The exact sense cannot be settled, but it is a technical term in this context, and comes again in verses 19, 22, 24 and 27.

21. *the priest shall here put the woman on oath*: this is a rubric, or liturgical instruction, set within the words of the priest, and so rightly put in brackets. *with an adjuration*: that is, he solemnly charges her to tell the truth. *miscarriage and untimely birth*: this is the most probable meaning of the words given literally in the footnote, which are a euphemism.

22. *'Amen, Amen'*: this is a strong expression of agreement, as 'Amen' often is in the New Testament too (cp. e.g. John 1: 51 for 'Amen, Amen'; N.E.B. 'In truth, in very truth'). The woman recognizes formally the effectiveness of the ordeal procedure.

23. *on a scroll*: a piece of parchment. In the same way in Tibet and India charms are written out and eaten and believed to be effective. In Israel itself Ezekiel was given a

scroll to eat 'written all over on both sides with dirges and laments and words of woe' (Ezek. 2: 9–10).

25. The account of the offering is probably a later addition to the story, which was then tied in by the awkward repetition of the priest making the woman drink the water (verse 26). While special forms of sacrifice are envisaged in this chapter, the *grain-offering* (see on 4: 16) is in accordance with the general rules in Lev. 2.

27–8. P assumes that the ordeal will 'work' by God's providential intervention. We could ourselves expect the woman to suffer no harm in any case unless through the effects of her own guilty mind working on her body.

29–31. The passage is rounded off by a tidy summary, which looks back to verses 12–14. ✲

THE LAW ON NAZIRITES: THE BASIC REGULATIONS

6 1, 2 The LORD spoke to Moses and said, Speak to the Israelites in these words: When anyone, man or woman, makes a special*a* vow dedicating himself to the LORD as a Nazirite,*b*
3 he shall abstain from wine and strong drink. These he shall not drink, nor anything made from the juice of
4 grapes; nor shall he eat grapes, fresh or dried. During the whole term of his vow he shall eat nothing that comes from the vine, nothing whatever, shoot or berry.*c*
5 During the whole term of his vow no razor shall touch his head; he shall let his hair grow long and plait it until he has completed the term of his dedication; he shall keep
6 himself holy to the LORD. During the whole term of his
7 vow he shall not go near a corpse, not even when his father or mother, brother or sister, dies; he shall not make

[a] makes a special: *or* performs a . . .
[b] *That is* separated one *or* dedicated one.
[c] *The two Hebrew words are of uncertain meaning.*

himself ritually unclean for them, because the Nazirite vow to his God is on his head. He shall keep himself holy 8 to the LORD during the whole term of his Nazirite vow.

If someone suddenly falls dead by his side touching 9 him and thereby making his hair, which has been dedicated, ritually unclean, he shall shave his head seven days later, on the day appointed for his ritual cleansing. On the 10 eighth day he shall bring two turtle-doves or two young pigeons to the priest at the entrance to the Tent of the Presence. The priest shall offer one as a sin-offering and the 11 other as a whole-offering and shall make expiation for him for the sin he has incurred through contact with the dead body; and he shall consecrate his head afresh on that day. The man shall re-dedicate himself to the LORD for 12 the term of his vow and bring a yearling ram as a guilt-offering. The previous period shall not be reckoned, because the hair which he dedicated became unclean.

✻ The Priestly writer goes on to set out the law about an institution whereby men could consecrate themselves to the service of God. This chapter is thus connected to the preceding one by the theme of the special holiness of the people of God.

The Nazirite is a man dedicated to God. The earliest instance we know of a man called by this title is that of Samson, 'a Nazirite consecrated to God from the day of his birth' (Judg. 13: 5). He is a Nazirite for life; a man devoted to God, rather than a pious man. His great renown is his long hair (worn because he is a Nazirite) which gives him his strength. Samuel, though he is not called a Nazirite, is given to God, and may not shave (1 Sam. 1: 11). Amos treats the existence of Nazirites, who do not drink wine, as due to a great act of God, parallel with the deliverance from Egypt and the institution of prophecy (Amos 2: 10f.). John the Baptist, called by

God from birth, living in the desert, never taking 'wine or strong drink' (Luke 1: 15), although he is not called a Nazirite, is a man in the same mould.

In this chapter we have a later development (after the exile) of this lifelong Naziriteship into a temporary vow. We cannot tell certainly when the change took place. It is not here presented as an innovation, but as established practice, and after the exile there is in fact no evidence that lifelong Naziriteship survived as an institution. Neither the circumstances in which men chose to be Nazirites, nor the period, are here mentioned. At the time of Christ we hear of Paul paying the expenses of a group of four men (Acts 21: 23f.) who are under a vow, although the word Nazirite is not used; and though the institution did not survive into Christianity (nor indeed into modern Judaism) the ideal of the man wholly devoted to God, standing apart from other men by abstinence and special clothing, has remained deeply embedded to this day in the monastic tradition of Christianity, and continues to evoke respect.

2. *as a Nazirite*: the footnote gives the literal meaning of the word.

3. The first specific condition is abstinence, not only from *strong drink*, but from everything connected with the grape. This condition does not apply directly to the lifelong Nazirite before the exile, but the mother of Samson had to abstain from wine and strong drink (see Judg. 13: 4, 14); and such abstinence is the special characteristic of the Rechabites, a group somewhat like the Nazirites, abstaining from wine and living in tents (see Jer. 35, especially verse 6).

5. The second condition is that (like Samson, cp. Judg. 13: 5; 16: 17) he remains untouched by a razor as a sign of his holiness. Hair occupies a special place in the thought of many nations, and in a religious context will either be kept uncut (as was the case with a high Roman priest of Jupiter, the Flamen Dialis) or shorn right off (as with Egyptian, or with modern Buddhist, priests).

6. *he shall not go near a corpse*: the third condition. The Nazirite is defiled by contact with any dead body. This rule is stricter than in the case of ordinary priests (for whom relatives are excepted, Lev. 21: 1–2), and is otherwise applied so strictly only to the high priest (Lev. 21: 11).

9. It is next laid down what the Nazirite shall do if he accidentally infringes these rules by touching a dead body. His vow is void, and he must offer sacrifice, and begin the vow again. His hair is shorn off, and (according to a later Jewish tradition) is so utterly unclean that it must be, not simply burned, but buried.

10. These birds are usually provided as a substitute for a more expensive form of sacrifice, for example by a woman in childbirth (Lev. 12: 8, cp. Luke 2: 24), or by a sufferer from a skin-disease as a purification offering (Lev. 14: 22). Here they are all that is required. It is not clear why.

11–12. A *sin-offering* is made to bring back into a right relationship with God a man who has come into contact with impurity, broken a taboo or violated a cultic law (that is, one about the manner or form of public worship). So here a sin-offering is required because the Nazirite's sin was inadvertent. The *whole-offering* is one in which the sacrificial animal is consumed completely, and not eaten at all by priest and worshipper. It is here required because the Nazirite is appearing before God. The *guilt-offering* is a punitive fine, paid to God for the loss of what was his due (cp. Lev. 14: 12). It is only incorporated in the sacrificial system at the time of P, but is clearly known earlier in Israel (so for instance Gen. 26: 10, translated there 'retribution'). It should be carefully noted that *sin-offering* and *guilt-offering*, similar though they sound in English, are quite different from one another, and that neither of them has the sense we might expect of an offering to atone for deliberate sin or for consequent guilt, but the more technical sense just explained. ✶

THE COMPLETION OF THE VOW

¹³ The law for the Nazirite, when the term of his dedication is completed, shall be this. He shall be brought to the
¹⁴ entrance to the Tent of the Presence and shall present his offering to the LORD: one yearling ram without blemish as a whole-offering, one yearling ewe without blemish as a sin-offering, one ram without blemish as a
¹⁵ shared-offering, and a basket of cakes made of flour mixed with oil, and of wafers smeared with oil, both unleavened, together with the proper grain-offerings and
¹⁶ drink-offerings. The priest shall present all these before the LORD and offer the man's sin-offering and whole-
¹⁷ offering; the ram he shall offer as a shared-offering to the LORD, together with the basket of unleavened cakes and
¹⁸ the proper grain-offering and drink-offering. The Nazirite shall shave his head at the entrance to the Tent of the Presence, take the hair which had been dedicated and put it on the fire where the shared-offering is burn-
¹⁹ ing. The priest shall take the shoulder of the ram, after boiling it, and take also one unleavened cake from the basket and one unleavened wafer, and put them on the palms of the Nazirite's hands, his hair which had been
²⁰ dedicated having been shaved. The priest shall then present them as a special gift before the LORD; these, together with the breast of the special gift and the leg of the contribution, are holy and belong to the priest. When this has been done, the Nazirite is again free to drink wine.
²¹ Such is the law for the Nazirite who has made his vow. Such is the offering he must make to the LORD for his

dedication, apart from anything else that he can afford. He must carry out his vow in full according to the law governing his dedication.

* The other interest of the author is in the ceremonies on completion of the vow. This comes in three parts: the Nazirite offers sacrifices (verses 13–17); he shaves his head and throws the hair in the fire (verse 18); and the priest takes his share of the sacrificial gifts (verses 19–20). It can be assumed that a sacrificial feast then followed, although this is not mentioned.

14. *his offering*: the Nazirite must bring all the regular forms of offering. *shared-offering*: a sacrifice of thanksgiving, in which only part of the animal is burnt on the altar, and the rest consumed by priest and offerer. It is seen as establishing a close communion with God, because God and the worshipper each have a part of the animal.

15. *drink-offerings*: offerings of wine poured out on the ground, not consumed by the worshipper.

18. *and put it on the fire*: this is not intended as another sacrifice, but as the total annihilation of the consecrated object once it has fulfilled its function, so that it cannot be profaned.

19. The priest's share is put in the hands of the offerer, so that he can present it back to the priest.

20. The breast and the leg are the priest's due from every offering (Lev. 7: 34); the other gifts are special to this occasion, and *special gift* is a technical term for them; it used to be translated 'wave offering' on the assumption that it was waved before the altar by the priest, but the view is now preferred that it does not imply movement, and is a term borrowed from Babylonia during the exile, with the sense of 'special contribution'.

21. *apart from anything else that he can afford*: this is only the minimum. The man can make extra offerings, as he can make extra vows for a longer period.

So the vow has been carried out in full, and the Nazirite returns to ordinary life, having given to God his period of special devotion. ✶

THE PRIESTS' BLESSING

22,23 The LORD spoke to Moses and said, Speak to Aaron and his sons in these words: These are the words with which you shall bless the Israelites:

24   The LORD bless you and watch over you;
25   the LORD make his face shine upon[a] you
            and be gracious to you;
26   the LORD look kindly on you and give you peace.

27 They shall pronounce my name over the Israelites, and I will bless them.

✶ This new section is perhaps included to show God's blessing as a response to acts of voluntary devotion like a Nazirite vow. It is one of the functions of the priests to bless (so Deut. 21: 5), to pray for God to favour and prosper those he is addressing, and in the act of so praying effectively to ensure it. The place for this is primarily in the sanctuary, when the participants are being dismissed after an act of worship (so Lev. 9: 22 or 2 Sam. 6: 18, an instance where the king takes on himself a priestly role). The blessing here given, which is addressed to 'you' in the singular, is not in typical P language, and is probably much older; older too than Ps. 67: 1, which is inspired by it. It is written in a cumulative metrical pattern (one verse of three words, one of five, one of seven), of lines each with two halves which complement one another. It is one of the finest pieces of poetry in P; and has passed into constant Christian use to this day.

[a] *Or* to.

22. *Aaron and his sons*: all the priests, down to the writer's time.

25. *make his face shine upon you*: a figure of speech for 'look (now) upon you with favour'. It is not a lasting state but an action.

26. *look kindly on you*: literally 'lift up his face to you', in friendship, as to 'hide the face' means to be angry (Deut. 31: 18 is an example). *and give you peace:* peace in the broadest sense, for which there is no single word in English, good health, prosperity, happiness; both this-worldly well-being and a right relationship with God. It is the regular word of greeting in Hebrew, *shālōm*, equivalent of the Arabic *salaam*.

27. *pronounce my name*: to claim the people as the people of God. In Israel God has a specific personal name, 'Yahweh'. Pronouncing this name over the people is itself felt to be effective as a blessing, because this indicates that they are his. ✳

THE OFFERINGS OF THE CHIEF MEN: WAGONS AND OXEN

On the day that Moses completed the setting up of the 7 Tabernacle, he anointed and consecrated it; he also anointed and consecrated its equipment, and the altar and its vessels. The chief men of Israel, heads of families – that 2 is the chiefs of the tribes, who had assisted in preparing the detailed lists – came forward and brought their offer- 3 ing before the LORD, six covered wagons and twelve oxen, one wagon from every two chiefs and from each one an ox.[a] These they brought forward before the Tabernacle; and the LORD spoke to Moses and said, 4 'Accept these from them: they shall be used for the 5 service of the Tent of the Presence. Assign them to the Levites as their several duties require.'

[a] *Or* a bull.

6 So Moses accepted the wagons and oxen and assigned
7 them to the Levites. He gave two wagons and four oxen
8 to the Gershonites as required for their service; four
   wagons and eight oxen to the Merarites as required for
   their service, in charge of Ithamar the son of Aaron the
9 priest. He gave none to the Kohathites because the service
   laid upon them was that of the holy things: these they
   had to carry themselves on their shoulders.

* Chs. 7–9 complete this section of P's work with a description of cultic preparations for the departure of the Israelites. The reason for the arrangement of the material is not
immediately obvious, but is probably by association of ideas.
The sacrifices and offerings of the Nazirite vow lead on here
to the thought of the offerings made before departure. First,
to make the move of the Ark possible, each chief gives an
ox and every two chiefs a wagon, which are divided between
the two groups who have to transport articles this way (this
refers back to 4: 21–33).

1. *On the day that Moses completed*: this dating takes us back
to one month before the beginning of the book of Numbers.
This is a flashback. It is not an instance of carelessness, for this
earlier date comes again in 9: 1 and 9: 15. *he anointed and
consecrated it*: this carries out the command given in Exod.
40: 9–10.

2. *The chief men of Israel*: these are the same chiefs already
listed in 1: 5–15, as is seen from the names given in verses 12,
18, etc.

3. *six covered wagons and twelve oxen*: two to pull each
wagon.

8. *four wagons and eight oxen to the Merarites*: 4: 31–3
assigned them a bulkier and heavier load than that of the
Gershonites.

9. *because the service laid upon them was that of the holy things*:
the special care that is proper to the Ark and the contents of

the Tabernacle is emphasized again. In fact the Ark was carried on a cart in the time of David (2 Sam. 6: 3). It is carried by men's arms in Jerusalem (2 Sam. 6: 13 and 15: 24), perhaps at first because carts could not be used there easily; and so the belief grew that it was too holy to be carried except by men (and, later, by specially appointed men, the Levites). ✳

OFFERINGS OF THE CHIEF MEN:
GIFTS FOR ALL THE DIFFERENT FORMS OF SACRIFICE

When the altar was anointed, the chiefs brought their gift 10 for its dedication and presented their offering before it. The LORD said to Moses, 'Let the chiefs present their 11 offering for the dedication of the altar one by one, on consecutive days.'

The chief who presented his offering on the first day 12 was Nahshon son of Amminadab of the tribe of Judah. His offering was one silver dish weighing a hundred and 13 thirty shekels by the sacred standard and one silver tossing bowl weighing seventy, both full of flour mixed with oil as a grain-offering; one saucer weighing ten gold 14 shekels, full of incense; one young bull, one full-grown 15 ram, and one yearling ram, as a whole-offering; one 16 he-goat as a sin-offering; and two bulls, five full-grown 17 rams, five he-goats, and five yearling rams, as a shared-offering. This was the offering of Nahshon son of Amminadab.

On the second day Nethaneel son of Zuar, chief of 18 Issachar, brought his offering. He brought one silver dish 19 weighing a hundred and thirty shekels by the sacred standard and one silver tossing-bowl weighing seventy, both full of flour mixed with oil as a grain-offering; one 20

21 saucer weighing ten gold shekels, full of incense; one
young bull, one full-grown ram, and one yearling ram, as
22, 23 a whole-offering; one he-goat as a sin-offering; and two
bulls, five full-grown rams, five he-goats, and five yearling rams, as a shared-offering. This was the offering of
Nethaneel son of Zuar.

24   On the third day the chief of the Zebulunites, Eliab
25 son of Helon, came. His offering was one silver dish
weighing a hundred and thirty shekels by the sacred
standard and one silver tossing-bowl weighing seventy,
26 both full of flour mixed with oil as a grain-offering, one
27 saucer weighing ten gold shekels, full of incense; one
young bull, one full-grown ram, and one yearling ram,
28, 29 as a whole-offering; one he-goat as a sin-offering; and
two bulls, five full-grown rams, five he-goats, and five
yearling rams, as a shared-offering. This was the offering
of Eliab son of Helon.

30   On the fourth day the chief of the Reubenites, Elizur
31 son of Shedeur, came. His offering was one silver dish
weighing a hundred and thirty shekels by the sacred
standard and one silver tossing-bowl weighing seventy,
32 both full of flour mixed with oil as a grain-offering; one
33 saucer weighing ten gold shekels, full of incense; one
young bull, one full-grown ram, and one yearling ram,
34, 35 as a whole-offering; one he-goat as a sin-offering; and
two bulls, five full-grown rams, five he-goats, and
five yearling rams, as a shared-offering. This was the
offering of Elizur son of Shedeur.

36   On the fifth day the chief of the Simeonites, Shelumiel
37 son of Zurishaddai, came. His offering was one silver
dish weighing a hundred and thirty shekels by the sacred

standard and one silver tossing-bowl weighing seventy,
both full of flour mixed with oil as a grain-offering;
one saucer weighing ten gold shekels, full of incense; 38
one young bull, one full-grown ram, and one yearling 39
ram, as a whole offering; one he-goat as a sin-offering; 40
and two bulls, five full-grown rams, five he-goats, and 41
five yearling rams, as a shared-offering. This was the
offering of Shelumiel son of Zurishaddai.

On the sixth day the chief of the Gadites, Eliasaph son 42
of Reuel,[a] came. His offering was one silver dish weighing 43
a hundred and thirty shekels by the sacred standard and
one silver tossing-bowl weighing seventy, both full of
flour mixed with oil as a grain-offering; one saucer 44
weighing ten gold shekels, full of incense; one young 45
bull, one full-grown ram, and one yearling ram, as a
whole-offering; one he-goat as a sin-offering; and two 46, 47
bulls, five full-grown rams, five he-goats, and five
yearling rams, as a shared-offering. This was the offering
of Eliasaph son of Reuel.[a]

On the seventh day the chief of the Ephraimites, 48
Elishama son of Ammihud, came. His offering was one 49
silver dish weighing a hundred and thirty shekels by the
sacred standard and one silver tossing-bowl weighing
seventy, both full of flour mixed with oil as a grain-
offering; one saucer weighing ten gold shekels, full of 50
incense; one young bull, one full-grown ram, and one 51
yearling ram, as a whole-offering; one he-goat as a 52
sin-offering; and two bulls, five full-grown rams, five 53
he-goats, and five yearling rams, as a shared-offering.
This was the offering of Elishama son of Ammihud.

[a] *So Sept. (cp. 1: 14; 2: 14); Heb.* Deuel.

59

54 On the eighth day the chief of the Manassites, Gamaliel
55 son of Pedahzur, came. His offering was one silver dish
weighing a hundred and thirty shekels by the sacred
standard and one silver tossing-bowl weighing seventy,
both full of flour mixed with oil as a grain-offering;
56, 57 one saucer weighing ten gold shekels, full of incense; one
young bull, one full-grown ram, and one yearling ram,
58, 59 as a whole-offering; one he-goat as a sin-offering; and
two bulls, five full-grown rams, five he-goats, and five
yearling rams, as a shared-offering. This was the offering
of Gamaliel son of Pedahzur.

60 On the ninth day the chief of the Benjamites, Abidan
61 son of Gideoni, came. His offering was one silver dish
weighing a hundred and thirty shekels by the sacred
standard and one silver tossing-bowl weighing seventy,
both full of flour mixed with oil as a grain-offering;
62 one saucer weighing ten gold shekels, full of incense;
63 one young bull, one full-grown ram, and one yearling
64 ram, as a whole-offering; one he-goat as a sin-offering;
65 and two bulls, five full-grown rams, five he-goats, and
five yearling rams, as a shared-offering. This was the
offering of Abidan son of Gideoni.

66 On the tenth day the chief of the Danites, Ahiezer
67 son of Ammishaddai, came. His offering was one silver
dish weighing a hundred and thirty shekels by the sacred
standard and one silver tossing-bowl weighing seventy,
both full of flour mixed with oil as a grain-offering;
68, 69 one saucer weighing ten gold shekels, full of incense; one
young bull, one full-grown ram, and one yearling ram,
70, 71 as a whole-offering; one he-goat as a sin-offering; and
two bulls, five full-grown rams, five he-goats, and five

yearling rams, as a shared-offering. This was the offering
of Ahiezer son of Ammishaddai.

On the eleventh day the chief of the Asherites, Pagiel 72
son of Ocran, came. His offering was one silver dish 73
weighing a hundred and thirty shekels by the sacred
standard and one silver tossing-bowl weighing seventy,
both full of flour mixed with oil as a grain-offering; one 74
saucer weighing ten gold shekels, full of incense; one 75
young bull, one full-grown ram, and one yearling ram,
as a whole-offering; one he-goat as a sin-offering; and 76,77
two bulls, five full-grown rams, five he-goats, and five
yearling rams, as a shared-offering. This was the offering
of Pagiel son of Ocran.

On the twelfth day the chief of the Naphtalites, Ahira 78
son of Enan, came. His offering was one silver dish 79
weighing a hundred and thirty shekels by the sacred
standard and one silver tossing-bowl weighing seventy,
both full of flour mixed with oil as a grain-offering; one 80
saucer weighing ten gold shekels, full of incense; one 81
young bull, one full-grown ram, and one yearling ram,
as a whole-offering; one he-goat as a sin-offering; and 82,83
two bulls, five full-grown rams, five he-goats, and five
yearling rams, as a shared-offering. This was the offering
of Ahira son of Enan.

This was the gift from the chiefs of Israel for the dedica- 84
tion of the altar when it was anointed: twelve silver dishes,
twelve silver tossing-bowls, and twelve golden saucers;
each silver dish weighed a hundred and thirty shekels, 85
each silver tossing-bowl seventy shekels. The total
weight of the silver vessels was two thousand four hundred shekels by the sacred standard. There were twelve 86

golden saucers full of incense, ten shekels each by the sacred standard: the total weight of the gold of the
87 saucers was a hundred and twenty shekels. The number of beasts for the whole-offering was twelve bulls, twelve full-grown rams, and twelve yearling rams, with the prescribed grain-offerings, and twelve he-goats for the
88 sin-offering. The number of beasts for the shared-offering was twenty-four bulls, sixty full-grown rams, sixty he-goats, and sixty yearling rams. This was the gift for the dedication of the altar when it was anointed.

* Each of the chiefs makes identical offerings on successive days to make possible the different forms of sacrificial worship, and with each the full details are repeated. Then the grand totals of the gifts are also given. The intention is no doubt to provoke the author's contemporaries to equally generous giving to the temple (as in the similar account of generous giving in 1 Chron. 29). Most modern taste finds the repetition without alteration of these verses tedious; but the author intends it as a gracious and satisfying way of underlining the generosity, which becomes ever more satisfying as it is repeated. The repetition is to have a cumulative effect, rather like the build-up of 'the Twelve Days of Christmas' or of 'One Man Went to Mow'. The setting in the wilderness can here be seen to be quite artificial; the richness of the offerings shows that the writer is thinking of the worship of the established temple of a later age.

10. *the altar* is for P at the very centre of the cult, and is what makes sacrifice possible.

12. *The chief*: the order of chiefs and of tribes is the same as in ch. 2.

13–17. The gifts make possible the first 'grain-offering', 'whole-offering', 'sin-offering' and 'shared-offering' (on these see respectively the notes on 4: 16; 6: 11; and 6: 14).

The animals are brought alive, the flour and oil for cereal offerings in costly vessels. The author does not of course turn to the question where all these can be obtained in the wilderness.

13f. *weighing a hundred and thirty shekels*: the silver dishes are roughly 1500 grams, the silver tossing-bowls 800 grams, and the gold saucers 115 grams. A *tossing-bowl* is used in the ritual of sacrifice to throw the animal's blood upon the altar. ✻

THE VOICE OF GOD SPEAKS TO MOSES

And when Moses entered the Tent of the Presence to 89 speak with God, he heard the Voice speaking from above the cover over the Ark of the Tokens from between the two cherubim: the Voice spoke to him.

✻ This verse is not closely connected with its context. Much is obscure about it, for it seems to be an account of a single incident, which does not however tell us what it was that the voice said. The voice must be the voice of God. It is clear that the verse is a counterpart to, and fulfilment of, Exod. 25: 22, where this meeting is promised. It may be simply put here to show that that promise was fulfilled, or it may be a fragment of a fuller narrative. ✻

THE SEVEN LAMPS OF THE LAMP-STAND

The LORD spoke to Moses and said, 'Speak to Aaron in **8** 1,2 these words: "When you mount the seven lamps, see that they shed their light forwards in front of the lamp-stand."' Aaron did this: he mounted the lamps, so as to 3 shed light forwards in front of the lamp-stand, as the LORD had instructed Moses. The lamp-stand was made 4 of beaten-work in gold, as well as the stem and the petals.

Moses made it to match the pattern which the LORD had shown him.

* Another detail is filled in before Israel is ready to depart. Exod. 25: 31–40 gave the instructions for making the lamps, and Exod. 37: 17–24 an account of their making. Now their installation is told. The lamp-stand stands within the Tabernacle, and is the only source of light there, while the Holy of Holies is in darkness.

The sacred light is ancient in Israel. Already at Shiloh there was a 'lamp of God' which burnt all night in Samuel's time (1 Sam. 3: 3), and in Solomon's temple there are ten lampstands of red gold (1 Kings 7: 48f.), replaced by the lampstands here described in the restored temple built after the exile. The basic shape is known from the Arch of Titus in Rome, which portrays a lamp-stand taken from the Jerusalem temple, with a central stem, and three branches on each side curving outwards. It is used today as a distinctive symbol of Judaism.

The lamp was lit only at night, according to Exod. 30: 8; Lev. 24: 1–3. In later times the lamp burns all the time and takes on a symbolic sense as a sign of the presence of God's glory. It is treated as having symbolic meaning in Zechariah's vision, though the lamp there may have a different structure (Zech. 4: 1–3, 11–14). As part of the same religious sense, lights have continued to be used in some churches as a sign of God's presence in them.

2. The lamps were small bowls of oil with wicks on top of the central stem, and of the three arms on either side. Aaron puts them in place after they have been lit. Seven is a number used very frequently, with symbolic overtones, in the Old Testament: cp. the seven days of the week, the seven pillars of wisdom (Prov. 9: 1), the seven-year cycle of famine and plenty (Gen. 41). The reason for this is no longer clear, but the number seven appears to indicate completeness and perfection.

3. *forwards in front of the lamp-stand*: to send light to where the table stood on the north side.

4. *beaten-work in gold*: this is what is known as repoussé work, hammered out of a solid plate of gold, as the trumpets are made of beaten silver (10: 2). *

THE PURIFICATION OF THE LEVITES

The LORD spoke to Moses and said: Take the Levites 5, 6 apart from the rest of the Israelites and cleanse them ritually. This is what you shall do to cleanse them. Sprinkle lustral 7 water over them; they shall then shave their whole bodies, wash their clothes, and so be cleansed. Next, 8 they shall take a young bull as a whole-offering[a] with its prescribed grain-offering, flour mixed with oil; and you shall take a second young bull as a sin-offering. Bring 9 the Levites before the Tent of the Presence and call the whole community of Israelites together. Bring the Levites 10 before the LORD, and let the Israelites lay their hands on their heads. Aaron shall present the Levites before the 11 LORD as a special gift from the Israelites, and they shall be dedicated to the service of the LORD. The Levites shall 12 lay their hands on the heads of the bulls; one bull shall be offered as a sin-offering and the other as a whole-offering to the LORD, to make expiation for the Levites. Then you 13 shall set the Levites before Aaron and his sons, presenting them to the LORD as a special gift. You shall thus separate 14 the Levites from the rest of the Israelites, and they shall be mine.

After this, the Levites shall enter the Tent of the Pres- 15 ence to serve in it, ritually cleansed and presented as a

[a] as a whole-offering: *prob. rdg.; Heb. om.*

16 special gift; for they are given and dedicated to me, out of all the Israelites. I have accepted them as mine in place of all that comes first from the womb, every first child

17 among the Israelites; for every first-born male creature, man or beast, among the Israelites is mine. On the day when I struck down every first-born creature in Egypt, I hallowed all the first-born of the Israelites to myself,

18,19 and I have accepted the Levites in their place. I have given the Levites to Aaron and his sons, dedicated among the Israelites to perform the service of the Israelites in the Tent of the Presence and to make expiation for them, and then no calamity will befall them when they come close to the sanctuary.

20 Moses and Aaron and the whole community of Israelites carried out all the commands the LORD had given to

21 Moses for the dedication of the Levites. The Levites purified themselves of sin and washed their clothes, and Aaron presented them as a special gift before the LORD and made expiation for them, to cleanse them.

22 Then at last they went in to perform their service in the Tent of the Presence, before Aaron and his sons. Thus the commands the LORD had given to Moses concerning the Levites were all carried out.

23,24 The LORD spoke to Moses and said: Touching the Levites: they shall begin their active work in the service of the Tent of the Presence at the age of twenty-five.

25 At the age of fifty a Levite shall retire from regular

26 service and shall serve no longer. He may continue to assist his colleagues in attendance in the Tent of the Presence but shall perform no regular service. This is how you shall arrange the attendance of the Levites.

✳ One further detail is mentioned before the departure. The account of 3: 5–13, which gave the duties of the Levites, is filled out with the addition of a rite of purification, in a desire to supply a formal parallel to the consecration of the priests in Lev. 8: 6–12. The Levites are cleansed from ceremonial pollution, but are not 'consecrated' or made holy as are the priests (Exod. 28: 41 and Lev. 8: 12).

7. *Sprinkle lustral water*: literally 'water of sin', water to clear away sin. The phrase only occurs here, so that we do not know if it means water treated in some way, or just pure water. *shave their whole bodies*: for cleanliness. Herodotus says that the Egyptian priests shaved all over their body every other day. *wash their clothes*: as a layman does, for instance before Sinai (Exod. 19: 14). The priests when consecrated have completely new robes (Exod. 29: 8 and Lev. 8: 13).

10. *lay their hands on their heads*: literally 'lean their hands', not in blessing but in identification, making them their representatives.

12. *as a sin-offering and the other as a whole-offering*: cp. on 6: 11f.

13. The Levites are given to the priests as their servants. *as a special gift*: see on 6: 20.

16–18. This largely repeats 3: 11–13, to emphasize that the LORD takes the Levites as a substitute for the first-born of Israel, who are his due.

19. *and to make expiation for them*: in this case not for past faults, but to prevent them in the future, and especially the intrusion of lay people into the sanctuary.

23–6. This is a later appendage to ch. 8. It enshrines the memory of a particular social situation in Israel after the exile, representing the middle stage in the lowering of the age for beginning service from the thirty of 4: 3 to the twenty of 1 Chron. 23: 24. ✳

THE FIRST PASSOVER AFTER THE EXODUS:
PROVISION FOR A SUPPLEMENTARY PASSOVER

9 In the first month of the second year after they came out of Egypt, the LORD spoke to Moses in the wilderness of
2 Sinai and said, 'Let the Israelites prepare the Passover at
3 the time appointed for it. This shall be between dusk and dark on the fourteenth day of this month, and you shall keep it at this appointed time, observing every rule and
4 custom proper to it.' So Moses told the Israelites to pre-
5 pare the Passover, and they prepared it on the fourteenth day of the first month, between dusk and dark, in the wilderness of Sinai. The Israelites did exactly as the LORD had instructed Moses.

6 It happened that some men were ritually unclean through contact with a corpse and so could not keep the Passover on the right day. They came before Moses and
7 Aaron that same day and said, 'We are unclean through contact with a corpse. Must we therefore be debarred from presenting the LORD's offering at its appointed time
8 with the rest of the Israelites?' Moses answered, 'Wait, and let me hear what commands the LORD has for you.'

9, 10 The LORD spoke to Moses and said, Tell the Israelites: If any one of you or of your descendants is ritually un-clean through contact with a corpse, or if he is away on a long journey, he shall keep a Passover to the LORD none
11 the less. But in that case he shall prepare the victim in the second month, between dusk and dark on the four-teenth day. It shall be eaten with unleavened cakes and
12 bitter herbs; nothing shall be left over till morning, and

no bone of it shall be broken. The Passover shall be kept
exactly as the law prescribes. The man who, being ritually 13
clean and not absent on a journey, neglects to keep the
Passover, shall be cut off from his father's kin, because
he has not presented the LORD's offering at its appointed
time. That man shall accept responsibility for his
sin.

When an alien is settled among you, he also shall keep 14
the Passover to the LORD, observing every rule and custom proper to it. The same law is binding on you all,
alien and native alike.

* To round off the cultic preparations for departure we have
the first feast celebrated after the great liturgical innovations
of Sinai, with rules for those who miss the Passover appended.
There is a parallel for this association of themes in Ezra 6:
16–22, where the Passover is celebrated following the dedication of the second temple and the re-establishment of its
ministry. The Passover is kept, and then a particular problem,
of people unable to keep the Passover on the right day because of ritual uncleanness, is cleared up by the occurrence of
the problem and the giving of a decision on the case by God
(verses 6–12). The pattern of solution of individual cases as a
guide to a principle is a pattern which is found elsewhere in
Numbers too (e.g. 27: 1–11 and 36: 1–12). Provision for a
Passover in the second month instead of in the first, and so
a full month late, is found otherwise only in Chronicles
(2 Chron. 30: 1–3) as having been made by Hezekiah when he
included the people of the northern kingdom in the observance
of the Passover. Finally the obligatory and all-embracing
character of the Passover is re-emphasized (verses 13–
14).

In origin the Passover is likely to have been a spring feast to keep off evil spirits; but from early days it was used to celebrate the miraculous departure of the Israelites from Egypt under Moses, and thus incorporated features which commemorated this. It was kept in March–April, and the Christian Easter has grown directly out of it.

1. *In the first month of the second year*: the story is again set in the month preceding the census of 1: 1, as it was in 7: 1.

2–5. The full rules of Exod. 12: 1–20, 43–9 are summarized.

6. *It happened*: an individual case becomes the occasion for receiving further guidance on the detailed application of the law from God. They could not take part in a sacrifice while unclean (so Lev. 7: 20f.) and contact with a dead body made them unclean (Num. 19: 11).

8. The case is adjourned until Moses can enter the sanctuary, where God will speak to him (Exod. 25: 22).

10. In addition to the cause under discussion, absence on a long journey is given as a reason for holding a Passover in the second month; but as verse 13 makes clear, these are the only two acceptable reasons.

11. *he shall prepare the victim*: a lamb, or failing that a sheep or goat. The *bitter herbs* are not identified, but are probably from earliest times an accompaniment of the lamb; but the *unleavened cakes* are from an originally separate feast of unleavened cakes held at the same time of year, which was early united with the Passover.

12. *and no bone of it shall be broken*: the perfection of the sacrificial lamb must be preserved. This is one of the passages drawn on in John 19: 36, and applied to Christ as the Passover lamb. The smearing of blood on door-posts and lintel, a part of the rite designed originally to frighten off evil spirits (Exod. 12: 22), is not mentioned here.

13. *shall be cut off from his father's kin*: he will die by divine agency, rather than by infliction of the death penalty. It is underlined that the severest penalty awaits those who unnecessarily miss the Passover.

14. *an alien*: this is not a passing foreigner, who may not eat the Passover (Exod. 12: 45), but a resident alien, who becomes a member of the community, and like the widow and the fatherless has a special status because he has no kin to protect him. ✶

The journey from Sinai to Edom

✶ The N.E.B. treats the second part of Numbers (9: 15–20: 13), the journey from Sinai to Edom, as beginning at this point. More commonly 9: 15–10: 10 has been included in the first section as being still preparatory to the departure, and still part of the continuous use of P, before J (see pp. 3f.) is drawn on for the first time. It is not a very serious point. The different ways of dividing the text represent different ways of interpreting its emphasis. The N.E.B. division leads us now to the heart of the book of Numbers, a story drawn from both P and J, which are combined to give a narrative of a journey, broken off for legal sections in chs. 15, 18 and 19. The course of this journey is dominated by two themes, both theological in character: God's gracious leading of his chosen people with tender care, under the hand of his servant Moses, and the sinful response to this of his people in grumbling, disobedience and rebellion, which provokes God's wrath and his postponement of the entry into the land until all the rebellious generation has died. The story is intended by its narrators to serve also as a warning to their hearers not to disobey God, and Paul uses it in the same way in 1 Cor. 10: 1–13 ('These events happened as symbols to warn us not to set our desires on evil things, as they did', verse 6). ✶

THE FIERY CLOUD OVER THE TABERNACLE

15 ON THE DAY WHEN they set up the Tabernacle, that is the Tent of the Tokens, cloud covered it, and in the evening a brightness like fire appeared over it till 16 morning. So it continued: the cloud covered it by day[a] 17 and a brightness like fire by night. Whenever the cloud lifted from the tent, the Israelites struck camp, and at the place where the cloud settled, there they pitched their 18 camp. At the command of the LORD they struck camp, and at the command of the LORD they encamped again, and continued in camp as long as the cloud rested over 19 the Tabernacle. When the cloud stayed long over the Tabernacle, the Israelites remained in attendance on the 20 LORD and did not move on; and it was the same when the cloud continued over the Tabernacle only a few days: at the command of the LORD they remained in camp, and 21 at the command of the LORD they struck camp. There were also times when the cloud continued only from evening till morning, and in the morning, when the cloud lifted, they moved on. Whether by day or by 22 night, they moved as soon as the cloud lifted. Whether it was for a day or two, for a month or a year, whenever the cloud stayed long over the Tabernacle, the Israelites remained where they were and did not move on; they 23 did so only when the cloud lifted. At the command of the LORD they encamped, and at his command they struck camp. At the LORD's command, given through Moses, they remained in attendance on the LORD.

[a] by day: *so Sept.; Heb. om.*

✻ Before the camp moves off, we are given a final note of how the fiery cloud accompanies the Israelites and acts as their guide. This section takes and expands Exod. 40: 34–8, and is by P again. The cloud is a theological representation of the accompanying presence of God in the form of a visible sign. It is found already in J, where from the exodus onwards the people are led by a column of cloud by day and of fire by night (Exod. 13: 21). In P the concept is slightly different: it is not a column, and it is not a guide going ahead, but covers the Tabernacle in the centre of the camp: it is the visible external sign of the 'glory' within. For P it first appears as part of the theophany or manifestation of God on Sinai (Exod. 24: 15–18). Now it serves as a clear indication of God's will for Israel to stay still or to move. His freedom to act exactly as he wills is thereby stressed: his holy nation complies with his will and obeys.

16. *by day*: the sense clearly demands the restoration of a word which is found in the Septuagint, and must have been left out in the Hebrew by accident.

17–18. This follows closely Exod. 40: 36–8.

19–23. This amplifies and expands verse 18, and follows out all its implications in detail.

22–3. Israel's total conformity to the will of God is thus stressed. ✻

THE SILVER TRUMPETS

The Lord spoke to Moses and said: Make two trumpets **10** 1, 2 of beaten silver and use them for summoning the community and for breaking camp. When both are sounded, 3 the whole community shall muster before you at the entrance to the Tent of the Presence. If a single trumpet 4 is sounded, the chiefs who are heads of the Israelite clans shall muster. When you give the signal for a shout, those 5 encamped on the east side are to move off. When the 6

signal is given for a second shout those encamped to the
south are to move off. A signal to shout is the signal to
7 move off. When you convene the assembly, you shall
8 sound a trumpet but not raise a shout. This sounding of
the trumpets is the duty of the Aaronite priests and shall
be a rule binding for all time on your descendants.

9　　When you go into battle against an invader and you
are hard pressed by him, you shall raise a cheer when the
trumpets sound, and this will serve as a reminder of
you before the LORD your God and you will be delivered
10 from your enemies. On your festal days and at your
appointed seasons and on the first day of every month,
you shall sound the trumpets over your whole-offerings
and your shared-offerings, and the trumpets shall be a
reminder on your behalf before the LORD[a] your God.
I am the LORD your God.

＊ The author moves naturally from the cloud as a signal for
the departure of the Israelites to the other signal to them to
assemble and move off, the silver trumpets. These are not like
the modern trumpet, but are long metal tubes flared at one
end, such as are shown on the Arch of Titus in Rome. The
trumpet was already known in Egypt before the time of the
exodus, but in Israel the horn is the more common instru-
ment, and the trumpet, though known in Hosea, only becomes common after the exile. It has two main uses, in war-
fare, alongside the shout or war-cry (so both are used in the
story of the fall of Jericho; Josh. 6: 1–20), and in worship to
summon the community and express joy and thanksgiving.
The trumpet becomes then the symbol of the time of the
end; it is prominent, used for summons and alarm, in the
War Rule of the Qumran community (one of the Dead Sea

[a] the LORD: *so some MSS.; others om.*

Scrolls) and is repeatedly sounded in the book of Revelation, while in 1 Cor. 15: 52 it is the sign for the resurrection of the dead. So this brief section has long echoes in the traditions of God's people.

3. *When both are sounded*: a blast on two trumpets summons all the people; on one, only the chiefs.

5. *When you give the signal for a shout*: this is a different signal from the sounding of verse 3, and is the signal for departure. Only those to east and south are mentioned: it is not necessary to spell out all the variations.

9. *and you are hard pressed by him*: an example of this in practice can be found in 2 Chron. 13: 12–16, where the men of Judah with the help of the trumpets and the shout defeat an ambush by the men of Israel.

10. *On your festal days*: the trumpet is to sound at great feasts and on the first of each month; 29: 1 speaks of the first day of the seventh month as a special day for this. ✳

THE ISRAELITES LEAVE SINAI

In the second year, on the twentieth day of the second 11 month, the cloud lifted from the Tabernacle of the Tokens, and the Israelites moved by stages from the wilderness 12 of Sinai, until the cloud came to rest in the wilderness of Paran. The first time that they broke camp at the 13 command of the LORD given through Moses, the standard 14 of the division of Judah moved off first with its tribal hosts: the host of Judah under Nahshon son of Amminadab, the host of Issachar under Nethaneel son of Zuar, 15 and the host of Zebulun under Eliab son of Helon. 16 Then the Tabernacle was taken down, and its bearers, 17 the sons of Gershon and Merari, moved off.

Secondly, the standard of the division of Reuben 18 moved off with its tribal hosts: the host of Reuben under

19 Elizur son of Shedeur, the host of Simeon under Shelu-
20 miel son of Zurishaddai, and the host of Gad under
21 Eliasaph son of Reuel.*a* The Kohathites, the bearers of the
holy things,*b* moved off next, and on their arrival found
the Tabernacle set up.

22   Thirdly, the standard of the division of Ephraim moved
off with its tribal hosts: the host of Ephraim under
23 Elishama son of Ammihud, the host of Manasseh under
24 Gamaliel son of Pedahzur, and the host of Benjamin
under Abidan son of Gideoni.

25   Lastly, the standard of the division of Dan, the rear-
guard of all the divisions, moved off with its tribal hosts:
26 the host of Dan under Ahiezer son of Ammishaddai, the
27 host of Asher under Pagiel son of Ocran, and the host of
Naphtali under Ahira son of Enan.

28   This was the order of march for the Israelites, mustered
in their hosts, and in this order they broke camp.

★ The Israelites now move off from Sinai in processional
array for the journey which will bring them in the end, by
way of Edom and Moab, to the promised land itself. The
story is told by P, who picks up the instructions of ch. 2,
and represents them being carried out. The order of the tribes
and the names of the leaders are exactly the same as in that
chapter. Only verses 17 and 21 are not based on ch. 2, but
give detail about the Levites carrying the Tabernacle added
from ch. 4: the clans of Gershon and Merari are to go before
the Reubenites to prepare the new site for the Tabernacle.

      11. *on the twentieth day of the second month*: nineteen days
therefore have passed since 1: 1, and ten months and nineteen
days since the arrival at Sinai (cp. Exod. 19: 1) on P's reckon-

[a] *So Sept.* (*cp.* 2: *14*); *Heb*. Deuel.
[b] holy things: *so Sept.; Heb*. sanctuary.

ing. *the cloud lifted from the Tabernacle of the Tokens*: the cloud
has been explained already in 9: 17–22. The Tabernacle of
the Tokens is the (late) name given the Tabernacle in 1: 50.

12. *in the wilderness of Paran*: we do not know exactly
where this is, but it must be in the northern part of the Sinai
peninsula.

28. *and in this order they broke camp*: the orderly fulfilment
of the command is part of P's grand conception of the move
forward of Israel under God. ✳

HOBAB AND THE ARK

And Moses said to Hobab son of Reuel the Midianite, 29
his brother-in-law, 'We are setting out for the place
which the LORD promised to give us. Come with us, and
we will deal generously with you, for the LORD has
given an assurance of good fortune for Israel.' But he 30
replied, 'No, I will not; I would rather go to my own
country and my own people.' Moses said, 'Do not 31
desert us, I beg you; for you know where we ought to
camp in the wilderness, and you will be our guide. If you 32
will go with us, then all the good fortune with which
the LORD favours us we will share with you.'

Then they moved off from the mountain of the LORD 33
and journeyed for three days, and the Ark of the Covenant of the LORD kept a day's journey[a] ahead of them to
find them a place to rest. The cloud of the LORD hung 34
over them by day when they moved camp. Whenever 35
the Ark began to move, Moses said,

> 'Up, LORD, and may thy enemies be scattered
> and those that hate thee flee before thee.'

[a] So Pesh.; Heb. a three days' journey.

77

36 When it halted, he said,

> 'Rest, LORD of the countless thousands of Israel.'

* For the first time in Numbers the work of the older source, J, appears. We do not have an alternative continuous account of the departure from Sinai (this was pushed out when the older material was taken into P), but only a few events told by J in connection with the departure from Sinai. Moses proposes an alliance with his brother-in-law Hobab, a Midianite. This is not simply the story of the acquisition of a temporary guide, but of the making of an alliance with the Kenites, of whom Hobab is one (Judg. 1: 16), and of whom the Israelites later remembered that 'you were friendly to Israel when they came up from Egypt' (1 Sam. 15: 6). The Kenites are a nomadic tribe in the Negeb to the south of Judah, a branch of the Midianites. The Midianites are an important tribal group, occupying a substantial area to the north and east of the Gulf of Akaba, and frequently mentioned in the Old Testament: Moses married one of them (Exod. 2: 16–21). Israel is not on good terms with the Midianites generally, but only with the Kenites. Then follows the older material's version of the departure of the Ark, and a recording of two no doubt very ancient cries used in connection with the movement of the Ark.

29. *Hobab son of Reuel the Midianite*: the story of Moses' marriage to the daughter of Reuel the Midianite is told in Exod. 2: 16–21. There are variant traditions about the name of Moses' father-in-law, for in Exod. 18 he is called Jethro: but this verse links up with the tradition of Exod. 2.

30. *I would rather go to my own country*: Israel is to go forward in a different direction from that by which Hobab would go home.

31. *and you will be our guide*: this implies that we have here a tradition which does not know of the leading of the cloud; but it may be that the author does not see that there is an inconsistency.

32. *we will share with you*: it is implied that Hobab (and so the Kenites too) are to enter Canaan with Israel, and share its blessings. We are not told explicitly if Hobab accepts or refuses, but it must be implied that he accepts. The story would have to tell us if the answer were no, and Judg. 1: 16 and 4: 11 imply a tradition that Hobab goes with Israel.

33. *the Ark of the Covenant of the LORD kept a day's journey ahead of them*: the older material differs from P in ch. 9, in showing the Ark as the guide, and the cloud as just accompanying Israel.

35. *Whenever the Ark began to move*: these sayings are used regularly with the Ark, not just on this occasion, and are no doubt a memory of a very old tradition. They connect the Ark directly with the presence of God, of which it is a sign, but show too that it is already an object to be carried before the Israelites in battle, as in 2 Sam. 11: 11. *Up, LORD, and may thy enemies be scattered*: this prayer is taken up at the beginning of Ps. 68: 1 – unless it is itself a quotation from the Psalm. But that is less likely.

36. *Rest, LORD of the countless thousands of Israel*: the text as we have it runs 'Return, O LORD of . . .' *Rest* represents a way of reading the same consonants of the Hebrew with different vowels. The correction is probably right. The great size of Israel is more appropriate to the settled Israel of a later date, so perhaps this saying is, though ancient, not as old as the setting it is given. ✻

FIRE IN THE CAMP

There came a time when the people complained to the **11** LORD of their hardships. When he heard, he became angry and fire from the LORD broke out among them, and was raging at one end of the camp, when the people appealed 2 to Moses. He interceded with the LORD, and the fire died

3 down. Then they named that place Taberah,[a] because the
fire of the LORD had burned among them there.

* In the first event after the departure from Sinai, J picks up
the theme, already enunciated in Exod. 14: 11f., of rebellion
and punishment as characteristic of Israel's relation to her God
in the wilderness. It is equally typical of this theme as it recurs
that Moses intercedes for his people, and that God forgives
and delivers them. This time the theme is set out very
briefly. There is no explanation of what the people complain
about in particular, or of the nature of the fire; the story
moves as quickly as it can to the explanation of the name
Taberah, and it was in fact formed to provide this explanation, but on the basis of a rebellion and forgiveness pattern
typical of J's stories of the people in the wilderness. Stories
which explain place-names (which are called aetiologies) are
not in fact uncommon in the Old Testament; another one
follows immediately.

1. *fire from the LORD*: this is intended to be understood as
a supernatural phenomenon, not as (for instance) lightning.

2. *He interceded with the LORD*: it is one of the firmest
elements in the tradition about Moses that he intercedes.

3. *they named that place Taberah*: as the footnote explains,
this word is taken to mean 'Burning'; the name gives rise to
the story. *

QUAILS AND MANNA ARE SENT BY GOD,
AND HIS SPIRIT RESTS ON THE ELDERS

4 Now there was a mixed company of strangers who had
joined the Israelites. These people began to be greedy for
better things, and the Israelites themselves wept once
5 again and cried, 'Will no one give us meat? Think of it!
In Egypt we had fish for the asking, cucumbers and water-

[a] *That is* Burning.

melons, leeks and onions and garlic. Now our throats are 6
parched; there is nothing wherever we look except this
manna.' (The manna looked like coriander seed, the 7
colour of gum resin. The people went about collecting it, 8
ground it up in hand-mills or pounded it in mortars, then
boiled it in the pot and made it into cakes. It tasted like
butter-cakes. When dew fell on the camp at night, the 9
manna fell with it.) Moses heard the people wailing, all 10
of them in their families at the opening of their tents.
Then the LORD became very angry, and Moses was
troubled. He said to the LORD, 'Why hast thou brought 11
trouble on thy servant? How have I displeased the LORD
that I am burdened with the care of this whole people?
Am I their mother? Have I brought them into the world, 12
and am I called upon to carry them in my bosom,
like a nurse with her babies, to the land promised by thee
on oath to their fathers? Where am I to find meat to give 13
them all? They pester me with their wailing and their
"Give us meat to eat." This whole people is a burden 14
too heavy for me; I cannot carry it alone. If that is thy 15
purpose for me, then kill me outright. But if I have won
thy favour, let me suffer this trouble at thy hands*a* no
longer.'

The LORD answered Moses, 'Assemble seventy elders 16
from Israel, men known to you as elders and officers in
the community; bring them to me at the Tent of the
Presence, and there let them take their stand with you.
I will come down and speak with you there. I will take 17
back part of that same spirit which has been conferred
on you and confer it on them, and they will share with

[a] this trouble . . . hands: *prob. original rdg., altered in Heb. to* my trouble.

you the burden of taking care for the people; then you
18 will not have to bear it alone. And to the people you shall
say this: "Hallow yourselves in readiness for tomorrow;
you shall have meat to eat. You wailed in the LORD's
hearing; you said, 'Will no one give us meat? In Egypt
we lived well.' The LORD will give you meat and you
19 shall eat it. Not for one day only, nor for two days, nor
20 five, nor ten, nor twenty, but for a whole month you
shall eat it until it comes out at your nostrils and makes
you sick; because you have rejected the LORD who dwells
in your midst, wailing in his presence and saying, 'Why
did we ever come out of Egypt?'"

21 Moses replied, 'Here am I with six hundred thousand
men on the march around me, and thou dost promise
22 them meat to eat for a whole month. How can the sheep
and oxen be slaughtered that would be enough for them?
If all the fish in the sea could be caught, would they be
23 enough?' The LORD said to Moses, 'Is there a limit to the
power of the LORD? You will see this very day whether
or not my words come true.'

24 Moses came out and told the people what the LORD
had said. He assembled seventy men from the elders of
25 the people and stationed them round the Tent. Then the
LORD descended in the cloud and spoke to him. He took
back part of that same spirit which he had conferred on
Moses and conferred it on the seventy elders; as the spirit
alighted on them, they fell into a prophetic ecstasy, for
the first and only time.

26 Now two men named Eldad and Medad, who had
been enrolled with the seventy, were left behind in the
camp. But, though they had not gone out to the Tent,

the spirit alighted on them none the less, and they fell
into an ecstasy there in the camp. A young man ran and 27
told Moses that Eldad and Medad were in an ecstasy in
the camp, whereupon Joshua son of Nun, who had 28
served with Moses since he was a boy, broke in, 'My
lord Moses, stop them!' But Moses said to him, 'Are 29
you jealous on my account? I wish that all the LORD's
people were prophets and that the LORD would confer
his spirit on them all!' And Moses rejoined the camp 30
with the elders of Israel.

Then a wind from the LORD sprang up; it drove quails 31
in from the west, and they were flying all round the
camp for the distance of a day's journey, three feet[a]
above the ground. The people were busy gathering quails 32
all that day, all night, and all next day, and even the man
who got least gathered ten homers. They spread them
out to dry all about the camp. But the meat was scarcely 33
between their teeth, and they had not so much as bitten
it, when the LORD's anger broke out against the people
and he struck them with a deadly plague. That place was 34
called Kibroth-hattaavah[b] because there they buried the
people who had been greedy for meat.

✳ The oldest element in this chapter is a miracle story, of the
Israelites being fed with quails in the wilderness, which sees
them as a gift from God. J himself then attached to this older
story an explanation of the name Kibroth-hattaavah ('Graves
of Greed'), and so gave a negative slant to the story, seeing
the Israelites as punished for their greed. So he brings in again
his characteristic view of the wilderness period as a time of
rebellion. Finally a strikingly different story has grown on to

[a] *Lit.* two cubits.   [b] *That is* the Graves of Greed.

the original one in verses 11–12, 14–17, 24*b*–30, told by a later writer who is making additions to J, and who is especially interested in prophecy and in the Tent of the Presence. The point of this story is the unexpected coming of the spirit upon the two men who have stayed behind, and the attack made upon restrictive views of the gift of the spirit in the words of Moses. The chapter is rather complicated, and it will help to remember that it is made up of these different layers.

4. *a mixed company of strangers*: the Israelites are accompanied by a crowd of riff-raff (so it could be translated); they have been referred to already in Exod. 12: 38, 'And with them too went a large company of every kind'. What they are doing with the Israelites is unexplained, but they take the blame for the demand for food.

wept once again: we have not heard of weeping before; but perhaps the story of Taberah (11: 1–3) is in the author's mind. *Will no one give us meat?*: the tradition that Israel had its flocks and herds with it (e.g. Exod. 12: 32, 'take your sheep and cattle, and go') seems to be forgotten here. Perhaps the people are being over-dramatic.

5. *cucumbers and water-melons*: the fruit and vegetables here listed are still popular in Egypt, and Herodotus tells us of workers on the pyramids eating radishes, onions and leeks.

6. *except this manna*: manna is a sticky, sweet excretion by insects upon the tamarisk tree in late May and June, which can be collected, and tastes like honey. It is still to be found in the Sinai peninsula. The giving of the manna is not described in detail here, because it was told in Exod. 16, where it was seen as a miracle.

7. The description of the manna is close to that in Exod. 16: 13–14, 31, and is perhaps taken over and adapted from there. It would then be a later insertion here; but a helpful one. *coriander seed*: the coriander looks somewhat like parsley, and is technically an umbelliferous annual. The seed is still used in cooking.

11. *Why hast thou brought trouble on thy servant?*: here the later editor begins the theme of the burden on Moses, who complains in a rather full, almost rhetorical, style.

12. *like a nurse with her babies*: the word for nurse is in fact masculine, so the phrase might better be translated 'like a nurse with babies'.

15. *then kill me outright*: Moses' despair is dramatically underlined, just as Elijah in despair later said to God: 'It is enough... now, LORD, take my life' (1 Kings 19: 4).

16. The LORD in answer promises both meat and the spirit: this underlines that two stories are overlapping here. *seventy elders*: we have already heard in Exod. 18 of the institution of lay judges to help Moses, and the elders who are to 'share...the burden of taking care for the people' (verse 17) are senior and responsible men in the community who are to add to their judicial responsibility a pastoral one. *at the Tent of the Presence*: we have met this term already in 1: 1, referring to a very elaborate tent of the P tradition. Here we meet it for the first time in the older material, where just one strand, later than J himself, appears to refer to it (cp. Exod. 33: 7-11 and Num. 12) as a simple tent pitched outside the camp, to which Moses and others go out to seek God (that is, to get oracular decisions from him). It was perhaps thought to shelter the Ark, but we are not explicitly told so.

17. *I will take back part of that same spirit*: the spirit, God's inspiration of men, is conceived of almost materially as something quantitative that comes on a man from without. Moses has so much of it that some can be shared with the elders.

18. *And to the people you shall say this*: the older story is taken up again here. *Hallow yourselves*: they must rid themselves of ritual uncleanness to eat meat provided by God.

21. *six hundred thousand men*: this is J's figure for the number of Israelite men, given already in Exod. 12: 37. It is generally assumed to be an ideal figure: the number that came out with Moses will in fact have been a few hundreds or thousands.

22. Moses argues with God. By this the author keeps up the suspense. Note the rhetorical exaggeration of e.g. *all the fish in the sea*.

23. *Is there a limit to the power of the LORD?*: the Hebrew literally means 'Is the LORD's hand shortened?' and uses this striking anthropomorphism (see on 12: 8) to stress God's omnipotence.

24. Here the story of the elders is resumed, and comes to its climax.

25. *they fell into a prophetic ecstasy*: some early prophets delivered their message in an abnormal state of mind (*ecstasy*) which could be brought on by wild dancing or by music. An example is the prophets whom Saul met (1 Sam. 10: 5). *for the first and only time*: the ecstasy served as a mark of the beginning of their office, but was not needed again.

26–8. *were left behind in the camp*: we are not told why; they are needed in the camp to make the next part of the story possible. *Joshua son of Nun*: the future leader of the Israelites into the promised land as Moses' successor. He is mentioned here because for this source Joshua is Moses' young assistant, and never moves from the tent (so Exod. 33: 11).

29. *I wish that all the LORD's people were prophets*: this is the climax of the story. The author is attacking men in his own time who try to confine the right to prophesy to those who have been officially recognized as prophets. The openness of his approach is attractive, and sounds very modern; but the contrast of openness and exclusiveness is perhaps as old as man.

31–2. The story returns to its basic theme. *quails*, small birds of the same family as partridges and pheasants, migrate twice a year in large numbers, northwards from Africa to Europe in March and April, south again in September. They do the journey in short stages, and are easily caught when they stop to rest. So this is in fact a regular natural phenomenon, but understood as miraculous divine provision. *ten homers*: the homer is a dry measure of capacity. We do not know

86

exactly how large it was, but it is between 134 and 230 litres (4 to 6 bushels). So ten homers is an extremely large quantity.

33. Verses 33 and 34 are added by J to the original story to sound the note of God's punishment for greed.

34. *Kibroth-hattaavah*: 'Graves of Greed' is the apparent sense of this name. Though the place cannot be identified, there can be no doubt the name is authentic, and the negative twist has been given to the story in order to explain the place-name. ✲

THE UNIQUENESS OF MOSES IS VINDICATED BY GOD

From Kibroth-hattaavah the Israelites went on to Haze- 35 roth, and while they were at Hazeroth, Miriam and Aaron **12** began to speak against Moses. They blamed him for his Cushite wife (for he had married a Cushite woman), and they said, 'Is Moses the only one with*a* whom the 2 LORD has spoken? Has he not spoken with*a* us as well?' Moses was in fact a man of great humility, the most 3 humble man on earth. But the LORD heard them and 4 suddenly he said to Moses, Aaron and Miriam, 'Go out all three of you to the Tent of the Presence.' So the three went out, and the LORD descended in a pillar of cloud; he 5 stood at the entrance to the tent and summoned Aaron and Miriam. The two of them went forward, and he said, 6

'Listen to my words.
If he*b* were your prophet and nothing more,
I would make myself known to him in a vision,
  I would speak with him in a dream.
But my servant Moses is not such a prophet;   7

[a] Or by.   [b] *Prob. rdg.; Heb.* the LORD.

he alone is faithful[a] of all my household.

8   With him I speak face to face,
       openly and not in riddles.
       He shall see the very form of the LORD.
       How do you dare speak against my servant Moses?'

9 Thus the anger of the LORD was roused against them,
10 and he left them; and as the cloud moved from the tent,
there was Miriam, her skin diseased and white as snow.
Aaron turned towards her and saw her skin diseased.
11 Then he said to Moses, 'Pray, my lord, do not make us
pay the penalty of sin, foolish and wicked though we have
12 been. Let her not be like something still-born, whose
flesh is half eaten away when it comes from the womb.'
13 So Moses cried, 'Not this, O LORD! Heal her, I pray.'
14 The LORD replied, 'Suppose her father had spat in her
face, would she not have to remain in disgrace for seven
days? Let her be kept for seven days in confinement out-
15 side the camp and then be brought back.' So Miriam
was kept outside for seven days, and the people did not
16 strike camp until she was brought back. After this they
set out from Hazeroth and pitched camp in the wilderness of Paran.

* Miriam is punished for unjustly attacking Moses and his
special relationship with God, which Moses then illustrates
by interceding for her, so that she is healed and restored. The
central point of the story is to emphasize the uniqueness of
Moses as the humble man with whom (alone) God speaks
face to face. In this he differs from the typical prophet (or
prophetess, such as Miriam is). The story is built upon a
foundation of an earlier tradition of Miriam being smitten

[a] *Or* to be trusted.

with a skin-disease in a dispute with Moses, but its emphasis
has shifted in the developed version to the status of Moses. The
story comes to us from the older material; its final form however is due to the later writer who is specially interested in the
Tent of the Presence, whose hand is found also in Exod. 33:
7–11, and has just been noted in parts of Num. 11. He may be
responsible for the present form of at least verses 4, 5 and 9.
The story, though it is set in the wilderness, is not a wilderness story but a Moses story, and no doubt once had no fixed
place in the traditions. It has been brought in here perhaps to
balance out the teaching of 11: 26–9 with its implication that
all the prophets share in the prophetic work of Moses. Perhaps it rebukes prophetic groups which claimed too much
for themselves, claimed perhaps to be 'prophets like Moses'
(a phrase used in Deut. 18: 18 of a future prophet).

35. *went on to Hazeroth*: its whereabouts are unknown.

12: 1. *Miriam and Aaron began to speak against Moses*:
Miriam appears here for the first time in Numbers. She has
appeared already as a prophetess in Exod. 15: 20, where she
sings the refrain of the 'song of Moses', and she is there called
sister of Aaron. Aaron comes to be regarded as brother of
Moses (although this is probably not original, but part of the
process of relating the characters in the story together) and so
in Num. 26: 59 Miriam is treated as sister of both Aaron and
Moses. But it should not be presumed that the author of this
story regarded Miriam as sister of Aaron, still less of Moses,
although the story will imply that she is known as a prophetess. *They blamed him for his Cushite wife*: this is not likely
without further explanation to refer to a woman from the
Sudan or Ethiopia (the usual sense of Cush in the Old
Testament), and may mean 'from Cushan', which is referred
to in parallel with Midian in Hab. 3: 7, and must overlap it in
sense. Cushites are attested too in Palestine in 2 Chron. 14:
8–14, where they are defeated by King Asa, and the name comes
as well in lists of the Egyptian Pharaohs Rameses II and III
referring to southern Palestine. If this is what is meant *his*

Cushite wife could be a reference to Zipporah of Midian, whom we hear of as his wife in Exod. 2: 21. But it sounds like a new wife, since the story in Exod. 18 indicates that he had separated from Zipporah, and no name is given here. On the other hand if this chapter was originally a floating tradition, the reference may indeed be to Zipporah, and when it was placed here the link was not made explicit. *and they said*: the double fault-finding, first for the marriage, and then for Moses' special relation with God, suggests that the original story is here expanded.

2. *Has he not spoken with us as well?*: although Miriam is not in this chapter called a prophetess as she is in Exod. 15: 20, the tradition that she was one is clearly implied here. They do not deny Moses' inspiration by God, but claim equality with him, a claim denied by the story.

3. *a man of great humility*: the word is '*ānāw*, a key term in the religious language of the psalms for the ideal religious man (e.g. Ps. 25: 9 'He guides the humble man in doing right'), and from here inherited by Christianity (Matt. 5: 5, translated 'of a gentle spirit' in the N.E.B.). Absence of self-assertiveness in the presence of God gives the right relationship with him. Moses is here given the highest valuation that Israelite piety has.

4. *Go out all three of you to the Tent of the Presence*: it stands outside the camp (cp. the note on 11: 16).

5. *the LORD descended in a pillar of cloud*: the presence of God is understood very straightforwardly as localized, and movable. Whether he is still present in the heavens as well is not indicated, but it is probably assumed.

6. *and he said*: the oracle that follows is in rhythmic form, and is probably intended to be in verse, as it is set out in the text. *and nothing more*: this is an explanatory addition, which does not occur in the Hebrew text, but is implied by it. *in a vision*: it is implied that the usual form of prophetic revelation is through visions and dreams. In the work of the later classical prophets (those, that is, whose teaching is

preserved to us in the books named after them) visions continue to be an important medium of revelation, but dreams are not referred to except to be criticized when the false prophets boast of their dreams (cp. especially Jer. 23: 25–32).

7. *my servant Moses*: 'servant' is a title used especially of those who are close to God, of Moses and of David in particular, to indicate their following of his will; and used of Israel in Isa. 40–55 in some very famous sections of the book.

8. *I speak face to face*: this is literally 'mouth to mouth', which is a unique expression in the Old Testament, and implies a mode of direct contact only given to Moses (cp. Deut. 34: 10). *openly and not in riddles*: all the normal forms of prophetic revelation, this implies, contain necessarily an element of ambiguity, and the oracle given relies on the interpretative work of the prophet himself, and so has an element of uncertainty in it. *He shall see the very form of the LORD*: this is a remarkably bold assertion. In early Israelite thought God was conceived of as being like a man in form if only he could be seen (this way of thinking about God is called technically 'anthropomorphism') but it was believed that man could not see him and live (so e.g. Judg. 13: 22 'We are doomed to die, we have seen God'). Exod. 33: 23 has God letting Moses see his back, but saying he cannot see his face. So the present passage continues to stress uniquely the special position of Moses. The reference to the *form of the LORD* within what is an utterance of the LORD is odd; it may be carelessness, but it may be a sign that this is a later addition to the oracle. *How do you dare speak*: the verse form is lost here, and this may be a prosy further addition to the original oracle, spelling out the conclusion which in the verse is only implied.

9. *the anger of the LORD*: as in 11: 1 and 10, this human emotion is without hesitation ascribed to God.

10. *and as the cloud moved*: since God descended in a pillar of cloud, this is the visible form of his leaving them. *her*

skin diseased: N.E.B. rightly avoids the traditional translation 'leprous'. The Hebrew word used covers a wide variety of skin-diseases, some quite easily cured. There is a tradition in the Old Testament that men are smitten with skin-disease as a punishment by God, and we hear this of Gehazi, Elisha's servant, in 2 Kings 5: 27, and of King Uzziah in 2 Chron. 26: 16–21, where he is smitten for his pride.

13. *Heal her, I pray*: Moses is seen as interceding for her, as he often intercedes for Israel.

14. *Suppose her father*: the saying of God starts very abruptly, and some think that the original beginning is lost. *had spat in her face*: this probably refers to a custom of a father spitting in his daughter's face to disgrace her, as a punishment for her misdemeanour, although this is not attested elsewhere in the Old Testament. But in Deut. 25: 9 a woman spits in a man's face as a formalized mark of contempt. *Let her be kept for seven days*: it is implied that she is healed at once, but must then be kept outside for the usual seven days' period of segregation of skin-diseases; and this is her punishment.

15. *until she was brought back*: so the story ends with God's forgiveness and Moses' magnanimity triumphing over the jealousy of Miriam and Aaron. ✻

MEN ARE CHOSEN TO EXPLORE CANAAN

13 1,2 The LORD spoke to Moses and said, 'Send men out to explore the land of Canaan which I am giving to the Israelites; from each of their fathers' tribes send one man, 3 and let him be a man of high rank.' So Moses sent them from the wilderness of Paran at the command of the LORD, all of them leading men among the Israelites. 4 These were their names:

from the tribe of Reuben, Shammua son of Zaccur;
5 from the tribe of Simeon, Shaphat son of Hori;

from the tribe of Judah, Caleb son of Jephunneh;   7

from the tribe of Issachar, Igal son of Joseph;   6

from the tribe of Ephraim, Hoshea son of Nun;   8

from the tribe of Benjamin, Palti son of Raphu;   9

from the tribe of Zebulun, Gaddiel son of Sodi;   10

from the tribe of Joseph (that is from the tribe of 11
Manasseh), Gaddi son of Susi;

from the tribe of Dan, Ammiel son of Gemalli;   12

from the tribe of Asher, Sethur son of Michael;   13

from the tribe of Naphtali, Nahbi son of Vophsi;   14

from the tribe of Gad, Geuel son of Machi.   15

These are the names of the men whom Moses sent to 16
explore the land. But Moses called the son of Nun
Joshua, not Hoshea.

When Moses sent them to explore the land of Canaan, 17
he said to them, 'Make your way up by the Negeb, and
go on into the hill-country. See what the land is like, 18
and whether the people who live there are strong or weak,
few or many. See whether it is easy or difficult country 19
in which they live, and whether the cities in which they
live are weakly defended or well fortified;[a] is the land 20
fertile or barren, and does it grow trees or not? Go boldly
in and take some of its fruit.' It was the season when the
first grapes were ripe.

They went up and explored the country from the 21
wilderness of Zin as far as Rehob by Lebo-hamath. They 22
went up by the Negeb and came to Hebron, where
Ahiman, Sheshai and Talmai, the descendants of Anak,[b]
were living. (Hebron was built seven years before Zoan

[a] *Prob. rdg., cp. Sam. MSS.; Heb.* are in camps or in walled cities.
[b] descendants of Anak: *or* tall men.

23 in Egypt.) They came to the gorge of Eshcol,[a] and there they cut a branch with a single bunch of grapes, and they carried it on a pole two at a time; they also picked pome-
24 granates and figs. It was from the bunch of grapes which the Israelites cut there that that place was named the gorge of Eshcol.

✻ Chs. 13 and 14 tell how explorers are sent ahead into Palestine. They report back that the land is very fertile, but its inhabitants fearsome. The people lose heart, and wish they were back in Egypt. They are punished for their faithlessness by not being allowed themselves to enter the promised land, but only their children. They nevertheless attempt this, and are heavily defeated.

These two chapters have a key position in the book, and set out in classic form the theme of faithlessness and its punishment, which is made the cause of the forty years' delay before they can enter Canaan. This strongly theological theme, *the* great theme of Numbers, underlies the whole narrative, and is responsible for the form it takes (cp. pp. 7f.).

The narrative is a combination of J and P material. P has retold J's story with characteristic differences of emphasis and strengthening of detail, and the two are then combined into a continuous story, in which the differences do not stand out very conspicuously (13: 1–17a, 21, 25, 32–3; 14: 1–3, 5–7, 10, 26–38 come from P, the rest from J).

1. Verses 1–17a are from P. *Send men out to explore the land*: usually, but less appropriately, known in earlier translations as 'spies'. Moses sends an advance party ahead, as later Joshua does (Josh. 2).

3. *leading men*: the word is the same as 'chiefs' in ch. 1. The names however are different.

4. *These were their names*: some of the names are early in form, and must be taken from old traditions, others are late.

[a] Eshcol: *that is* Bunch of Grapes.

from the tribe of Reuben: the tribes come again in the order of
1: 5–15, except that the pairs Manasseh–Ephraim and Naphtali–Gad are reversed here.

8. *Hoshea son of Nun*: this is Joshua. We have here an
interesting side-product of P's theology. Since he believed
the name 'Yahweh' for God was not revealed to Israel until
Exod. 6: 3, after Joshua had been born, he could not have
had a name formed with Yahweh as an element, as Joshua
(Hebrew *Yehōshua'*) is. So he renames him with a similar
name which does not display this element, *Hoshea*, and verse
16 attributes the name Joshua to Moses himself.

17. *the Negeb*: the flattish waste country on the southern
edge of Palestine, lying between the cultivable land and the
desert proper. It is still called the Negev by modern Israelis.
the hill-country: the undulating land to the north of the
Negeb.

18. *See what the land is like*: Canaan is quite unfamiliar to
the invading Israelites. The explorers are concerned to discover first the strength of the people and of their cities, and
secondly the fertility of the land.

20. *take some of its fruit*: a distant parallel is the dove of
Gen. 8: 11, bringing back an olive leaf as a sign of (restored)
fertility.

21. *the wilderness of Zin*: taken by P to be on the southern edge
of Canaan. *Rehob*: also called Beth-rehob, west of Hermon in
the far north of Israel. *by Lebo-hamath*: Lebo-hamath is a
city about 60 miles (96 km) further north-north-east from
Beth-rehob on the way to Hamath. The name was until
recently rendered 'entrance of Hamath', but this is wrong.
This verse and verse 25 are from P, and indicate a much more
extensive exploration than that envisaged by J, one which
extends right up to the traditional northern borders of Israel.

22. *and came to Hebron*: an ancient city 20 miles (32 km)
south of Jerusalem, where in the tradition all the patriarchs
had been buried. The special interest of Hebron to this story
is that Caleb is to be promised it. This is not made clear in the

story as we now have it, but is indicated in Judg. 1: 20. Ahiman, Sheshai and Talmai are perhaps figures of Israelite legends: *the descendants of Anak*: literally 'sons of a necklace', or possibly 'sons of a neck', 'long-necked, tall men', pre-Israelite inhabitants of the land, who are built up in later tradition as giants (so verses 32-3, which come from P, and Deut. 9: 2). We know from Egyptian texts that there was a tribe Anak in Palestine already about 2000 B.C. *Zoan in Egypt*: called Tanis in Greek, a city in the delta built by Rameses II (1301-1234), and for a while the capital of Egypt. Presumably an old local tradition of Hebron is preserved in this verse, and it may have as its foundation some true relation between the two cities; but it cannot be true as it stands, for Hebron was substantially older than this.

23. *to the gorge of Eshcol*: verses 23-4 are an addition to the text of J, put in as an explanation of the place-names given.   *

THE EXPLORERS REPORT

25 After forty days they returned from exploring the coun-
26 try, and came back to Moses and Aaron and the whole community of Israelites at Kadesh in the wilderness of Paran. They made their report to them and to the whole community, and showed them the fruit of the country.
27 And this was the story they told Moses: 'We made our way into the land to which you sent us. It is flowing
28 with milk and honey, and here is the fruit it grows; but its inhabitants are sturdy, and the cities are very strongly fortified; indeed, we saw there the descendants of Anak.
29 We also saw the Amalekites who live in the Negeb, Hittites,*a* Jebusites, and Amorites who live in the hill-country, and the Canaanites who live by the sea and along the Jordan.'

[a] *Or*, with Sam., Hivites.

Then Caleb called for silence before Moses and said, 30
'Let us go up at once and occupy the country; we are
well able to conquer it.' But the men who had gone with 31
him said, 'No, we cannot attack these people; they are
stronger than we are.' Thus their report to the Israelites 32
about the land which they had explored was discourag-
ing: 'The country we explored', they said, 'will swallow
up any who go to live in it. All the people we saw there
are men of gigantic size. When we set eyes on the Nephi- 33
lim*a* (the sons of Anak*b* belong to the Nephilim) we felt
no bigger than grasshoppers; and that is how we looked
to them.'

✻ 26. *Kadesh* is an important city in the northern part of the
Sinai peninsula; but it has perhaps been erroneously inserted
here, for the Israelites were in verse 3 in the wilderness of
Paran, as they still are in this verse, but Kadesh is in the wilderness of Zin (27: 14; Deut. 32: 51).

27. *And this was the story*: the men give an open report,
mentioning the strength of the inhabitants of the land, but not
seeking to discourage the Israelites from entering. *flowing
with milk and honey*: a traditional phrase, found in J and in
Deuteronomy and related writings, for great fertility.

29. The Amalekites are a strong nomadic group to the
south of the Negeb, old enemies of the Israelites, whom later
Saul attempts to wipe out (1 Sam. 15). *Hittites*: this is the
name of a great nation in southern Asia Minor, whose empire
was destroyed and their name largely forgotten soon after
1200 B.C. The reference is possibly to scattered offshoots of
the main Hittites. But it is better to read 'Hivites' with the
footnote, and take it as a name of one of the pre-Israelite
groups in Palestine. *Jebusites* are the inhabitants of Jebus,
identified with Jerusalem (e.g. Josh. 15: 8). *Amorites*: the text

[*a*] Or giants.   [*b*] sons of Anak: *or* tall men.

distinguishes them from Canaanites, but we do not know what the difference was, except that they are in the hill-country. Sometimes the word is treated as meaning the same as Canaanites, and the whole of Canaan was called Amurru by the Babylonians. *Canaanites*, often used as a general term for the inhabitants of Palestine, is here confined to the inhabitants of the coastal plain and of the Jordan valley.

30. *Caleb* is represented as in favour of the conquest, the others as opposed, to produce a dramatic confrontation.

32. *will swallow up*: because it is so large, or because it is so fertile, or because it has so many warring groups? It is not clear which is meant.

33. *the Nephilim*: these are referred to otherwise only in Gen. 6: 4, where the name refers to a race of semi-divine beings, offspring of marriage between 'the sons of the gods' and women. Israel had then a tradition of giants inhabiting the earth in early times, and the explorers despondently claim that the sons of Anak are of this size. The massive size of some Canaanite fortresses may have contributed to the growth of this tradition. *grasshoppers*: a typical Hebrew simile, meaning 'helpless and small'. *

THE PEOPLE REBEL

14 Then the whole Israelite community cried out in dismay;
2 all night long they wept. One and all they made complaints against Moses and Aaron: 'If only we had died in Egypt or in the wilderness!' they said. 'Far happier if
3 we had! Why should the LORD bring us to this land, to die in battle and leave our wives and our dependants to become the spoils of war? To go back to Egypt would be
4 better than this.' And they began to talk of choosing someone to lead them back.

5   Then Moses and Aaron flung themselves on the ground

before the assembled community of the Israelites, and 6
two of those who had explored the land, Joshua son of
Nun and Caleb son of Jephunneh, rent their clothes and 7
addressed the whole community: 'The country we
penetrated and explored', they said, 'is very good land
indeed. If the LORD is pleased with us, he will bring us 8
into this land which flows with milk and honey, and give
it to us. But you must not rebel against the LORD. You 9
need not fear the people of the land; for there we shall
find food.*a* They have lost the protection that they had:
the LORD is with us. You have nothing to fear from them.'
But by way of answer the assembled Israelites threatened 10
to stone them, when suddenly the glory of the LORD
appeared to them all in the Tent of the Presence.

* This section is a combination of J and P.

1. *the whole Israelite community: community* is a very characteristic word of the P source to describe Israel, viewing it
as a religious unity.

3. *To go back to Egypt would be better than this*: the rebellion
goes very deep. They would rather be slaves in Egypt than
attempt to win Canaan by battle. This is a very strong statement. Neh. 9: 17, retelling this story, actually says they did
choose a leader to take them back to Egypt.

5f. Only those four who do not rebel attempt to change the
mind of the Israelites. *rent their clothes*: a traditional expression
of great grief in the ancient Near East. Jacob does it when he
believes Joseph is dead (Gen. 37: 34).

7. *very good land indeed*: the land is contrasted with the
people of the land. The situation is bleak only because of the
size of the people: the land itself is good, and God will bring
the Israelites in safely if (verse 8) he is pleased with them.

[a] *Lit.* for they are our food.

9. *the protection that they had*: literally 'their shadow', a metaphor, typical of a hot country, for the protection of their gods.

10. *threatened to stone them*: a typical action in a rebellion, as later all Israel stoned to death Adoram, who was Rehoboam's commander of the forced levies (1 Kings 12: 18). *the glory of the LORD*: the glory of God is in visible form as P envisages it, and looks like 'a devouring fire' (Exod. 24: 17). ✲

THE LORD THREATENS TO DESTROY ISRAEL,
BUT MOSES INTERCEDES FOR THEM SUCCESSFULLY

11 Then the LORD said to Moses, 'How much longer will this people treat me with contempt? How much longer will they refuse to trust me in spite of all the signs I have
12 shown among them? I will strike them with pestilence. I will deny them their heritage, and you and your descendants I will make into a nation greater and more
13 numerous than they.' But Moses answered the LORD, 'What if the Egyptians hear of it? It was thou who didst
14 bring this people out of Egypt by thy strength. What if they tell the inhabitants of this land? They too have heard of thee, LORD, that thou art with this people, and art seen face to face, that thy cloud stays over them, and thou goest before them in a pillar of cloud by day and in a
15 pillar of fire by night. If then thou dost put them all to death at one blow, the nations who have heard these tales
16 of thee will say, "The LORD could not bring this people into the land which he promised them by oath; and so he destroyed them in the wilderness."

17 'Now let the LORD's might be shown in its greatness,
18 true to thy proclamation of thyself – "The LORD, long-

suffering, ever constant, who forgives iniquity and rebellion, and punishes sons to the third and fourth generation for the iniquity of their fathers, though he does not sweep them clean away." Thou hast borne with this 19 people from Egypt all the way here; forgive their iniquity, I beseech thee, as befits thy great and constant love.'

The LORD said, 'Your prayer is answered; I pardon 20 them. But as I live, in very truth the glory of the LORD 21 shall fill the earth. Not one of all those who have seen 22–23 my glory and the signs which I wrought in Egypt and in the wilderness shall see the country which I promised on oath to their fathers. Ten times they have challenged me and not obeyed my voice. None of those who have flouted me shall see this land. But my servant Caleb 24–25 showed a different spirit: he followed me with his whole heart. Because of this, I will bring him into the land in which he has already set foot, the territory of the Amalekites and the Canaanites who dwell in the Vale, and put his descendants in possession of it. Tomorrow you must turn back and set out for the wilderness by way of the Red Sea.'[a]

The LORD spoke to Moses and Aaron and said, 'How 26, 27 long must I tolerate[b] the complaints of this wicked community? I have heard the Israelites making complaints against me. Tell them that this is the very word of the 28 LORD: As I live, I will bring home to you the words I have heard you utter. Here in this wilderness your bones 29 shall lie, every man of you on the register from twenty years old and upwards, because you have made these

[a] Or the Sea of Reeds.   [b] must I tolerate: *prob. rdg.; Heb.* for.

30 complaints against me. Not one of you shall enter the land
which I swore with uplifted hand should be your home,
except only Caleb son of Jephunneh and Joshua son of
31 Nun. As for your dependants, those dependants who, you
said, would become the spoils of war, I will bring them
in to the land you have rejected, and they shall enjoy
32 it. But as for the rest of you, your bones shall lie in this
33 wilderness; your sons shall be wanderers in the wilderness
forty years, paying the penalty of your wanton disloyalty
34 till the last man of you dies there. Forty days you spent
exploring the country, and forty years you shall spend –
a year for each day – paying the penalty of your iniquities.
You shall know what it means to have me against you.[a]
35 I, the LORD, have spoken. This I swear to do to all this
wicked community who have combined against me.
There shall be an end of them here in this wilderness;
36 here they shall die.' But the men whom Moses had sent to
explore the land, and who came back and by their report
37 set all the community complaining against him, died of
the plague before the LORD; they died of the plague be-
38 cause they had made a bad report. Of those who went to
explore the land, Joshua son of Nun and Caleb son of
Jephunneh alone remained alive.

* The debate in verses 11–21 appears to be a late expansion
of J's story, in part borrowed directly from Exod. 32: 9–
14; 34: 6, 7, 9.

11. *all the signs*: these are God's miraculous interventions.
It is often suggested that Israel made no clear distinction between the miraculous and the non-miraculous, as we understand them, and that signs are therefore just specially striking

[a] *Or* to thwart me.

instances of God's action, which is at all times a presupposition of what happens in the world. But in fact they had a view of miracle as an event suspending normal natural laws which is not substantially different from ours.

12. *you and your descendants*: as a whole nation had been made of the descendants of Abraham, so a new nation would be made of the descendants of Moses alone.

13-16. Now a theological debate begins, in which Moses appeals to God's honour, which he believes is at stake, and so persuades God to change his mind and pardon Israel. The theme of the intercession of Moses, found elsewhere too in Numbers (for instance 11: 2; 12: 13), comes out strongly here.

18. This is a clearly deliberate quotation of Exod. 34: 6-7 (slightly shortened), where in the remaking of the Sinai covenant God proclaims himself to be in his essential nature loving and forgiving. It is a strong statement of a view of God's nature which is often quite falsely said not to be in the Old Testament, but only in the New. *to the third and fourth generations*: older Israelite thought embodied in this phrase its awareness that the strength of family ties carried both blessing and misfortune on from one generation to another.

20. God changes his mind to pardon, as he could for instance again in Amos 7: 3: 'Then the LORD relented and said, "This shall not happen."' Expressions like this stand alongside a belief in principle in the unchangeableness of God (see on 23: 19).

22-3. A central idea of Numbers is enunciated in these verses, that none of the generation who rebelled will be allowed to enter the promised land except Caleb (and, of course, Joshua, verse 30). *Ten times they have challenged me*: we do not have ten stories of rebellion. *Ten times* may mean just 'often', as when Jacob says 'you changed my wages ten times over' in Gen. 31: 41.

24f. *my servant Caleb*: Caleb stands for the house of Caleb, a tribal group in the south of Judah, with a separate history of their own, who are later swallowed up in Judah. Probably, as this tradition suggests, they entered Canaan from the south, not from the east as the main line of Israelites according to tradition did. In an older form of this tradition Caleb was promised Hebron in particular; cp. the note on 13: 22, and Judg. 1: 20. *the territory of the Amalekites and the Canaanites who dwell in the Vale*: this phrase is not repeated in Deut. 1: 40, which otherwise gives the substance of this verse. It is a later addition to the text of Numbers, one which does not completely fit in with 13: 29. *set out for the wilderness by way of the Red Sea*: because of their complaints they are not allowed to move directly towards Canaan, but must go round in a big detour to the south.

26. *The LORD spoke to Moses and Aaron*: this new introduction to the LORD's words shows that P now takes up the narrative down to verse 38. He condemns all those who complained to die in the wilderness, while the actual explorers die of the plague. This punishment is at the core of the understanding of the wilderness period as forty years of chastisement. We would disagree now profoundly with this picture of God's justice; but we must recognize the sense of the majesty of God and of the seriousness of disobedience to his will, which is reflected in this passage.

27f. *How long must I tolerate?*: the textual alteration indicated by the footnote is in Hebrew not as far-reaching as it looks in translation. For the obscure phrase 'how long for the complaints' is substituted 'how long to me for the complaints' on the assumption that just two letters have dropped out; and this is idiomatically translated as in our text. *the very word of the LORD*: this is the characteristic introduction to the utterance of a prophet, borrowed here to stress the seriousness of God's words.

29. *on the register*: that is, who were listed in the census of ch. 1. *from twenty years old*: because only those over twenty were included in the census.

30. *which I swore with uplifted hand*: the promise originally

made to Abraham in Gen. 17: 8. It is quite common for God
to be spoken of as if he had a body with parts like a man,
although this is known to be metaphorical (cp. on 12: 8).
The hand is lifted up in the regular gesture of an oath.

31. *your dependants*: your children. This refers back to verse 3.

33. *shall be wanderers*: the Hebrew text has 'shepherds'.
The N.E.B. reads it with different vowels, but no change in
the older consonantal text, to give a stronger sense. *forty
years*: this is the origin of the tradition of forty years of wandering in the wilderness. For its theological significance cp.
the introduction to 13: 1–24 and the note on verse 26 above;
and for its historical value see the introduction, p. 5. 'Forty
years' is often used as a round number to indicate a fairly
long period of human life, and here is thought of as the time
needed for one generation of men to die off. *wanton disloyalty*:
this gives the true sense of the Hebrew 'your acts of prostitu-
tion', a term often used in the prophets about religious
faithlessness.

37. *died of the plague*: the LORD's condemnation works
itself out in a spectacular and terrible form. This is the kind
of way people naturally expected God to behave, but then as
now the actual working of God's ways is much more difficult
than this to discern. ✳

A VAIN ATTEMPT TO DEFEAT THE ENEMY

When Moses reported the LORD's words to all the Israel- 39
ites, the people were plunged in grief. They set out early 40
next morning and made for the heights of the hill-
country, saying, 'Look, we are on our way up to the
place the LORD spoke of. We admit that we have been
wrong.' But Moses replied, 'Must you persist in dis- 41
obeying the LORD's command? No good will come of
this. Go no further; you will not have the LORD with you, 42
and your enemies will defeat you. For in front of you are 43

the Amalekites and Canaanites, and you will die by the
sword, because you have ceased to follow the LORD, and
44 he will no longer be with you.' But they went recklessly
on their way towards the heights of the hill-country,
though neither the Ark of the Covenant of the LORD
45 nor Moses moved with them out of the camp; and the
Amalekites and Canaanites from those hills came down
and fell upon them, and crushed them at Hormah.

* The people misguidedly attempt now, too late, to win
God's favour by attacking the Amalekites and Canaanites,
ignoring the sentence of verse 25, and attempting to come
straight up into Canaan from the south. In the absence of
God's support they are crushingly defeated. The author
(who is J) wishes to make the point for his own day that a
people which lacks God's favour cannot prosper.

44. *the Ark of the Covenant of the LORD*: the Ark (in the
older source too) was seen as leading the people in battle, and
acting as a token of success.

45. *and crushed them at Hormah*: it may be that a memory
of an actual defeat at Hormah in the northern Negeb underlies this: but Hormah in 21: 1–3 is the basis of a story which
plays on a possible meaning of the name, 'total destruction'
(for the sense see on 21: 2), and an allusion to this meaning
may underlie the mention of it here too. *

RULES ON THE PROPER FORM OF OFFERINGS TO THE LORD

15 1,2 The LORD spoke to Moses and said, Speak to the Israelites in these words: When you enter the land where you
3 are to live, the land I am giving you, you will make food-
offerings to the LORD; they may be whole-offerings or

any sacrifice made in fulfilment of a special*ᵃ* vow or by way of freewill offering or at one of the appointed seasons. When you thus make an offering of soothing odour from herd or flock to the LORD, the man who 4 offers, in presenting it, shall add a grain-offering of a tenth of an ephah of flour mixed with a quarter of a hin of oil. You shall also add to the whole-offering or 5 shared-offering a quarter of a hin of wine as a drink-offering with each lamb sacrificed.

If the animal is a ram, the grain-offering shall be two 6 tenths of an ephah of flour mixed with a third of a hin of oil, and the wine for the drink-offering shall be a third 7 of a hin; in this way you will make an offering of soothing odour to the LORD.

When you offer to the LORD a young bull, whether as 8 a whole-offering or as a sacrifice to fulfil a special*ᵇ* vow, or as a shared-offering, you shall add a grain-offering of 9 three tenths of an ephah of flour mixed with half a hin of oil, and for the drink-offering, half a hin of wine; the 10 whole will thus be a food-offering of soothing odour to the LORD. This is what must be done in each case, for 11 every bull or ram, lamb or kid, whatever the number of 12 each that you offer. Every native Israelite shall observe 13 these rules in each case when he offers a food-offering of soothing odour to the LORD.

When an alien residing with you or permanently 14 settled among you offers a food-offering of soothing odour to the LORD, he shall do as you do.*ᶜ* There is one 15

[*a*] in fulfilment of a special: *or* to discharge a . . .
[*b*] fulfil a special: *or* discharge a . . .
[*c*] *So Pesh.; Heb. adds* the assembly.

and the same rule for you and for the resident alien, a
rule binding for all time on your descendants; you and
16 the alien are alike before the LORD. There shall be one
law and one custom for you and for the alien residing
with you.

✻ A collection of priestly laws on different subjects follows,
although no reason has yet been found why it was placed
here in particular. Perhaps the final editor felt that narratives
should alternate with laws. The laws in this chapter are late
in their formulation, probably later than P, and intended as a
supplement to it; but the rules they enshrine can be much
older. The first section lays down the quantities of flour,
oil and wine that are to accompany different forms of public
and private sacrifices. The amounts, which are related to the
size of the animal, are perhaps late, but the offering of such
accompaniments to sacrifice is undoubtedly old. Hannah for
instance takes to Shiloh 'a bull three years old, an ephah of
meal, and a flagon of wine' (1 Sam. 1: 24). The text says
nothing about the significance of such gifts. If there was once
an idea that they are to give the deity a full meal, it is long
lost in Israel. Possibly they sought deliberately to represent
the different forms of man's use of the natural resources of the
land (as Deuteronomy uses 'your corn and new wine and oil'
to describe 'the fruit of your land' (Deut. 7: 13)). This
passage is concerned not to describe sacrifice in general, but to
prescribe quantities. Phoenician 'sacrificial tariffs' have actually been found at Marseilles and at Carthage, and these are
the nearest parallel to the directions here. The fundamental
and significant concern of this text is its concern to make to
God a full and worthy offering.

3. *food-offerings*: this is a general term in the Priestly
Writer for offerings which are consumed by fire. It may
actually mean 'fire-offerings'. *whole-offerings*: offerings
totally destroyed by fire, with no part kept back to be eaten.

an offering of soothing odour: the phrase reflects the old idea
that the deity actually smells and takes delight in the sacrifice.
It is no longer a living idea when this is written, but has become a vivid metaphor for acceptable worship.

4. *a tenth of an ephah*: modern equivalents to these quantities
must be regarded as very approximate, but one suggestion
is that with the lamb they are about $7\frac{1}{2}$ pints (4.5 litres) of
flour and 3 pints (1.8 litres) each of oil and wine. The same
quantities are found again in other late sacrificial rules in
Exod. 29: 40 and in Num. 28–9. The flour is united with the
other offerings and then burnt; the wine is poured out at the
foot of the altar.

5. *shared-offering*: one from which the priest and wor-
shippers eat after it has been offered.

6. *two tenths of an ephah*: with a ram this is about 15 pints
(9 litres) of flour and 4 pints (2.5 litres) each of oil and wine.

9. *three tenths of an ephah*: with a bull this is about $22\frac{1}{2}$ pints
(13.5 litres) of flour and 6 pints (3.75 litres) each of oil and
wine.

14–16. *an alien*: this is a provision scrupulously concerned
for justice, and surprising to those with a fixed idea of Israel's
concern as self-centred. The alien (that is, the resident alien)
is subject to the same laws as the native Israelite, and shares
their privileges, but also their duties (cp. 9: 14). *

MISCELLANEOUS PROVISIONS ABOUT
DELIBERATE AND INADVERTENT SINS

The LORD spoke to Moses and said, Speak to the Israelites 17, 18
in these words: After you have entered the land into
which I am bringing you, whenever you eat the bread 19
of the country, you shall set aside a contribution for the
LORD. You shall set aside a cake made of your first 20
kneading of dough, as you set aside the contribution
from the threshing-floor. You must give a contribution 21

to the LORD from your first kneading of dough; this rule is binding on your descendants.

22 When through inadvertence you omit to carry out any
23 of these commands which the LORD gave to Moses – any command whatever that the LORD gave you through Moses on that first day and thereafter and made binding
24 on your descendants – if it be done inadvertently, unnoticed by the community, then the whole community shall offer one young bull as a whole-offering, a soothing odour to the LORD, with its proper grain-offering and drink-offering according to custom; and they shall add
25 one he-goat as a sin-offering. The priest shall make expiation for the whole community of Israelites, and they shall be forgiven. The omission was inadvertent; and they have brought their offering, a food-offering to the LORD; they have made their sin-offering before the LORD
26 for their inadvertence; the whole community of Israelites and the aliens residing among you shall be forgiven. The inadvertence was shared by the whole people.

27 If any individual sins inadvertently, he shall present a
28 yearling she-goat as a sin-offering, and the priest shall make expiation before the LORD for the said individual,
29 and he shall be forgiven. For anyone who sins inadvertently, there shall be one law for all, whether native Israel-
30 ite or resident alien. But the person who sins presumptuously, native or alien, insults the LORD. He shall be cut
31 off from his people, because he has brought the word of the LORD into contempt and violated his command. That person shall be wholly cut off; the guilt shall be on his head alone.

32 During the time that the Israelites were in the wilder-

ness, a man was found gathering sticks on the sabbath
day. Those who had caught him in the act brought him 33
to Moses and Aaron and all the community, and they 34
kept him in custody, because it was not clearly known
what was to be done with him. The LORD said to Moses, 35
'The man must be put to death; he must be stoned by all
the community outside the camp.' So they took him 36
outside the camp and all stoned him to death, as the
LORD had commanded Moses.

The LORD spoke to Moses and said, Speak to the Israel- 37, 38
ites in these words: You must make tassels like flowers
on the corners of your garments, you and your children's
children. Into this tassel you shall work a violet thread,
and whenever you see this in the tassel, you shall remem- 39
ber all the LORD's commands and obey them, and not go
your own wanton ways, led astray by your own eyes
and hearts. This token is to ensure that you remember all 40
my commands and obey them, and keep yourselves
holy, consecrated to your God.

I am the LORD your God who brought you out 41
of Egypt to become your God. I am the LORD your
God.

✻ 17–21. This rule deals with a small regular levy for the
priests on food made from dough. It is not an annual offering
of first-fruits, but is charged on all food, perhaps at each new
baking. Provision for the priests is one of the (clearly appropriate!) concerns of the Priestly Writer (cp. Num. 18).

22–31. In verses 22–31 provisions follow for inadvertent
transgressions by the community (verses 22–6) or by individuals (verses 27–9). No detailed instance of inadvertence is
given. There are similar provisions, with a more complicated

scheme, in Lev. 4–5. This version is late, and expands the detail of the sacrifice to be made.

30. It will be seen that no sacrifice can atone for deliberate sin; nothing but the mercy of God can take this away. When Heb. 10: 11 talks of 'sacrifices, which can never remove sins' the author was not disagreeing with, but was faithful to, the Old Testament's own concept of sacrifice.

32–6. An individual case arises for which the penalty is not known, and this is used as the occasion for receiving more detailed guidance from the LORD, as happened in Num. 9: 6–13. In Exod. 35: 3 kindling fire on the sabbath day is specifically forbidden (as is the carrying of loads in Jer. 17: 24–7). This may have been something which was done naturally by many people continuously down to the period after the exile, and which the priestly group is trying hard to stamp out. In that case this story would be designed to be exemplary, for it clearly attempts to assimilate sabbath-breaking to great sins against God like blasphemy or idolatry, which are punished with death. We may doubt whether this new provision was ever literally enforced; the point being made is that infringement of what is seen as a basic require-ment (cp. Exod. 20: 8–11) brings danger to the whole com-munity if the offender is not removed from it. For a similar emphasis, cp. the story of Achan's sin and its disastrous consequences in Josh. 7.

37–40. As the final section of this chapter we have the command to wear *tassels* on garments as a reminder of the LORD's commandments. It may possibly have been included here to indicate how faults of inadvertence could be avoided by using this reminder of the law. The wearing of tassels is an ancient custom among other nations too, and already mentioned in Deut. 22: 12 ('You shall make twisted tassels on the four corners of your cloaks'); but P gives it a new significance, because of which the wearing of tassels is im-portant to Jews in the New Testament (Matt. 23: 5, 'with large tassels on their robes'), and to this day.

38. *a violet thread*: used also e.g. on the high priest's turban (Exod. 28: 37). Violet is such a common dyed colour that it is unlikely to have any special significance here.

41. The language is in the characteristic style of the Holiness Code of Lev. 17–26 (cp. the note on 3: 13). This section may be modelled on the Code, or is possibly an excerpt from it. ✶

TWO REBELLIONS, SECULAR AND RELIGIOUS

Now Korah son of Izhar, son of Kohath, son of Levi, **16** with the Reubenites Dathan and Abiram sons of Eliab and On son of Peleth, challenged the authority of Moses. 2 With them in their revolt were two hundred and fifty Israelites, all men of rank in the community, conveners of assembly and men of good standing. They confronted 3 Moses and Aaron and said to them, 'You take too much upon yourselves. Every member of the community is holy and the LORD is among them all. Why do you set yourselves up above the assembly of the LORD?' When 4 Moses heard this, he prostrated himself, and he said to 5 Korah and all his company, 'Tomorrow morning the LORD shall declare who is his, who is holy and may present offerings to him. The man whom the LORD chooses shall present them. This is what you must do, you, 6 Korah, and all your company: you must take censers and put fire in them, and then place incense on them be- 7 fore the LORD tomorrow. The man whom the LORD then chooses is the man who is holy. You take too much upon yourself, you sons of Levi.'

Moses said to Korah, 'Now listen, you sons of Levi. 8 Is it not enough for you that the God of Israel has set 9

you apart from the community of Israel, bringing you near him to maintain the service of the Tabernacle of the LORD and to stand before the community as their
10 ministers? He has brought you near him and your brother Levites with you; now you seek the priesthood
11 as well. That is why you and all your company have combined together against the LORD. What is Aaron that you should make these complaints against him?'

12 Moses sent to fetch Dathan and Abiram sons of Eliab,
13 but they answered, 'We are not coming. Is it a small thing that you have brought us away from a land flowing with milk and honey to let us die in the wilderness? Must
14 you also set yourself up as prince over us? What is more, you have not brought us into a land flowing with milk and honey, nor have you given us fields and vineyards to inherit. Do you think you can hoodwink*a* men like
15 us? We are not coming.' This answer made Moses very angry, and he said to the LORD, 'Take no notice of their murmuring. I have not taken from them so much as a single ass; I have done no wrong to any of them.'

16 Moses said to Korah, 'Present yourselves before the LORD tomorrow, you and all your company, you and
17 they and Aaron. Each man of you is to take his censer and put incense on it. Then you shall present them before the LORD with their two hundred and fifty censers, and you
18 and Aaron shall also bring your censers.' So each man took his censer and put fire in it and placed incense on it; Moses and Aaron took their stand at the entrance to the

[a] *Lit.* gouge out the eyes of . . .

Tent of the Presence,[a] and Korah gathered his[b] whole 19
company together and faced them at the entrance to the
Tent of the Presence.

Then the glory of the LORD appeared to the whole
community.

☆ This chapter is unusually perplexing. Two stories of rebellion have been knitted into one another to give a complex
continuous story of the simultaneous rebellion of Korah,
Dathan and Abiram. J told a story of a purely secular rebellion
against the authority of Moses by Dathan and Abiram. This is
found, with its beginning missing, in verses 12–15, 25,
27b, 28–31, 34. Deut. 11: 6 and Psalm 106: 17 refer to
Dathan and Abiram being swallowed up, with no mention of Korah, and this confirms that there are originally two
different stories here. P tells an independent story of Korah
rebelling, and maintaining that the tribe of Levi was not
more sacred than the other tribes of Israel. But within this
story there is another strand, probably added later, which
represents Korah and his followers as Levites who try to
secure the rights of the priests (so 7b–11, 16–17, 19–21 and
36–40). The final editor has drawn together the different
threads in such a way as to produce a readable continuous
story; but it has awkward transitions which reveal that it is a
compilation. The main strand of P reflects a need to assert
the pre-eminence of the Levites against men denying a special
position to them; the later strand a struggle within the priestly
orders in which the Korahites are worsted. This can be confirmed: in some material written after the exile the Korahites are one of the two great guilds of temple singers, and
their name stands in the headings of many of the psalms (these
headings are not unfortunately included in the N.E.B.);
but in a later version Korah is dropped altogether, and

[a] *So some MSS.; others* they stood at the entrance to the Tent of the
Presence, and Moses and Aaron . . .   [b] *So Sept.; Heb.* the.

replaced by Heman (1 Chron. 6: 33-48). These struggles for religious power appear to have been constant in Israel after the exile. There is an interesting parallel to the claims here rejected in a successful demand of the Levite singers made in A.D. 64 to wear the white linen robes of the priests, and of the Levite temple servants to 'be taught to sing hymns', so that they should stand on a level with the Levitical singers (Josephus, *Antiquities* xx. 9. 6 (216-18); Josephus too condemns the insolence of the Levites!). On the other hand the J rebellion gives another instance of a theme that is constant in Numbers of straight rebellious disobedience (e.g. ch. 14). Underlying J's story may be an earlier tradition of a group that refused to join in an entry into the land from the south. 'We will not go up' (the correct translation in verses 12 and 14) is a survival of this tradition. The fate of Dathan and Abiram is perhaps based on a natural phenomenon of the wilderness which could be taken to explain their disappearance (verse 30). Jude 11 shows us a New Testament writer comparing heretics of his day with Korah.

1-11 are from P, with 1*b* added to tie J and P together.

1. *and On son of Peleth*: he does not come into the story, and since in 26: 8f. Dathan and Abiram are called sons of Eliab son of Pallu it is possible that we should correct the texts to read here 'sons of Eliab son of Pallu' (or Peleth, as an alternative form).

2. *two hundred and fifty Israelites*: Korah is accompanied in his rebellion by a group of men of standing. His failure is the more striking.

3. *You take too much upon yourselves*: the line of thought is reminiscent of Num. 12: 2, where Aaron himself with Miriam complains against Moses 'Is Moses the only one with whom the LORD has spoken?'

4. *he prostrated himself*: this time not in intercession (as in 14: 5), but in despair, or else to acknowledge that it is God who must make the decision.

5. *The man whom the LORD chooses*: the theme of God

choosing between two groups is recurrent in the Old Testament: Isaac and Ishmael, Jacob and Esau, David and not one of his brothers.

6. *you must take censers*: flat pans, in shape like shovels, on which incense can be burnt; not enclosed like a modern censer.

8–11. This is the addition to P, in which the Levites are represented as seeking the status of priesthood.

11. *What is Aaron*: i.e. what is the matter with Aaron, what has he done?

12–15 is from J. A preceding part of the story, in which Moses is first told of the rebellion of Dathan and Abiram, was evidently left out when the stories were brought together.

12. *We are not coming*: although this is the only translation that makes sense in the context, the text properly means 'we will not go up', and this implies an earlier stage in the tradition (see above).

13. *flowing with milk and honey*: we have had this already as a standard phrase used of Canaan, in 13: 27 and 14: 8. Here it is used most unusually of Egypt, to suggest the irony of the rebels regarding Egypt as equivalent to the promised land.

14. *hoodwink*: cp. the footnote. 'Stop us seeing the truth' might be a better paraphrase.

15. *I have not taken from them so much as a single ass*: cp. the similar claim made by Samuel in 1 Sam. 12: 3.

16–24 resumes the P story (verses 16–17, 19–21 at least are from the later strand in P): the test spoken of in verse 7 is now carried out.

18. *the Tent of the Presence*: see the comment on 1: 1.

19. *the glory of the LORD appeared*: in visible form (cp. on 14: 10). ✻

GOD PUNISHES THE REBELS

And the LORD spoke to Moses and Aaron and 20 said, 'Stand apart from this company, so that I may 21

22 make an end of them in a single instant.' But they prostrated themselves and said, 'O God, God of the spirits of all mankind, if one man sins, wilt thou be angry with 23 the whole community?' But the LORD said to Moses, 24 'Tell them to stand back from the dwellings of Korah, Dathan and Abiram.'

25 So Moses rose and went to Dathan and Abiram, and the 26 elders of Israel followed him. He said to the whole community, 'Stand well away from the tents of these wicked men; touch nothing of theirs, or you will be 27 swept away because of all their sins.' So they moved away from the places occupied by Korah, Dathan and Abiram. Now Dathan and Abiram, holding themselves erect, had come out to the entrance of their tents with 28 their wives, their sons, and their dependants. Then Moses said, 'This shall prove to you that it is the LORD who sent me to do all these things, and it was not my own 29 heart that prompted me. If these men die a natural death and share the common fate of man, then the LORD 30 has not sent me; but if the LORD makes a great chasm, and the ground opens its mouth and swallows them and all that is theirs, and they go down alive to Sheol, then you will know that these men have held the LORD in contempt.'

31 Hardly had Moses spoken when the ground beneath 32 them split; the earth opened its mouth and swallowed them and their homes – all the followers of Korah and all 33 their property. They went down alive into Sheol with all that they had; the earth closed over them, and they 34 vanished from the assembly. At their cries all the Israelites round them fled, shouting, 'Look to yourselves! the

earth will swallow us up.' Meanwhile fire had come out 35
from the LORD and burnt up the two hundred and fifty
men who were presenting the incense.

* 22–4. *God of the spirits of all mankind*: literally, of all flesh.
A phrase stressing God's relationship to all men, this is found
also in 27: 16, but not otherwise. Its form (beginning in
Hebrew with *El*) suggests the possibility that it is an old
Canaanite title for their high god El, who is identified with
Yahweh. *if one man sins, wilt thou be angry with the whole
community?*: the answer is no: God tells the others to *stand
back*. There is perhaps here a deliberate rejection of an idea
that was once current in Israel, that many suffer for the guilt
of one, which later is felt to be unjust (cp. Gen. 18: 16–33,
Abraham's intercession for Sodom, which argues this).

25–34 are largely from J again.

27. *Korah* is added here in the final editing.

29. *then the LORD has not sent me*: a miracle is to be the
proof of Moses' authority. For another example see Exod.
7: 16–18, where the plagues of Egypt show Moses' support by
God.

30. *if the LORD makes a great chasm*: the idea is probably
taken from a natural phenomenon, the *kewir*, a morass of
clay covered with a hard crust of salt, which can collapse
suddenly when rain falls, and becomes impassable. *alive to
Sheol*: Sheol is the underworld where the dead go, conceived
of as being actually beneath the earth. There is something
particularly horrible in the idea of being swallowed up by
Sheol still alive.

32. *all the followers of Korah and all their property*: this is
added in to tie the two stories together.

35. The punishment of Korah's followers is the same as
that of Nadab and Abihu, sons of Aaron, whose sin was similar (Lev. 10. 1–2). Presumably Korah dies too (this is implied
by verse 40); but it is not explicitly said. *Meanwhile* is inserted

by the N.E.B. to link the two stories, but it is not in the Hebrew. ✶

THE CENSERS ARE USED AS A COVERING FOR THE ALTAR

36,[a] 37 Then the LORD spoke to Moses and said, 'Bid Eleazar son of Aaron the priest set aside the censers from the burnt remains, and scatter the fire from them far and wide, 38 because they are holy. And the censers of these men who sinned at the cost of their lives you shall make into beaten plates to cover the altar; they are holy, because they have been presented before the LORD. Let them be a sign to the 39 Israelites.' So Eleazar the priest took the bronze[b] censers which the victims of the fire had presented, and they were beaten into plates to make a covering for the altar, 40 as a reminder to the Israelites that no person unqualified, not descended from Aaron, should come forward to burn incense before the LORD, or his fate would be that of Korah and his company. All this was done as the LORD commanded Eleazar through Moses.

✶ The next three sections of this chapter are late additions to P, filling out ideas which supplement the story of 16: 1–35. The different chapter division in the Hebrew (see the N.E.B. footnote) shows an awareness of the separate nature of this material, though the chapter divisions are late. The Hebrew manuscripts have division marks at both points. This section explains the origins of the bronze plates which cover the altar of whole-offering: they are the censers of Korah and his company, re-used because they have become holy. According to Exod. 27: 2 and 38: 2 (P) the altar is

[a] *17: 1 in Heb.*   [b] *Or copper.*

already covered with bronze; we have here a later and diver-
gent tradition, which has perhaps forgotten the presence of
the account there. Since verse 40 takes the use of the plates
as a reminder that the priests are superior to the Levites,
not the Levites to the rest, this passage comes from the later
strand we have already met in 16: 7–11, 16–21.

37. *scatter the fire from them*: so that it will go out. This is
to make sure that no ordinary fire can be kindled from it: it
is holy fire.

38. *they are holy*: they have become for all time the property
of God, and must be re-used for sacred purposes. We have
here an early idea of holiness as a belonging to God, without
moral overtones. *Let them be a sign*: not in the sense of a
miracle, but a warning or portent. ✳

THE PEOPLE COMPLAIN,
BUT AARON MAKES EXPIATION FOR THEM

Next day all the community of the Israelites raised com- 41
plaints against Moses and Aaron and taxed them with
causing the death of some of the LORD's people. As they 42
gathered against Moses and Aaron, they turned towards
the Tent of the Presence and saw that the cloud covered
it, and the glory of the LORD appeared. Moses and Aaron 43
came to the front of the Tent of the Presence, and the 44
LORD spoke to Moses and Aaron[a] and said, 'Stand well 45
clear of this community, so that in a single instant I
may make an end of them.' Then they prostrated themselves, and Moses said to Aaron, 'Take your censer, put 46
fire from the altar in it, set incense on it, and go with it
quickly to the assembled community to make expiation
for them. Wrath has gone forth already from the presence

[a] and Aaron: *so Sept.; Heb. om.*

47 of the LORD. The plague has begun.' So Aaron took
his censer, as Moses had said, ran into the midst of the
assembly and found that the plague had begun among the
people. He put incense on the censer and made expiation
48 for the people, standing between the dead and the living,
49 and the plague stopped. Fourteen thousand seven hundred
died of it, in addition to those who had died for the
50 offence of Korah. When Aaron came back to Moses at the
entrance to the Tent of the Presence, the plague had
stopped.

* The people complain again, and are again punished with
plague (cp. 11: 33 or 14: 11–12, 36f.). But Aaron burns
incense and makes expiation for the people by it, and so the
plague stops. Only a priest can make expiation, usually by
sacrifice; and it means not an action to propitiate God, or
placate his anger, but one which covers over, and so obliter-
ates, sin. We know no other instance of the burning of
incense effecting this, and it is perhaps a development from
reflection upon the preceding story, rather than testimony
to an otherwise unknown ritual. The penalty for complaining
again seems severe to us; but it tells us, not about the ways of
God himself, but about the ideas of a writer who took with
deep seriousness the majesty and power of God.

41. *and taxed them with causing the death of some of the
LORD's people*: this rendering reduces the strength of the
Hebrew, which is literally 'and said, "You have caused the
death of the LORD's people"'. The writer means us to see in
this an absurd, and reprehensible, exaggeration.

45. *Then they prostrated themselves*: there is no time for
intercession; the plague takes immediate effect.

46. *Wrath has gone forth*: the wrath of God is spoken of as
if it were an independent force which proceeds almost

automatically when it is evoked. *The plague has begun*: no detail is given about what kind of plague it is.

49. *Fourteen thousand seven hundred*: if the author had in mind the numbers given in ch. 1, this would be about a fortieth of the whole congregation.

50. *the plague had stopped*: the intervention of the authorized priest is effective. ✶

AARON'S STAFF BLOSSOMS
TO SHOW THE SUPERIORITY OF LEVI

The LORD spoke to Moses and said, 'Speak to the Israel- **17** 1,ᵃ 2
ites and tell them to give you a staff for each tribe, one
from every tribal chief, twelve in all, and write each
man's name on his staff. On Levi's staff write the name of 3
Aaron, for there shall be one staff for each head of a tribe.
You shall put them all in the Tent of the Presence before 4
the Tokens, where I meet you, and the staff of the man I 5
choose shall sprout. I will rid myself of the complaints
of these Israelites, who keep on complaining against
you.'

Moses thereupon spoke to the Israelites, and each of 6
their chiefs handed him a staff, each of them one for his
tribe, twelve in all, and Aaron's staff among them. Moses 7
put them before the LORD in the Tent of the Tokens, and 8
next day when he entered the tent, he found that Aaron's
staff, the staff for the tribe of Levi, had sprouted. Indeed,
it had sprouted, blossomed, and produced ripe almonds.
Moses then brought out the staffs from before the LORD 9
and showed them to all the Israelites; they saw for themselves, and each man took his own staff. The LORD said to 10

[a] 17: 16 in Heb.

Moses, 'Put back Aaron's staff in front of the Tokens
to be kept as a warning to all rebels, so that you may rid
me once and for all of their complaints, and then they
11 shall not die.' Moses did this; as the LORD had commanded him, so he did.

12   The Israelites said to Moses, 'This is the end of us!
13 We perish, one and all! Every single person who goes
near the Tabernacle of the LORD dies. Is this to be our
final end?'

* In the last of these late additions to ch. 16, P shows God
giving a lasting sign of the superiority of the Levites to the
other tribes, in order to put an end to their complaints. The
chiefs of the twelve tribes put staffs in the Tent of the Presence before the Tokens, and the staff of Levi sprouts with
almonds. God commands that it should be kept as a warning.
It is possible that a metal image of a sprouting staff existed
in the temple and that this story is intended to explain it.
More probably it never in fact existed, for if it had once
been there and subsequently lost, we might have expected
the writer to say so.

2. *a staff for each tribe*: these are official staffs of the chiefs,
rather than newly-cut rods. A new rod might in any case
sprout after cutting, with no miracle involved. The word
used for staff can also mean a tribe, and the play on words is
used deliberately.

3. *On Levi's staff*: Aaron is the most important descendant
of Levi, and stands for all the tribe.

4. *before the Tokens*: the tablets of the ten commandments
(cp. on 1: 50).

8. *and produced ripe almonds*: almonds can blossom overnight,
but to produce the fruit already ripe is clearly thought of as
miraculous. Cp. Jer. 1: 11, for a word-play involving 'an
almond in early bloom'.

10. *Put back Aaron's staff*: so it is implied that it continued to be kept in the temple.

12–13. The Israelites are exasperated and in despair.

13. *Every single person*: it is indicated that it is fatal to come near to God's presence (cp. on 1: 53). *

THE PRIESTS ARE TO HAVE CHARGE OF THE ALTAR

The LORD said to Aaron: You and your sons, together **18** with the members of your father's tribe, shall be fully answerable for the sanctuary. You and your sons alone shall be answerable for your priestly office; but you shall 2 admit your kinsmen of Levi, your father's tribe, to be attached to you and assist you while you and your sons are before the Tent of the Tokens. They shall be in attend- 3 ance on you and fulfil all the duties of the Tent, but shall not go near the holy vessels and the altar, or they will die and you with them. They shall be attached to you and 4 be responsible for the maintenance of the Tent of the Presence in every detail; no unqualified person shall come near you. You yourselves shall be responsible for 5 the sanctuary and the altar, so that wrath may no more fall on the Israelites. I have myself taken the Levites your 6 kinsmen out of all the Israelites as a gift for you, given to the LORD for the maintenance of the Tent of the Presence. But only you and your sons may fulfil the duties of your 7 priestly office that concern the altar or lie within the Veil. This duty is yours; I bestow on you this gift of priestly service. The unqualified person who intrudes on it shall be put to death.

* Instruction by God on the duties and dues of the priests and Levites are given in this chapter in the form of an address by God to Aaron. The whole chapter is in the Priestly style, and is probably a later addition to P; it was felt to come in appropriately after the picture of disputes over duties and privileges in chs. 16 and 17. First in a general statement we are told that the priests are in sole charge of the sanctuary, and the Levites exist to serve and help them, but may not touch the altar or the holy vessels, while no layman may approach on pain of death. What is said here has already been stated in 1: 50–3; 3: 5–10 and parts of ch. 16; but these ideas are deliberately drawn together here in summary form. This standard post-exilic interpretation attests the high value the Priestly school attached to the worthy service of God by those duly commissioned to it, and so to their deep awareness of his holiness. If we prefer to stress God's nearness and openness to man, we must not lose what is still of value in this profound awareness of his holiness.

1. *The LORD said to Aaron*: usually Aaron is addressed by God through Moses; this direct address is a sign of a late date within the Priestly school. The only other example is Lev. 10: 8. *You and your sons*: all the priests, for all the priests, and they alone, trace their descent from Aaron. *the members of your father's tribe*: the Levites are the sole members of the tribe of Levi. *shall be fully answerable*: literally, 'shall bear the iniquity of', shall be responsible for any faults committed in the sanctuary.

2. *to be attached to you*: a play on words which cannot be felt in English. The verb *lawah* (to attach, unite) is used to explain why they are called *lewi* (Levites). This may well not be the original sense of *lewi*, but it is found again in Gen. 29: 34, where Leah says: '"my husband and I will surely be united." So she called him Levi.'

3. *or they will die*: in the thought of the writer they will be struck dead by God, rather than subjected to the death penalty.

4. *unqualified person*: the word normally means stranger,

and is here used for anyone who is not a priest or a Levite: a
layman.

7. *or lie within the Veil*: the first hanging at the entrance to
the Holy Place. According to Lev. 16: 2, 17 only the high
priest could go within the Veil, and that only once a year, on
the Day of Atonement. This is alluded to here; it is not
proposed that access should be widened to all priests. *this gift
of priestly service*: the priests have done nothing to merit this
privilege; it is a free gift of God. ✳

THE GIFTS DUE TO THE PRIESTS FROM THE PEOPLE

The LORD said to Aaron: I, the LORD, commit to your 8
control the contributions made to me, that is all the holy-
gifts of the Israelites. I give them to you and to your sons
for your allotted portion due to you in perpetuity. Out 9
of the most holy gifts kept back from the altar-fire
this part shall belong to you: every offering, whether
grain-offering, sin-offering, or guilt-offering, rendered
to me as a most holy gift, belongs to you and to your sons.
You shall eat it as befits most holy gifts; every male may 10
eat it. You shall regard it as holy.

This also is yours: the contribution from all such of 11
their gifts as are presented as special gifts by the Israelites.
I give them to you and to your sons and daughters with
you as a due in perpetuity. Every person in your household who is ritually clean may eat them.

I give you all the choicest of the oil, the choicest of 12
the new wine and the corn, the firstfruits which are given
to the LORD. The first-ripe fruits of all produce in the 13
land which are brought to the LORD shall be yours.
Everyone in your household who is clean may eat them.

14   Everything in Israel which has been devoted to God shall be yours.

15   All the first-born of man or beast which are brought to the LORD shall be yours. Notwithstanding, you must accept payment in redemption of any first-born of man

16   and of unclean beasts: at the end of one month you shall redeem it at the fixed price of five shekels of silver by the

17   sacred standard (twenty gerahs to the shekel). You must not, however, allow the redemption of the first-born of a cow, sheep, or goat; they are holy. You shall fling their blood against the altar and burn their fat in sacrifice

18   as a food-offering of soothing odour to the LORD; their flesh shall be yours, as are the breast of the special gift and the right leg.

19   All the contributions from holy-gifts, which the Israelites set aside for the LORD, I give to you and to your sons and daughters with you as a due in perpetuity. This is a perpetual covenant of salt before the LORD with you and your descendants also.

20   The LORD said to Aaron: You shall have no patrimony in the land of Israel, no holding among them; I am your holding in Israel, I am your patrimony.

---

* Next the rights of priests and Levites are stated. They are set apart because of their cultic duties, and so have no land; but instead they have the right to support from the people who use their services, for spiritual goods are greater than material goods. This comes to them in the form of portions from sacrifices, firstfruits and first-born of beasts, and tithes. The section is in detail rather complicated, and has undergone some additions before reaching its present form. Complicated though the details are, support of this sort is necessary to any kind of ordered ministry, and Paul emphatically claims the same rights for the Christian ministry ('those who preach the Gospel should earn their living by the Gospel', 1 Cor. 9: 14). The mutual dependence of ministers and people on each other and on God is thus brought out.

8. First comes a general statement: *all the holy-gifts* (gifts of any sort to God, cp. on 5: 9) are committed to the priest. This is then set out in detail in the following verses. *to your control*: or better, 'all that is reserved of'.

9. First come portions of sacrifices other than the whole-offering and the shared-offering, both of which were consumed in the sacred meal. The part kept back is of the grain-offering a handful, and of other offerings parts of the fat (set out in detail in Lev. 2 and 3).

10. *as befits most holy gifts*: it may not be clear on first reading, but this means 'as befits extremely holy gifts', not 'as befits most of the holy gifts'.

11–18 go on to deal with offerings from the world of nature.

11. *to you and to your sons and daughters with you*: it is here made clear that the appropriate parts of *special gifts* are not eaten in the sanctuary, but shared with the whole household of the priest.

12–13. *oil* and *wine* and *corn* are regularly joined together in Israelite thought: cp. the offerings in 15: 4, and the regular phrase 'your corn and new wine and oil' (e.g. Deut. 7: 13). *firstfruits*: earlier in P there was a technical distinction between this and *first-ripe fruits* (verse 13), which was a narrower term, though both refer to some of the new produce of the year, that is dedicated to God. But in this chapter the two appear to mean the same. Note that the quantities of firstfruits are not laid down.

14. *which has been devoted to God*: this is the 'ban' under which objects are wholly given to God and cannot be redeemed (cp. on 21: 2). In war in early Israel they were destroyed; now they are claimed by the priesthood.

15. The first-born of man and beast are God's; this is a very

widespread religious concept. Both perhaps at a very primitive time were sacrificed to him; but it is of very old standing in Israel that a payment could be made instead, for *man* and for *unclean beasts*, as specified in verse 16. But clean animals could not be redeemed: they are holy, and belong to the priests. *unclean beasts*: on cleanness and uncleanness generally cp. the introduction to 5: 1–4. This distinction is also applied to animals, and detailed lists of clean and unclean beasts are found in P. The reasons for the allocations are often obscure, but there clearly are reasons. The distinction is found already in J (Gen. 7: 2) and is no doubt very ancient.

16. This verse is a later addition, interrupting the context. *silver by the sacred standard*: cp. the note on 3: 47.

17. *You shall fling their blood*: though not a sacrifice the animals are treated like one. But the whole of the flesh is given to the priests, not only part of it.

18. *the breast of the special gift and the right leg*: this refers to the provision about the shared-offering in Lev. 7: 30–4.

19 summarizes verses 11–18. A *perpetual covenant of salt* is a rare phrase, meaning one guaranteed by the bond of eating a meal together. The phrase occurs again only in the very late 2 Chron. 13: 5, 'the Lord the God of Israel gave the kingship over Israel to David and his descendants in perpetuity by a covenant of salt'. Thus both the divine role through David and the priestly order are regarded as established for ever.

20. *You shall have no patrimony*: the priests possess no landed property, but receive these dues instead. ✳

THE DUES OF THE LEVITES

21 To the Levites I give every tithe in Israel to be their patrimony, in return for the service they render in maintaining
22 the Tent of the Presence. In order that the Israelites may not henceforth approach the Tent and thus incur the
23 penalty of death, the Levites alone shall perform the

service of the Tent, and they shall accept the full responsibility for it. This rule is binding on your descendants for all time. They shall have no patrimony among the Israelites, because I give them as their patrimony the tithe 24 which the Israelites set aside as a contribution to the LORD. Therefore I say to them: You shall have no patrimony among the Israelites.

* We move on to the Levites, who are supported by a tithe (a fixed charge of one tenth) on agricultural produce. In this form the law is late, for in Deut. 14: 22–9, while the Israelites were enjoined not to neglect the Levites, these shared the tithe in two years out of three with the offerer, and in the third year with the poor, with 'the aliens, orphans, and widows' (Deut. 14: 29). Their demands gradually increased; and at a later stage still (Lev. 27: 30–3) they required tithes of cattle and sheep as well. Whether there was a tithe before the time of Deuteronomy is uncertain.

21. This *tithe* is seen as a return for the service done by the Levites in taking upon themselves the duty and the risk involved in approaching God's presence. They, like the priests, have no territorial possessions as their *patrimony*, but depend entirely on the tithe. *

THE DUES OF THE LEVITES TO THE PRIESTS

The LORD spoke to Moses and said, Speak to the Levites 25,26 in these words: When you receive from the Israelites the tithe which I give you from them as your patrimony, you shall set aside from it the contribution to the LORD, a tithe of the tithe. Your contribution shall count for you as 27 if it were corn from the threshing-floor and juice from the vat. In this way you too shall set aside the contribution 28

due to the LORD out of all tithes which you receive from
the Israelites and shall give the LORD's contribution to
29 Aaron the priest. Out of all the gifts you receive you shall
set aside the contribution due to the LORD; and the gift
which you hallow*ᵃ* must be taken from the choicest of
them.

30   You shall say to the Levites: When you have set aside
the choicest part of your portion, the remainder shall
count for you as the produce of the threshing-floor and
31 the winepress, and you may eat it anywhere, you and
your households. It is your payment for service in the
32 Tent of the Presence. When you have set aside its choicest
part, you will incur no penalty in respect of it, and you
will not be profaning the holy-gifts of the Israelites; so
you will not die.

✶ In another still later development the Levites in turn are to
pay to the priests a tithe on their tithe. For the Levites these
stand in the place of property, and the priests are therefore
entitled to be supported by a tithe of this too.

25. *The LORD spoke to Moses*: the address to Moses indicates that we have a new beginning here.

27 shows that the tithe paid to the Levites is to them what the
basic crop is to the people.

29. *you hallow*: it will be seen from the N.E.B. footnote
that this is the probable reading. The Hebrew as it stands
means 'his hallowed thing', but this does not fit. Originally
the consonants only were written, the vowels added later.
This correction keeps the consonants of the Hebrew text, and
assumes that the wrong vowels were added in.

30. There is a new introduction here, and so another
addition. The N.E.B. has made the text more logical. As it

[a] you hallow: *prob. rdg.; Heb. obscure.*

stands the Hebrew says 'You shall say to them', and later
continues 'the remainder shall count for the Levites'. If the
word translated 'set aside' is instead translated 'demanded',
it is possible to take this section as addressed to the priests, on
how they are to deal with the offerings of the Levites. It would
be easier to follow the N.E.B., but it does involve a forced
understanding of the wording, and the alternative is probably
better. The passage is not in any case very well phrased in the
Hebrew. ✻

THE RITUAL OF THE RED COW

The LORD spoke to Moses and Aaron and said: This is a **19** 1, 2
law and a statute which the LORD has ordained. Tell the
Israelites to bring you a red cow without blemish or
defect, which has never borne the yoke. You shall give 3
it to Eleazar the priest, and it shall be taken outside the
camp and slaughtered[a] to the east of it. Eleazar the priest 4
shall take some of the blood on his finger and sprinkle it
seven times towards the front of the Tent of the Presence.
The cow shall be burnt in his sight, skin, flesh, and blood, 5
together with the offal. The priest shall then take cedar- 6
wood, marjoram, and scarlet thread, and throw them into
the heart of the fire in which the cow is burning. He shall 7
wash his clothes and bathe his body in water; after which
he may enter the camp, but he remains ritually unclean
till sunset. The man who burnt the cow shall wash his 8
clothes and bathe his body in water, but he also remains
unclean till sunset. Then a man who is clean shall collect 9
the ashes of the cow and deposit them outside the camp
in a clean place. They shall be reserved for use by the
Israelite community in the water of ritual purification;

[a] *Or* he shall take it outside the camp and slaughter it . . .

10 for the cow is a sin-offering. The man who collected the ashes of the cow shall wash his clothes, but he remains unclean till sunset. This rule shall be binding for all time on the Israelites and on the alien who is living with them.

* The Priestly Writer now appends another chapter on how the people is to be kept ritually pure. A red cow without fault is to be killed and burnt entire, and its ashes used to make a water of ritual purification used especially in the case of those who have touched a corpse. The ritual is without parallel in Israel, and is something of a mystery. It is not a sacrifice: it is not done in the temple, and the cow itself is not given to God, but totally burnt, and used to provide the ashes in the water. The ritual is in origin magical, and perhaps Canaanite. We do not hear of any belief in Israel before the exile that contact with a corpse defiles (see for instance Gen. 46: 4 and 50: 1), but abhorrence of dead bodies is very widespread, and so are rituals to avert uncleanness from touching them, and these sometimes (e.g. in India) involve the use of cows. The insistence that the cow should be red, the accompanying objects, and the odd way of making the water, no doubt go back to this magical stage. But as the ritual is taken into Israelite practice by the Priestly school, it is subordinated to their beliefs about the LORD. The ritual uncleanness is an offence against his holiness, and must be taken away. The chapter comes from a late stage of P, and has itself gone through a long process of development, and had some late additions made to it, as a result of which its sequence of thought is at times rather jerky.

2. *a red cow*: red to suggest blood, a powerful cleansing agent; or possibly 'red-brown', like the earth in which the dead are buried. *cow* is traditionally translated 'heifer' (a cow which has not borne a calf), and so already in the Septuagint and in Heb. 9: 13, which refers briefly to this chapter. But the word actually used here is not so narrow. *which has never*

borne the yoke: like the heifer used in a ritual in cases of un-detected murder in Deut. 21: 1–9.

3. *to Eleazar the priest*: so it is given in later times to a priest of the line of Aaron. But perhaps Eleazar is singled out to be given the cow in order to safeguard the purity of Aaron himself.

4. The sprinkling of blood *seven times* is found in the ritual of sacrifice in Lev. 4: 3–12, and is perhaps a late adaptation of that rite into one previously unfamiliar with it, to assimilate it to a sacrifice.

5. There is no parallel in sacrifices proper to this total consumption.

6. *cedar-wood, marjoram, and scarlet thread*: these are also used in the purification of those suffering from skin-disease (Lev. 14: 6–7), and have symbolic significance there as part of the cleansing process. Their point here is not clear, and they may be borrowed from that ritual. Marjoram has cleansing quali-ties; this is a better translation than the traditional hyssop, which is not a native of Palestine.

7, 8 and 10 arc probably borrowed from the ritual in the laws on purity (Lev. 11: 25; 15: 8; 16: 28). Why are they unclean? Probably the cow becomes unclean in advance of its actual use to remove uncleanness.

9. It is not until now that the purpose of the ritual is stated.

10. *and on the alien*: see the note on 9: 14. ✻

THE USE OF THE WATER OF PURIFICATION

Whoever touches a corpse shall be ritually unclean for 11 seven days. He shall get himself purified with the water of 12 ritual purification on the third day and on the seventh day, and then he shall be clean. If he is not purified both on the third day and on the seventh, he shall not be clean. Everyone who touches a corpse, that is the body of a 13 man who has died, and does not purify himself, defiles the

Tabernacle of the LORD. That person shall be cut off from Israel. The water of purification has not been flung over him; he remains unclean, and his impurity is still upon him.

14 When a man dies in a tent, this is the law: everyone who goes into the tent and everyone who was inside the
15 tent shall be ritually unclean for seven days, and every open vessel which has no covering tied over it shall also
16 be unclean. In the open, anyone who touches a man killed with a weapon or one who has died naturally, or who touches a human bone or a grave, shall be unclean for
17 seven days. For such uncleanness, they shall take some of the ash from the burnt mass of the sin-offering and add
18 fresh water to it in a vessel. Then a man who is clean shall take marjoram, dip it in the water, and sprinkle the tent with all the vessels in it and all the people who were there, or the man who has touched a human bone, a corpse (whether the man was killed or died naturally), or a grave.
19 The man who is clean shall sprinkle the unclean man on the third day and on the seventh; on the seventh day he shall purify him; then the man shall wash his clothes and
20 bathe in water, and at sunset he shall be clean. If a man who is unclean does not get himself purified, that person shall be cut off from the assembly, because he has defiled the sanctuary of the LORD. The water of purification has
21 not been flung over him: he is unclean. This rule shall be binding on you[a] for all time. The man who sprinkles the water of purification shall also wash his clothes, and whoever touches the water shall be unclean till sunset.
22 Whatever the unclean man touches shall be unclean, and any person who touches that shall be unclean till sunset.

[a] *So some MSS.; others* them.

* Now the use of the water of purification is set out. Verses 11–13 indicate in a legal style the law on impurity from contact with a corpse; verses 14–16 list particular instances requiring purification; verses 17–19 describe a particular ritual of purification, and verses 20–2 restate rules already given.

13. *shall be cut off from Israel*: he must live outside the camp (cp. on 5: 1–4). It is not clear what this means in terms of life in the promised land itself. *The water of purification has not been flung over him*: it is implied that if this is done he will be purified.

14. *in a tent*: or, presumably, when they are in the promised land, in a house.

17–19. This is a second, different ritual, using the water of purification, and giving another means of cleansing, which is also no doubt ancient in origin.

17. *the burnt mass of the sin-offering*: that is, the ashes of the cow (verse 9). *fresh water*: from a running stream. It is assumed that it is always fresh water that is added to make the water of purification, and this too has roots in older ideas of a magical character.

18. *a man who is clean*: it is noteworthy that a priest is not required.

20 restates the rule given in verses 11–13.

21–2 similarly restate the rules of verses 7, 8 and 10, which were a later addition in 1–10.

With the ritual of purification given, Israel has been prepared ritually for the task ahead, and is now ready to think about moving on towards the promised land. *

THE PEOPLE DISPUTE AT THE WATERS OF MERIBAH

In the first month the whole community of Israel reached **20** the wilderness of Zin and stayed some time at Kadesh; there Miriam died and was buried.

There was no water for the community; so they 2

3 gathered against Moses and Aaron. The people disputed with Moses and said, 'If only we had perished when our
4 brothers perished in the presence of the LORD! Why have you brought the assembly of the LORD into this
5 wilderness for us and our beasts to die here? Why did you fetch us up from Egypt to bring us to this vile place, where nothing will grow, neither corn nor figs, vines nor pomegranates? There is not even any water to
6 drink.' Moses and Aaron came forward in front of the assembly to the entrance of the Tent of the Presence. There they fell prostrate, and the glory of the LORD appeared to them.

7, 8   The LORD spoke to Moses and said, 'Take a^a staff, and then with Aaron your brother assemble all the community, and, in front of them all, speak to the rock and it will yield its water. Thus you will produce water for the community out of the rock, for them and their beasts
9 to drink.' Moses left the presence of the LORD with the
10 staff, as he had commanded him. Then he and Aaron gathered the assembly together in front of the rock, and he said to them, 'Listen to me, you rebels. Must we get
11 water out of this rock for you?' Moses raised his hand and struck the rock twice with his staff. Water gushed out in
12 abundance and they all drank, men and beasts. But the LORD said to Moses and Aaron, 'You did not trust me so far as to uphold my holiness in the sight of the Israelites; therefore you shall not lead this assembly into the land
13 which I promised to give them.' Such were the waters of Meribah,^b where the people disputed with the LORD and through which his holiness was upheld.

[a] *Or* the.   [b] *That is* Dispute.

✳ After the sedentary period represented by chs. 15–19, Israel's journey is now resumed. The death of Miriam is mentioned first. Then, before Israel moves off, there is one last incident of rebellion, a complaint of the lack of water at Meribah, which Moses remedies by striking the rock with his staff. But Moses and Aaron have themselves offended God (see the comment on verse 12), and are told that they will not lead the people into the promised land. This is the origin of 'the waters of Meribah', or 'of dispute'. Exod. 17: 1–7 has already told a J version of a miracle at Meribah in which the staff of Moses and the striking of the rock have a place in the story. So we have here P's re-use of the same story, with the distinctive motif of Moses' distrust incorporated. This makes it different enough for the final editor to wish to keep both stories rather than leave one out. The underlying theme is again of the faithlessness of man and the faithfulness of God, shown classically in the wilderness experience.

1. *In the first month*: March–April, but the year is not given; we are in the fortieth year for P, who sees Israel only then arrive at Kadesh, but not for J, who has them go straight to there from Egypt (Num. 12: 16; 13: 26). So the redactor (see p. 9) responsible for this verse leaves out any indication of the year altogether. *wilderness of Zin*: cp. the notes on 13: 21 and 26. *there Miriam died*: this is probably put in by the final redactor. Miriam is not otherwise mentioned in P, but the redactor wishes to present Miriam and Aaron as dying successively before Moses, as he comes to the end of his story.

3. *when our brothers perished*: the reference is to Korah and his company (16: 35 and 49).

5. *corn nor figs, vines nor pomegranates*: typical of Canaan, not of Egypt: the explorers in 13: 23 bring back grapes, pomegranates and figs.

6. *and the glory of the LORD appeared to them*: cp. the note on 14: 10.

8. *Take a staff*: elsewhere in P it is Aaron who has the staff, but here the author thinks of the staff with which in the older

tradition Moses struck the Nile, turning water into blood, and divided the sea (Exod. 7: 20; 14: 16). *speak to the rock*: this was no doubt a well-known landmark at Kadesh. Note that Moses is simply to speak to it.

10. *Listen to me, you rebels*: Moses's behaviour differs from his previous patience and readiness to intercede, and prepares us for a new turn to be taken in this story.

11. *and struck the rock twice*: he had only been told to speak to it (verse 8).

12. *You did not trust me*: God's sudden anger is a puzzle unless it is caused by Moses' failure simply to speak to the rock without striking it. The striking twice is a sign of lack of faith in God. Moses will not trust his word, but wants a specific material action. Underlying this tradition is the need for P to explain why Moses and Aaron did not in fact enter the promised land (for there was no tradition of their presence there): it must be because of a grievous fault of theirs.

13. *Such were the waters of Meribah*: the name (which is no doubt of an actual place near Kadesh, referred to also as Meribah-by-Kadesh in Deut. 32: 51 and Ezek. 47: 19) is made to explain the story, just as the underlying story in Exod. 17: 1–7 was originally built round the name Meribah ('Dispute': see footnote). So it is an aetiology: cp. the introduction to 11: 1–3. *his holiness was upheld*: this is another play on words; the place-name Kadesh is formed from the root which means 'be holy', and the author is alluding to this. ✳

The approach to the promised land

EDOM REFUSES TO ALLOW ISRAEL TO PASS THROUGH THEIR LAND

14 FROM KADESH MOSES sent envoys to the king of Edom: This is a message from your brother Israel.
15 You know all the hardships we have encountered, how

our fathers went down to Egypt, and we lived there for
many years. The Egyptians ill-treated us and our fathers
before us, and we cried to the LORD for help. He listened 16
to us and sent an angel, and he brought us out of Egypt;
and now we are here at Kadesh, a town on your frontier.
Grant us passage through your country. We will not 17
trespass on field or vineyard, or drink from your wells.
We will keep to the king's highway; we will not turn
off to right or left until we have crossed your territory.'
But the Edomites answered, 'You shall not cross our 18
land. If you do, we will march out and attack you in
force.' The Israelites said, 'But we will keep to the main 19
road. If we and our flocks drink your water, we will
pay you for it; we will simply cross your land on foot.'
But the Edomites said, 'No, you shall not', and took the 20
field against them with a large army in full strength.
Thus the Edomites refused to allow Israel to cross their 21
frontier, and Israel went a different way to avoid a
conflict.

* From now to the end of the book Israel is on the move
again, to the very border of the promised land, passing to the
south of Edom and then north to the east of Moab to reach
the Jordan from the east. This section tells of an approach to
the king of Edom for permission to pass through his country,
which is refused. It is probably a later addition to J, modelled
on the very similar earlier account of the challenge to Moab
(21: 21–4), which however ends in Israel conquering Moab.
It is created to fill a gap which the editor has realised, namely
that the old traditions contain no indication one way or the
other of how Israel fared in contact with Edom. This gap is
historically due to the fact that there was no such contact:
those who came out of Egypt entered Palestine from the

south, others quite separately from the east. Edom is a traditional enemy of Israel, but though this does come out in the story, it is not made a central point in it.

14. *your brother Israel*: Edom is identified with Esau, twin brother of Jacob, whose other name is Israel (Gen. 25: 23–6). The two nations are very close, and speak the same language, but fight, too, like brothers. The hostility was at its greatest after the exile, when Edom gained territory at the expense of Judah (cp. the book of Obadiah, where Israel's hatred of Edom is clearly seen).

15. *how our fathers went down to Egypt*: verses 15–16 recite in summary the story of how God has brought Israel out of Egypt. Creed-like recitals of this sort (cp. Deut. 26: 5–9 or Josh. 24: 2–13) are now thought to be relatively late (as creeds are late in Christianity). It is only appropriate here because of the supposed close relationship of Israel and Edom.

16. *and sent an angel*: angels in the Old Testament are manifestations of the presence of God in human form. They can appear and disappear suddenly, but look just like men: there is no thought of wings or a shining appearance (this is a much later, post-biblical concept). They bring to men directly God's word and will (cp. the appearances of angels in Judg. 6: 11–24 and 13: 2–23).

17. *the king's highway*: this is usually thought to be a specific road (so better 'the King's Highway'), mentioned three times in the Old Testament (cp. 21: 22 and Deut. 2: 27), which runs from Damascus down through Jordan to the gulf of Akaba, and which used to have a row of fortresses along it. The modern Arabic name for it still means 'road of the ruler'.

19. The plea is repeated and again refused: not a sign of two sources, but a repetition to make the point more sharply.

20. *took the field against them*: and presumably fought with them, although this is not said.

21. *went a different way*: Israel must make a very awkward detour to the south and then east of Edom (it is assumed the

power of Edom did not extend as far south as the Gulf of
Akaba, or they could not have got past at all); but they
accept without complaint, because they are the weaker
group. *

THE DEATH OF AARON

The whole community of Israel set out from Kadesh and 22
came to Mount Hor. At Mount Hor, near the frontier of 23
Edom, the LORD said to Moses and Aaron, 'Aaron shall 24
be gathered to his father's kin. He shall not enter the
land which I promised to give the Israelites, because
over the waters of Meribah you rebelled against my command. Take Aaron and his son Eleazar, and go up Mount 25
Hor. Strip Aaron of his robes and invest Eleazar his son 26
with them, for Aaron shall be taken from you: he shall
die there.' Moses did as the LORD had commanded him: 27
they went up Mount Hor in sight of the whole community, and Moses stripped Aaron of his robes and invested 28
his son Eleazar with them. There Aaron died on the
mountain-top, and Moses and Eleazar came down from
the mountain. So the whole community saw that Aaron 29
had died, and all Israel mourned him for thirty days.

* P as he comes to the end of his story tells of the death of
Aaron before that of Moses, and the story includes the passing
on of his sacred office. It is the importance of the high priesthood after the exile that leads to this emphasis.

22. *and came to Mount Hor*: the site is uncertain (as so many
are). The traditional identification with Jebel Harun ('Mount
of Aaron'), the tallest mountain in the middle of the area of
Edom, although it goes back as far as Josephus (first century
A.D.), is due to a later tradition, since Hor cannot be within the
area of Edom.

24. *He shall not enter the land*: we are explicitly reminded of verse 12.

26. *Strip Aaron of his robes*: the special garments of the high priest which are described in Lev. 8: 7–9, including a striking breastplate with twelve precious stones on it. The investing of Eleazar with the robes is the mark of the transfer of authority to him. This stresses the continuity and abiding authority of the true priestly line.

29. *and all Israel mourned him for thirty days*: mourning usually lasted for seven days, but because of their importance Aaron and Moses (Deut. 34: 8) are mourned for thirty days, a month instead of a week. Now Moses alone is left of Israel's leaders. ✶

VICTORY AT HORMAH

21 When the Canaanite king of Arad who lived in the Negeb heard that the Israelites were coming by way of Atharim, he attacked them and took some of them 2 prisoners. Israel thereupon made a vow to the LORD and said, 'If thou wilt deliver this people into my power, I will 3 destroy their cities.' The LORD listened to Israel and delivered the Canaanites into their power.*ᵃ* Israel destroyed them and their cities and called the place Hormah.*ᵇ*

✶ Israel vows to attack the Canaanites, defeats them and destroys Hormah. Hormah means 'destruction' (cp. 14: 45), and this part of the story is an aetiology (cp. the introductory note to 11: 1–3). But the story with its mention of 'their cities' is older than the reference to Hormah in particular, and reflects a tradition of a conquest of part of Canaan from the south. The same is true of Num. 13–14 and 16 in their original form. But J has superimposed on these older traditions his view that Israel entered Canaan only from the east, and so this

[a] into their power: *so Sam.; Heb. om.*   [b] *That is* Destruction.

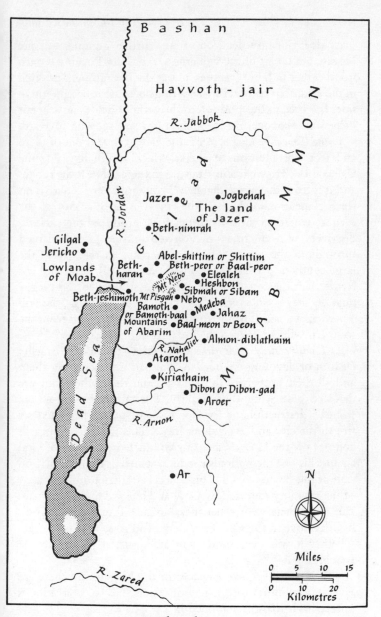

2. Moab and Ammon

story does not now lead on to any further conquests in the Negeb, but is part of the wilderness traditions. Possibly it once stood earlier in J, but has been put at the last moment possible in the traditions of Israel's wanderings because it has a positive side. It is used in this position to show the Israelites now at last successfully conquering the Canaanites and moving forward.

1. *the Canaanite king of Arad*: the *king of Arad* is out of place and is a late addition to a text which originally said 'the Canaanites'. Hormah and Arad are juxtaposed in Josh. 12: 14, and it is from that verse that he is brought in here. There is no further mention of him in the story. Arad is a city in the Negeb, where recent excavations have produced the exciting discovery of a sanctuary of Yahweh outside Jerusalem used throughout the period of the monarchy. *in the Negeb*: the large southern part of Canaan (see map, p. 12), drier and less fertile than the rest of Israel, which is still called the Negev now. *by way of Atharim*: or 'by the Way of Atharim', naming a particular road. It is not known, but must have led from the southern wilderness into the Judaean hill-country.

2. *I will destroy their cities*: this refers to an old Israelite custom of devoting enemies to 'the ban', consecrating them and all their properties to Yahweh, and then when they are defeated destroying them utterly. For another example cp. Joshua's destruction of Jericho, Josh. 6: 24: 'They then set fire to the city and everything in it.' This is a part of Israel's concept of 'the Holy War', war conducted on behalf of God against his and the nation's enemies, which as enemies of God cannot but be destroyed. This reflects a rather primitive view of the morality required by God, and one we find repugnant. But it conflicts with other ideas already found about God's limitless love in the Old Testament; and it is far from certain whether it was ever more than an idealized picture to the Israelites.

3. *and called the place Hormah*: in the Negeb, but there are several possibilities for the identification, and so its location is uncertain. It is also mentioned in 14: 45. ✳

146

THE BRONZE SERPENT

Then they left Mount Hor by way of the Red Sea to 4
march round the flank of Edom. But on the way they
grew impatient and spoke against God and Moses. 5
'Why have you brought us up from Egypt', they said,
'to die in the desert where there is neither food nor
water? We are heartily sick of this miserable fare.'
Then the LORD sent poisonous snakes among the people, 6
and they bit the Israelites so that many of them died.
The people came to Moses and said, 'We sinned when we 7
spoke against the LORD and you. Plead with the LORD to
rid us of the snakes.' Moses therefore pleaded with the
LORD for the people; and the LORD told Moses to make a 8
serpent*a* of bronze*b* and erect it as a standard, so that
anyone who had been bitten could look at it and recover.
So Moses made a bronze serpent and erected it as a stand- 9
ard, so that when a snake had bitten a man, he could
look at the bronze serpent and recover.

✻ The people rebel yet again, and are punished with poisonous
snakes. Moses prays for them, and is told to make a serpent of
bronze; those bitten will recover if they look at it. This story
was developed to explain the origin of a bronze serpent which
stood in the temple of Jerusalem down to the reign of Hezekiah, who had it destroyed (2 Kings 18: 4: '. . . and broke up
the bronze serpent that Moses had made; for up to that time
the Israelites had been burning sacrifices to it; they called it
Nehushtan'). The word Nehushtan is formed from *neḥosheth*,
'bronze', but sounds as if it ought to be connected with *naḥash*,
'serpent', and would therefore be thought particularly appro-

[a] *Or* snake.
[b] a serpent of bronze: *so some Sept. MSS.; Heb.* a poisonous thing.

priate. This bronze serpent very probably in fact goes back in Jerusalem to pre-Israelite times, and was a fertility symbol in the temple of the Jebusites in Jerusalem. Several other bronze serpent images have been found in Palestine, for instance at Gezer, Hazor and Megiddo; one has recently been discovered in the excavation of a temple at Timnah in the Arabah, near Elat, dated to about 1200–900 B.C. and assumed to be Midianite in origin, so it was known in the wilderness area as well as in Palestine. But the story here looks like an explanatory story built upon the existence of the snake in the temple in Jerusalem. While Hezekiah must have recognized its Canaanite origin and destroyed it for this reason, it was earlier regarded as legitimate but in need of explanation, and so the story we have was developed. The serpent moves from its fertility context to being understood as having healing and protective properties for those bitten by snakes, and so is a sign of the LORD's protective power. The story takes up the standard themes of rebellion and punishment in the wilderness, without developing them, and is perhaps written later than most of J, and very probably at the earliest after the building of Solomon's temple. J places this story last in his picture of the wilderness, to lay once more great emphasis on the deep-seated rebellion of the people, on Moses' intercession, and on God's readiness to forgive and to heal.

4. *Then they left Mount Hor*: this verse is added by the final editor to give a context to the story.

5. *Why have you brought us up?*: a familiar complaint, cp. 14: 3; 16: 13. *this miserable fare*: literally 'bread of emptiness'. This is a deeply contemptuous reference to the manna, which God himself had given.

6. *poisonous snakes*: literally 'fiery snakes'. The word translated 'poisonous' is used for the seraphs, the flying creatures of Isa. 6: 2, and so is sometimes translated 'flying serpents'. But probably 'fiery' refers to a particularly stinging and venomous bite. Poisonous snakes (mostly vipers) are found both in Palestine and in the Sinai peninsula.

1 Corinthians 10: 9 refers to this punishment by serpents as being a warning to Christians.

8. *could look at it and recover*: a rich re-use of this theme is found in John 3: 14, 'This Son of Man must be lifted up as the serpent was lifted up by Moses in the wilderness', where it refers to the saving power of Christ on the cross, to whom men look in faith.

9. The instructions of verse 8 are carried out precisely.

So for the last time in the wilderness Israel rebels and is forgiven; and the advance resumes. ✶

THE JOURNEY TO THE EAST OF MOAB

The Israelites went on and encamped at Oboth. They 10, 11 moved on from Oboth and encamped at Iye-abarim in the wilderness on the eastern frontier of Moab. From there 12 they moved and encamped by the gorge of the Zared. They moved on from the Zared and encamped by the 13 farther side of the Arnon in the wilderness which extends into Amorite territory, for the Arnon was the Moabite frontier; it lies between Moab and the Amorites. That is 14 why the Book of the Wars of the LORD speaks of Vaheb[a] in Suphah and the gorges:

> Arnon and the watershed of the gorges 15
> that falls away towards the dwellings at Ar
> and slopes towards the frontier of Moab.

From there they moved on to Beer:[b] this is the water-hole 16 where the LORD said to Moses, 'Gather the people together and I will give them water.' It was then that 17 Israel sang this song:

[a] *Name meaning* Watershed.   [b] *Name meaning* Water-hole.

18   Well up, spring water! Greet it with song,
          the spring unearthed by the princes,
          laid open by the leaders of the people
             with sceptre and with mace,
          a gift from[a] the wilderness.

19 And they proceeded from Beer[b] to Nahaliel, and from
20 Nahaliel to Bamoth; then from Bamoth to the valley in
    the Moabite country below the summit of Pisgah over-
    looking the desert.

* Israel advances by stages past Moab to the east up to the
borders of the Amorites. A travel narrative forms the framework here, with a list of the places the Israelites stop at on the
way; and it contains within it two ancient songs, neither of
them originally belonging in this setting. J probably contained
a travel narrative as it showed the Israelites moving nearer to
Palestine (Num. 11: 35 and 12: 16 are surviving parts of it),
but this has mostly been replaced by P's version of it, and the
details here may be secondary borrowing from other passages,
rather than original parts of J's narrative. So we may have here
not material from J itself, but details added to the older
material to fill a gap in its picture.

10f. are almost identical with Num. 33: 43–4, and are borrowed from there, and (incorrectly) placed here. *on the eastern
frontier of Moab*: for the probable location of Oboth and of
Iye-abarim see the map (p. 12).

12–13 trace Israel's movements by the rivers marking the
borders, the first between Edom and Moab, the second
between Moab and the Amorites. Both details are probably
taken over from Deut. 2: 13f., 24. Zared is the southernmost
tributary of the Dead Sea from the east (see the map, p. 145).

14. *the Book of the Wars of the LORD*: this is not referred to

[a] *So Sam.; Heb.* and from.   [b] *Prob. rdg.; Heb.* from a gift.

otherwise, but was no doubt a collection of songs celebrating
the victories of Israel over its enemies. We know of a similar
book called the Book of Jashar (or, of the upright man)
(Josh. 10: 13 and 2 Sam. 1: 18), which recorded David's
lament for Saul and Jonathan. The song is quoted here because
of the mention of Arnon, to confirm by a quotation that it
was the border of Moab. *of Vaheb in Suphah and the gorges*:
this is usually (and probably rightly) treated as the first line of
the poem. The place-names are out of place as a part of the
prose text. It would then read not *speaks of* but 'says:
Vaheb...' Vaheb and Suphah are in any case unknown. Then
read 'and the gorges of Arnon'.

15. *the watershed of the gorges*: the watershed is the line of
separation between systems of water flowing down into
different valleys. In a country with many gorges, like that to
the east of the Jordan, watersheds come frequently. *the
dwellings at Ar*: Ar was a city in Moab, referred to at other
times too in the Old Testament, and by some thought to be
the capital of Moab.

16. *they moved on to Beer*: this is a particular place, whose
name means 'waterhole' (perhaps it is abbreviated from a
longer name on the pattern of Beer-sheba). *this is the water-
hole*: the name 'Beer' is used as a peg on which to hang a
traditional song celebrating the springing up of well-water
when the well has been newly dug. It is usually thought to be
a work-song, perhaps of great antiquity. Water can often be
found quite near the surface in the wadis of valleys east of the
Jordan. The Bedouin sing such songs to this day, and one that
is recorded runs:

> 'Flow, water, spread abundantly!
> Wood, camel, do not scorn it!
> With sticks we have dug it!'

18. *unearthed by the princes*: it is odd that the workmen
singing the song do not themselves take credit for it, but give
it to their leaders. Perhaps after all it is nearer to a court song

than a workman's song. *with sceptre and with mace*: the signs of office of the leaders. They would not of course actually have been used as digging implements. This phrase continues to give them credit for the work.

19. Nahaliel and Bamoth must be on the central plateau of Moab, but have not been located with certainty; though Bamoth may be the Bamoth-baal of 22: 41 (footnote). *Bamoth* is a word used several times as an element in Moabite place-names in particular. It has traditionally been rendered 'high-places', but it has recently been persuasively argued that it means 'open-air, man-made cultic platforms' which were sometimes, but not always, on heights.

20. *below the summit of Pisgah*: found again in Num. 23: 14, probably in the range of the Abarim mountains opposite Jericho, and a promontory of a particular mountain from which the promised land could well be viewed (Deut. 3: 27; 34: 1). *the desert*: i.e. the wilderness of Judah, the desert region north-west of the Dead Sea. The word used, *jeshimon*, is also used as a place-name, and may possibly be one here too (cp. 23: 28). ✳

ISRAEL DEFEATS SIHON KING OF THE AMORITES

21 Then Israel sent envoys to the Amorite king Sihon and
22 said, 'Grant us passage through your country. We will not trespass on field or vineyard, nor will we drink from your wells. We will travel by the king's highway till
23 we have crossed your territory.' But Sihon would not grant Israel passage through his territory; he mustered all his people and came out against Israel in the wilderness.
24 He advanced as far as Jahaz and attacked Israel, but Israel put them to the sword, giving no quarter, and occupied their land from the Arnon to the Jabbok, the territory of the Ammonites, where the country became difficult.

So Israel took all these Amorite cities and settled in them, 25
that is in Heshbon and all its dependent villages. Heshbon 26
was the capital of the Amorite king Sihon, who had
fought against the former king of Moab and taken from
him all his territory as far as the Arnon. Therefore the 27
bards say:

> Come to Heshbon, come!
> Let us see the city of Sihon rebuilt and restored!
>> For fire blazed out from Heshbon,   28
>> and flames from Sihon's city.
>> It devoured Ar of Moab,
>> and swept the high ground at Arnon head.
>
>> Woe to you, Moab;   29
>> it is the end of you, you people of Kemosh.
>> He has made his sons fugitives
> and his daughters the prisoners of Sihon the Amorite
>>> king.
> From Heshbon to Dibon their very embers are burnt out 30
>>> and they are extinct,
>> while the fire*a* spreads onward to Medeba.

Thus Israel occupied the territory of the Amorites.   31

* A story of Israel's continued victorious advance, total defeat
of the Amorites, and conquest of their land, including Heshbon. This comes from J, and was drawn on when 20: 14-21
was composed. It leads on to a song celebrating a victory over
the king of Moab, which is brought in because of its mention
of Heshbon. This song is a considerable problem, for it looks
at first like a song of Sihon's own followers celebrating an
early victory over Moab. But the reference to 'Sihon the

[a] *So Sam.; Heb.* which.

Amorite king' in verse 29 sounds as if it is spoken by a third party. Most probably Israel sings the song, at a time when they have themselves occupied or reoccupied Heshbon, and call upon themselves to rebuild it. Since verses 28–9 are also found in Jer. 48: 45–6, which quotes a song considerably older than Jeremiah himself, it is possible that these two verses have been borrowed from there, and given a new heading in verse 27 to make sense of them here, and an ending perhaps added in verse 30, which is now too obscure for us to understand.

21. *the Amorite king*: the term 'Amorites' is sometimes used of Canaanites generally, but sometimes of a particular tribe or tribes occupying land both east and west of the Jordan; it is used in the latter sense here.

22. *the king's highway*: cp. on 20: 17.

23. For Jahaz see the map (p. 145).

24. *and occupied their land*: this is Israel's first conquest of land east of the Jordan which they keep.

25. *and settled in them*: this is based on the fact that there were Israelites settled east of the Jordan, as well as west of it, and that Heshbon was one of their main centres.

Heshbon: the site is still known, and it is called Hisban.

26 is a historical note giving a setting for verses 27–30, but based primarily on what can be deduced from these verses.

27 is a call to help in the rebuilding of Heshbon.

28 explains why Heshbon is a significant place, as a past site of defeat of Moab. *the high ground at Arnon head*: but this may be a place-name, Bamoth-Arnon, meaning 'the cultic platform by the Arnon'; cp. on verse 19.

29. *you people of Kemosh*: Kemosh is the national God of Moab, as Yahweh is of the Israelites. On almost the only surviving written record of the kingdom of Moab, the 'Moabite stone' (see p. 224), the king of Moab speaks of Kemosh's dealings with Moab in language very reminiscent of Israel's language about Yahweh (e.g. 'Kemosh was angry with his land . . . Kemosh drove him out before me . . . Kemosh said to me . . .').

30. The text is very corrupt and obscure. The N.E.B. makes

a good effort, but it is impossible to reconstruct the true text with confidence. *Dibon*: a leading city of Moab: see the map (p. 145). *Medeba* lies between Heshbon and Dibon. ✶

OG KING OF BASHAN IS ALSO DEFEATED

Moses then sent men to explore Jazer; the Israelites cap- 32 tured it together with its dependent villages[a] and drove out the Amorites living there. Then they turned and 33 advanced along the road to Bashan. Og king of Bashan, with all his people, took the field against them at Edrei. The LORD said to Moses, 'Do not be afraid of him. I have 34 delivered him into your hands, with all his people and his land. Deal with him as you dealt with Sihon the Amorite king who lived in Heshbon.' So they put him to the 35 sword with his sons and all his people, until there was no survivor left, and they occupied his land.

✶ This section agrees almost word for word with Deut. 3: 1–3. This comes in a part of Deuteronomy most of which is a summary by the Deuteronomist of material in the older sources, but it does not usually agree closely with the wording of the earlier version. Furthermore this section of Numbers contains some typically deuteronomic phrases ('Do not be afraid of him'; 'I have delivered him into your hands'). So it is almost certainly borrowed here from Deuteronomy to fill in what was felt to be a gap in the story. Sihon and Og became famous as a pair defeated by Israel, of whom for instance Pss. 135: 11 and 136: 19 and 20 sing as defeated by the LORD. The story is told in Deuteronomy to indicate how Israel conquered the lands it later held. Here it interrupts their orderly move forward by a sudden dash to the north-east.

[a] *So Sept.; Heb.* captured its dependent villages.

32. *Jazer* is on the way to the north. Verse 32 is filled in as an introduction to verses 33–5.

33. *Bashan* is to the north-east of where Israel has now reached (see map, p. 145), on both sides of the river Yarmuk. *Og* is not known before the deuteronomic narrative, in which he is more famous as a giant with a sarcophagus of basalt (other translations have 'bedstead of iron') 14 foot long and 6 foot wide (Deut. 3: 11). *at Edrei*: about 30 miles (48 km) east of the Sea of Galilee.

35. Again the people are totally destroyed, under the principle of the 'ban' (cp. on 21: 2). *

Israel in the plains of Moab

* In the last fifteen chapters of Numbers Israel is stationary again, marking time until it should be ready actually to enter the promised land. The book stops short of telling the story of this, and the theme is taken up again in the book of Joshua. But the insertion of Deuteronomy, and the distinguishing of the first five books as a separate group, the Pentateuch, covering the period down to the death of Moses and then stopping short, has separated Numbers from its original continuation. We have here stories of the king of Moab bringing a foreign prophet in the vain hope that he would curse Israel, of renewed shortcomings on the part of Israel, and of a new census conducted by Moses, who appoints his successor Joshua, of a war against Midian and the securing of the lands east of the Jordan, interspersed with further (late) additions to the Jewish law, brought in here before the telling of the period of lawgiving should be finished. We see here a picture, mainly from the Priestly writer, of the people of God, now completely renewed, having no member who had taken part

in the sin in the desert, blessed by God, and preparing itself, down to the smallest details, for the entry into the Promised Land. *

THE PROPHECIES OF BALAAM

* We begin with a very striking and unusual story. Balak king of Moab calls in a (non-Israelite) prophet of great reputation, Balaam, in the hope that he will curse Israel for him, and so do them harm; but Balaam disappoints him again and again, in his inspired state pouring out blessing and prediction of future prosperity. The prophecies are the very heart of the story, and to underline this it breaks off very abruptly after the last of them. The prophecies and the story are usually divided up between the two supposed early narratives of the Pentateuch, J and E, E being responsible for the two oracles in ch. 23 (verses 7–10 and 18–24), and the other, J, for the two in ch. 24 (verses 3–9 and 15–19). But this division misses an important feature of the narrative, that there is a steadily increasing firmness and confidence in the prophecies of Balaam. It would be quite impossible to reverse them, and put the prophecies of ch. 23 in ch. 24 and those of ch. 24 in ch. 23. Similarly Balaam's actual behaviour develops in the story. So something of importance is lost if the story is split up between two continuous sources, J and E. It was, rather, written as a continuous whole, and will be treated as such in this commentary. There is one exception to this, 22: 22–35 (the story of Balaam and the ass that speaks), which is an originally independent folktale incorporated rather loosely in the whole, for reasons which will be suggested later.

There are problems about the origin of the material used here. The story is no doubt written to provide a setting for the prophecies, but it is most likely that the prophecies were written by the same author as the narrative, and never existed separately from the narrative framework. Balaam must have been a figure of some importance, perhaps in the traditions of the East Jordanian shrine of Baal of Peor (23: 28; 31: 16), of alien origin, coming according to 22: 5 from Mesopotamia. He is a prophet, a man of a type found in Israel, but also in the nations round about (known as a *baru* or seer among the Babylonians, as a *kahin* among the pre-Islamic Arabs). He is like the early prophets in Israel, Samuel or Elijah, in that he does not write his prophecies down or give them to a school of disciples, but is regarded with great fear and reverence as being very close to God, receiving from him his word in a trance state or through means of divination, and can be very oddly dressed and behave in an abnormal way (cp. further on verse 5).

But if Balaam is a real figure he is re-used here by the author. It would be difficult to claim that there is here a reliable recollection of events of the time of the entry into the promised land. The author's intention is to speak to us by means of the oracles of Balaam. These show a fierce pride in Israel's nationhood. They speak of a star from Jacob smiting Moab and conquering Edom. This fits in well with David's conquest of these countries, and they were lost to Israel soon after. The prophecies do not appear to be urging Israel to recapture these states. So the date is most probably in David's reign, about 1000–960 B.C., or else quite early on in the reign of Solomon. The reference to Agag, the king of Amalek, Saul's captive whom Samuel slew (1 Sam. 15: 7–33), in 24: 7, also makes sense most readily fairly soon after that event. The prophecies then would be composed by J himself, the author-collector of the older material in the Pentateuch, who here builds up his picture of Israel in the wilderness to a grand climax in the dramatic scene of the heathen prophet looking forward to the great empire of King David.

The oracles themselves are pieces of poetry of great strength and beauty, and are perhaps from a literary point of view the highest achievement of the book of Numbers. ✶

MOAB IN TERROR

THE ISRAELITES went forward and encamped in the **22**
lowlands of Moab on the farther side of the Jordan
from Jericho.

Balak son of Zippor saw what Israel had done to the ₂
Amorites, and Moab was in terror of the people because ₃
there were so many of them. The Moabites were sick
with fear at the sight of them; and they said to the elders ₄
of Midian, 'This horde will soon lick up everything
round us as a bull crops the spring grass.' Balak son of
Zippor was at that time king of Moab. He sent a deputa- ₅
tion to summon Balaam son of Beor, who was at Pethor
by the Euphrates in the land of the Amavites, with this
message, 'Look, an entire nation has come out of Egypt;
they cover the face of the country and are settling at my
very door. Come at once and lay a curse on them, be- ₆
cause they are too many for me; then I may be able to
defeat them and drive them from the country. I know
that those whom you bless are blessed, and those whom
you curse are cursed.'

* Balak king of Moab is terrified of the Israelites, knowing
they have destroyed the Amorites, and plans therefore to
overcome them not by military might, but by supernatural
means. He sends for a prophet, who can both bless and curse,
seeing this as a surer way to overcome Israel.

1. This verse is part of the framework provided by P. The
lowlands of Moab are a wide plain that opens out on the east
side of the Jordan just north of the Dead Sea, about 5–7 miles
(8–11 km) broad. We have here the first mention in the Bible
of Jericho, known from excavation to be one of the oldest

cities of the world, dating back to about 7000 B.C., with an important part to play from time to time in the biblical narrative.

2. Here the older story begins. Balak is king of Moab (verse 4). He is not known outside these chapters, except for a passing reference in Judg. 11: 25. Very probably the name comes from a real tradition, though the role given him here is the work of the narrator. *Zippor* is the Hebrew for a small bird. Names based on words for animals occur in Hebrew; and Moabite was a language very close to Hebrew.

3. *The Moabites were sick with fear*: this repeats the content of 'Moab was in terror', and so has often been taken to be a sign of the presence of two separate sources. While there are instances where this is rightly recognized, especially in longer repetitions, we may see here a device, common in Hebrew, both in poetry and prose, by which the same thought is stated twice for emphasis. The fear is the starting-point for calling in Balaam.

4. The *elders of Midian* are only mentioned in the story here and in verse 7. They come in as Moab's neighbours to the south who share their fears. But some think they are a late addition to the story, based on the connection of Balaam with Midian which is made in 31: 8. *as a bull crops*: a very striking metaphor. It is more often locusts that are used as a symbol of complete destruction in the Bible.

5. Balaam is a seer from the Euphrates valley. Prophets or seers are known not only in Israel, but in many of its neighbours, and in very many peoples both ancient and modern. They are men who in an abnormal state of mind, often completely detached from the outside world (in 'ecstasy'), deliver a message which they believe has come from their god. Sometimes they are asked for this, sometimes they do it spontaneously. Sometimes they are paid for it, at other times they give it free; sometimes it is a declaration or a prohibition, sometimes a prediction of the future. They trace their special work to a specific call from their god; they may dress and

behave oddly, and are regarded by other men with both respect and fear, which can spill over into contempt. They are seen as specially close to God, and called 'men of God'. In the Christian Church too, which has had no formal place for them in its ministry, they have appeared again and again at irregular intervals, and in the Middle Ages were even acclaimed and listened to by popes. Balaam is represented as a man of this kind. While in fact he will have worshipped a god of his own, the story represents him as knowing the LORD (that is, the God whose name is Yahweh), because Israel thinks of Yahweh as lord of the whole world; so if Balaam has access to the divine world it is in fact to Yahweh that he has access. Later on, by the time P is writing in 31: 16, he is supposed to have led Israel to sin, and this view of him is taken over in the New Testament in Jude 11, and 2 Pet. 2: 15, 16. But there is no sign of disapproval of him in these chapters at all. *son of Beor*: it is rather odd that in Gen. 36: 32 we have a king of Edom, Bela son of Beor. They can hardly be the same person, however, and perhaps the name Beor has been borrowed either by Genesis from Numbers or by Numbers from Genesis. Pethor is on the west bank of the Euphrates, about 12 miles (19 km) south of Carchemish, and is found in Assyrian annals as Pitru. It is about 400 miles (nearly 644 km) from Moab, and the journey would take perhaps 25 days. The storyteller feels no interest in such details. *the land of the Amavites*: the Hebrew text reads 'land of the sons of his people'. But this would tell us nothing. A reference has been found in a fifteenth-century B.C. inscription at Alalakh in North Syria to *'amau* as part of the land of Alalakh, in the Sajur valley between Aleppo and Carchemish. This interpretation needs no alterations to the Hebrew letters; they are read with slightly different vowels. It is surprising that so local a name is known by the Israelites; but the fit seems too neat to be coincidental.

6. Balaam's blessing and *curse* are known to be automatically effective; like magic they just work. The Israelites thought that provided the person speaking had the right to

utter a blessing or a curse, it would indeed once spoken be effective. ✻

BALAAM REFUSES TO COME, BUT IN THE END
GOD BIDS HIM GO

7 The elders of Moab and Midian took the fees for augury with them, and they came to Balaam and told him what
8 Balak had said. 'Spend this night here,' he said, 'and I will give you whatever answer the LORD gives to me.'
9 So the Moabite chiefs stayed with Balaam. God came to Balaam and asked him, 'Who are these men with you?'
10 Balaam replied, 'Balak son of Zippor king of Moab has
11 sent them to me and he says, "Look, a people newly come out of Egypt is covering the face of the country. Come at once and denounce them for me; then I may be able to
12 fight them and drive them away."' God said to Balaam, 'You are not to go with them or curse the people, be-
13 cause they are to be blessed.'[a] So Balaam rose in the morning and said to Balak's chiefs, 'Go back to your own country; the LORD has refused to let me go with you.'
14 Then the Moabite chiefs took their leave and went back to Balak, and told him that Balaam had refused to come
15 with them; whereupon Balak sent a second and larger
16 embassy of higher rank than the first. They came to Balaam and told him, 'This is the message from Balak son of Zippor: "Let nothing stand in the way of your
17 coming. I will confer great honour upon you; I will do whatever you ask me. But you must come and denounce
18 this people for me."' Balaam gave this answer to Balak's messengers: 'Even if Balak were to give me all the silver

[a] *Or* are blessed.

and gold in his house, I could not disobey the command
of the LORD my God in anything, small or great. But stay 19
here for this night, as the others did, that I may learn
what more the LORD has to say to me.' During the night 20
God came to Balaam and said to him, 'If these men have
come to summon you, then rise and go with them, but
do only what I tell you.' So in the morning Balaam rose, 21
saddled his ass and went with the Moabite chiefs.

* Balaam at first refuses to go, but after his second refusal
God tells him to go with the men. The narrator draws out the
story to build up the tension, in a way well known in folk-
tales too.

7. *fees* were regularly paid for *augury*, that is, divination,
prediction of the future by watching the flight of birds, and
were paid in advance. Compare 1 Sam. 9: 7f., where Saul
wants to approach Samuel, and says 'If we do go, what shall
we offer him?'

8. *the LORD*: in this part of the story the narrator himself
says 'God', but makes Balaam say 'the LORD', even though
he is not an Israelite. Balaam here emphasizes his total dependence on God.

11. This repetition of the substance of an earlier verse
(verse 5) is made to emphasize the point. This is quite common
in Hebrew narrative, though it produces a fulness which we
find strange.

12. God forbids Balaam to go. Why, if he is going to let
him go in the end? The narrator wishes to spin out the story
and increase the suspense.

14. One might think from the narrative that the journey
took only a day: the story is not interested in the details of
how long it will take.

15. *of higher rank*: to impress Balaam by treating him with
greater respect. Balak will not take no for an answer.

17. *great honour*: this implies financial reward, as the silver and gold of verse 18 confirms. But Balaam insists on his total obedience to God.

20. *During the night* God comes to Balaam; this is usually assumed to be in a dream, although it is not explicitly indicated that it is. Night visions are frequently said to be a source of divine revelation; cp. for instance Job 4: 12–16 or Zech. 1: 8.

21. Balaam goes off after all. It is typical of this sort of storytelling that no question is raised about what went on in Balaam's mind; whether he wondered why God had changed his mind and let him go. *

THE TALE OF BALAAM AND THE SPEAKING ASS

22 But God was angry because Balaam was going, and as he came riding on his ass, accompanied by his two servants, the angel of the LORD took his stand in the road to bar
23 his way. When the ass saw the angel standing in the road with his sword drawn, she turned off the road into the fields, and Balaam beat the ass to bring her back on to the
24 road. Then the angel of the LORD stood where the road ran through a hollow, with fenced vineyards on either
25 side. The ass saw the angel and, crushing herself against the wall, crushed Balaam's foot against it, and he beat
26 her again. The angel of the LORD moved on further and stood in a narrow place where there was no room to
27 turn either to right or left. When the ass saw the angel, she lay down under Balaam. At that Balaam lost his
28 temper and beat the ass with his stick. The LORD then made the ass speak, and she said to Balaam, 'What have I done? This is the third time you have beaten me.'
29 Balaam answered the ass, 'You have been making a fool

of me. If I had had a sword here, I should have killed
you on the spot.' But the ass answered, 'Am I not still the   30
ass which you have ridden all your life? Have I ever
taken such a liberty with you before?' He said, 'No.'
Then the LORD opened Balaam's eyes: he saw the angel   31
of the LORD standing in the road with his sword drawn,
and he bowed down and fell flat on his face before him.
The angel said to him, 'What do you mean by beating   32
your ass three times like this? I came out to bar your way
but you made straight for me, and three times your ass   33
saw me and turned aside. If she had not[a] turned aside,
I should by now have killed you and spared her.' Balaam   34
replied to the angel of the LORD, 'I have done wrong. I
did not know that you stood in the road confronting me.
But now, if my journey displeases you, I am ready to go
back.' The angel of the LORD said to Balaam, 'Go on with   35
these men; but say only what I tell you.' So Balaam went
on with Balak's chiefs.

* This story comes in oddly here. It does not fit in at either
end. God has just told Balaam to go, but now he is angry that
he is going. And the whole implication of the story is that
God will stop Balaam, but at the end he tells him to go on.
The story has been added, then, to a Balaam story which was
complete without it. This is a once independent folktale,
told about someone else, in which the hero is in fact stopped
and sent back by God. But it has been transferred to Balaam,
and inserted here to provide added delay and tension. This was
done by a later editor, perhaps to bring out a heightened sense
of God's action in the story by using the folktale. The story is
best known for the speaking ass, a feature almost unparalleled
in the Old Testament (the serpent of Gen. 3 is the only other

[a] *So Sept.; Heb.* Perhaps she had . . .

animal that talks in the Old Testament). But it is not here underlined as a great miracle, for in a folktale such occurrences are common.

22. Balaam is not accompanied by the Moabite embassy, as in verse 21. The following verses show him travelling through cultivated land, with fenced vineyards, not across the desert. This emphasizes that the story here is not continuous with what has preceded it. *the angel of the LORD*: in some Old Testament stories the angel of the LORD is a form of God himself and the two terms are interchanged, as for example in Judg. 6: 11–24. In this story verse 31 seems to indicate a definite separation. The angel is in human form (cp. on 20: 16), but is invisible to men who do not have 'their eyes open'. Balaam cannot see him until verse 31. *to bar his way*: the Hebrew means literally 'to be an adversary', or 'Satan'. But the word *satan* refers to an emissary of God (as also for instance in Job chs. 1 and 2), not a malevolent spirit, as he appears in the period after the completion of the Old Testament (1 Chron. 21, written very late in the Old Testament period, shows some movement towards this picture).

23. The fields have no fences.

26. This is the third time, and the third time is the decisive one. This is a very common pattern in folktale material.

28. The ass speaks out in self-defence.

30. Note that the ass does not tell Balaam that the angel is there. It just defends itself against the charge of taking liberties.

31. *he bowed down*: because he knew himself to be in the presence of the supernatural.

34. With Balaam's confession of error we expect him now to return home.

35. Instead we get a verse inserted to make the transition. No really adequate reason is given why Balaam should be allowed to go on after all. ✳

BALAK MEETS BALAAM

When Balak heard that Balaam was coming, he came out 36
to meet him as far as Ar of Moab by the Arnon on his
frontier. Balak said to Balaam, 'Did I not send time and 37
again to summon you? Why did you not come? Did
you think that I could not do you honour?' Balaam 38
replied, 'I have come, as you see. But now that I am
here, what power have I of myself to say anything?
Whatever the word God puts into my mouth, that is
what I will say.' So Balaam went with Balak till they 39
came to Kiriath-huzoth, and Balak slaughtered cattle 40
and sheep and sent them to Balaam and to the chiefs
who were with him.

* Balak goes to meet Balaam, doing him great honour by
this, and upbraids him for his slowness in coming. Balaam
again stresses his total dependence on God.

36. It is only to meet a vitally important guest that the king
would go as far as his frontier. *Ar of Moab* is read with a slight
correction from 'the City of Moab' to bring in the place-name
already found in 21: 28. The Arnon is Moab's northern
frontier.

37. Balak is a little domineering, for he is the king. This is
emphasized to make his disappointment later the stronger.
honour: financial reward is again implied in the word.

38. Balaam again emphasizes that he can only do what God
wants.

39. Kiriath-huzoth is mentioned only here, and we do not
know exactly where it was.

40. The king can sacrifice (as apparently the earlier kings in
Israel had the right to: it is recorded of Saul, David and
Solomon that they did), and does so near, but not in the
presence of, Balaam and the chiefs. *

BALAAM'S FIRST ORACLE

41 In the morning Balak took Balaam and led him up to the Heights of Baal,[a] from where he could see the full extent
23 of the Israelite host. Then Balaam said to Balak, 'Build me here seven altars and prepare for me seven bulls and seven rams.' Balak did as he asked and offered[b] a bull
3-4 and a ram on each altar. Then he said to him, 'I have prepared the seven altars, and I have offered the bull and the ram on each altar.' Balaam said to Balak, 'Take your stand beside your sacrifice, and let me go off by myself. It may happen that the LORD will meet me. Whatever he reveals to me, I will tell you.' So he went forthwith,
5 and God met him. The LORD put words into Balaam's mouth and said, 'Go back to Balak and speak as I tell
6 you.' So he went back, and found Balak standing by his
7 sacrifice, and with him all the Moabite chiefs. And Balaam uttered his oracle:

> From Aram,[c] from the mountains of the east,
> Balak king of Moab has brought me:
> 'Come, lay a curse for me on Jacob,
> come, execrate Israel.'

8   How can I denounce whom God has not denounced?
> How can I execrate whom the LORD has not
>   execrated?

9   From the rocky heights I see them,
> I watch them from the rounded hills.
> I see a people that dwells alone,

[a] Heights of Baal: *Heb*. Bamoth-baal.
[b] *So some MSS.; others* and Balak and Balaam offered.
[c] *Or* Syria.

that has not made itself one with the nations.
Who can count the host*a* of Jacob   10
or number the hordes*b* of Israel?
Let me die as men die who are righteous,
grant that my end may be as theirs!

Then Balak said to Balaam, 'What is this you have done? 11
I sent for you to denounce my enemies, and what you
have done is to bless them.' But he replied, 'Must I not 12
keep to the words that the LORD puts into my mouth?'

☆ Balak takes Balaam where he can see the Israelite host, and
carries out all his instructions. But Balaam delivers an oracle
which refuses to curse Israel, and stresses that they dwell alone
and are countless in number (though he does not yet explicitly
bless them). The theme of the story is here struck, and it will
be heard again and again in the following oracles: Israel is
God's.

41. *the Heights of Baal*: this is perhaps better translated 'the
cultic platforms of Baal' (see the note on 21: 19) but it is
probably meant as a place-name, Bamoth-baal, having that
sense. Its site in that case is unknown to us.

23: 1. *seven altars*: there must have been an altar of Baal here
already, but this is ignored in the story. Seven is a common
number in religious symbolism among many peoples; cp. the
seven days of the week, or the seven days of many festivals.

4. *God met him*: presumably face to face. The narrator feels
no puzzle in this, so he does not tell us how he conceives of it.

5. *The LORD put words in Balaam's mouth*: Balaam is a
prophet, and his prophesying is understood as a faithful
repetition of the words of God himself (cp. 'I put my words
into your mouth', Jer. 1: 9).

7. *From Aram*: i.e. Syria, as the footnote indicates. The
oracle is in poetry, as early prophecy usually is. Prophecy and

[a] *Or* dust.   [b] *Or* quarter *or* sands.

poetic inspiration are closely linked. *the mountains of the east* are the ranges of the Syrian desert, reaching as far as Pethor. *Jacob* both here and subsequently in the oracles is used as an alternative title for the nation, not as a reference to the patriarch.

9. Compare Deut. 33: 28 in the somewhat similar poem, known as the Blessing of Moses: 'Israel lives in security, the tribes of Jacob by themselves.' But this poem may have been composed after the exile, and may display a knowledge of the oracle of Balaam.

10. *host . . . hordes*: literally each word means 'dust'. This is used metaphorically of the great numbers of the Israelites. *Let me die*: this is a tailpiece to the oracle, in which Balaam invokes upon himself a blessing that he may come to the end of his life in such splendour as belongs to Israel, the *men . . . who are righteous*.

11. Balak is understandably upset. But Balaam, as he points out (verse 12), has acted in the only way a prophet can (cp. the sense of prophetic compulsion in Jer. 20: 7–12). *

BALAK'S SECOND ATTEMPT, AND BALAAM'S SECOND ORACLE

13 Balak then said to him, 'Come with me now to another place from which you will see them, though not the full extent of them; you will not see them all. Denounce

14 them for me from there.' So he took him to the Field of the Watchers[a] on the summit of Pisgah, where he built seven altars and offered a bull and a ram on each altar.

15 Balaam said to Balak, 'Take your stand beside your sacri-

16 fice, and I will meet God over there.' The LORD met Balaam and put words into his mouth, and said, 'Go

17 back to Balak, and speak as I tell you.' So he went back,

[a] *Or* Field of Zophim.

and found him standing beside his sacrifice, with the
Moabite chiefs. Balak asked what the LORD had said, and 18
Balaam uttered his oracle:

> Up, Balak, and listen:
> hear what I am charged to say, son of Zippor.
> God is not a mortal that he should lie,   19
> not a man that he should change his mind.[a]
> Has he not spoken, and will he not make it good?
> What he has proclaimed, he will surely fulfil.
> I have received command to bless;   20
> I will bless[b] and I cannot gainsay it.
> He has discovered no iniquity in Jacob   21
> and has seen no mischief in Israel.[c]
> The LORD their God is with them,
> acclaimed among them as king.[d]
> What its curving horns are to the wild ox,   22
> God is to them, who brought them out of Egypt.
> Surely there is no divination in[e] Jacob,   23
> and no augury in[e] Israel;
> now is the time to say of Jacob
> and of Israel, 'See what God has wrought!'
> Behold a people rearing up like a lioness,   24
> rampant like a lion;
> he will not couch till he devours the prey
> and drinks the blood of the slain.

✻ It was common in the ancient world when consulting oracles or omens to persist until a favourable one was

[a] *Or* feel regret.   [b] *So Sam.; Heb.* he blessed.
[c] *Or* None can discover calamity in Jacob nor see trouble in Israel.
[d] *Or* royal care is bestowed on them.   [e] *Or* against.

obtained. This is what Balak tries to do, for he does not know the true nature of Yahweh and his commitment to Israel. But Balaam's second oracle emphasizes that the LORD will not change his mind; that he has directed Balaam to bless and not to curse; and that Israel is free from sin, and victorious. This oracle is longer and more explicit than the first.

13. *you will not see them all*: Balak seems to think that it was the sight of the mass of Israel that distorted Balaam's prophesying. The narrator perhaps puts this in to bring out Balak's simple misunderstanding of the work of a prophet.

14. *the Field of the Watchers*, or 'of Zophim', is unknown. For Pisgah see the note on 21: 20.

16. *The LORD met Balaam*: it is again stressed that Balaam's oracle is direct from the mouth of God.

19. This declaration is perhaps a standardized statement of principle in early Israel. It comes again in very similar form in prose in 1 Sam. 15: 29. Although the men of the Old Testament tell stories which imply that God can change his mind (so e.g. in the visions of Amos 7: 1–6, when the prophet appeals to God to have mercy), they know that in principle he is a God who is of unchanging purpose.

21. This is a very striking statement of the ethical superiority of Israel, and not at all in accord with the many traditions of Israel sinning in the wilderness. Nevertheless it may be what the writer wanted to say in this context. It should be noticed that an alternative translation is possible (see the footnote) which does not assert that there is no iniquity in Israel; although in turn it would in this form imply that Israel is free from trouble.

acclaimed among them as king: in its early days Israel is without an earthly king, but not without a king altogether, for the title is given to Yahweh.

22. The translation given here is the best that can be made of a difficult clause. The *wild ox* is known also from ancient Mesopotamia, and is related to the aurochs of Europe, the wild ancestor of domestic cattle; both wild ox and aurochs are

now extinct. Again there is a similar metaphor in the Blessing of Moses, Deut. 33: 17: 'In majesty he shall be like a first-born ox, his horns those of a wild ox.' *horns* are a symbol of royal status: cp. Ps. 89: 17, which is literally 'through thy favour our horn is high' (said by the king).

23. *divination*: consulting God through omens, for instance by casting lots with arrows; cp. Ezek. 21: 21, of the king of Babylon: 'he casts lots with arrows, consults teraphim and inspects the livers of beasts'. *augury*: making deductions about God's will from the flight of birds. It is true that these were not found in Israel, except illegally, for they were forbidden (Deut. 18: 11). But why is it said here? Either to stress that Israel is worthy of God's care because it does not resort to them, or (if the translation in the footnote is correct) to emphasize that they are powerless against Israel.

24. *rearing up like a lioness* is a simile used again of Israel later (e.g. Micah 5: 8, 'All that are left of Jacob . . . shall be . . . like a young lion loose in a flock of sheep'). The terrifying strength of Israel is emphasized, as if to imply by way of a climax that it might well attack Moab, and would defeat it. *

BALAAM'S THIRD ORACLE

Then Balak said to Balaam, 'You will not denounce 25 them; then at least do not bless them'; and he answered, 26 'Did I not warn you that I must do all the LORD tells me?' Balak replied, 'Come, let me take you to another 27 place; perhaps God will be pleased to let you denounce them for me from there.' So he took Balaam to the 28 summit of Peor overlooking Jeshimon, and Balaam told 29 him to build seven altars for him there and prepare seven bulls and seven rams. Balak did as Balaam had said, 30 and he offered a bull and a ram on each altar.

But now that Balaam knew that the LORD wished him **24**

to bless Israel, he did not go and resort to divination as
2 before. He turned towards the desert; and as he looked,
he saw Israel encamped tribe by tribe. The spirit of God
3 came upon him, and he uttered his oracle:

> The very word of Balaam son of Beor,
> the very word of the man whose sight is clear,
4 the very word of him who hears the words of God,
> who with staring eyes sees in a trance
> the vision from the Almighty:
5   how goodly are your tents, O Jacob,
> your dwelling-places, Israel,
6 like long rows of palms,
> like gardens by a river,
> like lign-aloes planted by the LORD,
> like cedars beside the water!
7 The water in his vessels shall overflow,
> and his seed shall be like great waters
> so that his king may be taller than Agag,
> and his kingdom lifted high.
8 What its curving horns are to the wild ox,
> God is to him, who brought him out of Egypt;
> he shall devour his adversaries the nations,
> crunch their bones, and smash their limbs in pieces.
9 When he reclines he couches like a lion,
> like a lioness, and no one dares rouse him.
> Blessed be they that bless you,
> and they that curse you be accursed!

✶ Balak is becoming disillusioned with Balaam, since he will
not curse Israel. But he is prepared to risk a last (third)
attempt, and makes the same preparations as before, but at a

new place. The third oracle is wholly directed as a blessing to Israel, and emphasizes yet more its strength and warlike character. Balak goes unmentioned in the last two oracles, both of which begin with what is apparently a formula for oracles. There are several places in the oracle where the meaning of the Hebrew is very difficult to establish, and the N.E.B. makes a very good attempt at the difficulties.

28. *the summit of Peor overlooking Jeshimon*: we do not know exactly where this was, but it was presumably near the abode of the Baal of Peor (25: 3, 5), on the east bank of the lower Jordan valley. Jeshimon, elsewhere a word for other particular desert regions (e.g. 1 Sam. 23: 19), here refers to the desert-like lower Jordan valley. Cp. the use of the word in 21: 20 where the N.E.B. translates it as 'the desert'.

24: 1. *he did not go and resort to divination as before*: this is something of a puzzle, for we have not previously been told that Balaam used divination (cp. on 23: 23). It is the journey to meet the LORD that is omitted this time. Does the author mean to imply that this meeting was achieved by divination? The story is not wholly consistent here. Perhaps there is something wrong with the word rendered 'divination' in the text.

2. *The spirit of God came upon him*: this has not been mentioned before. The spirit of God in the Old Testament is not usually understood as an abiding presence with men, like the Holy Spirit of the New Testament, but as an inrush of God's power for a limited period and purpose, experienced by mighty men (e.g. Samson in Judg. 14: 6), or kings (e.g. 1 Sam. 11: 6) or prophets (1 Sam. 10: 10).

3. *the very word*: the word used is one which occurs frequently in prophetic oracles in the Old Testament, in the phrase 'says the LORD', but only once at the beginning of an oracle (Isa. 1: 24; and elsewhere at the beginning of Ps. 110: 1 and in 2 Sam. 23: 1). It has not yet been used by Balaam.

4. *who with staring eyes sees in a trance*: literally 'falling down (i.e. in a trance), but opened as to his eyes' (presumably i.e. seeing with his inner eye what could not normally be seen).

the Almighty: the word used is *Shaddai*, an old title of God, of which the true sense is unknown.

6. *lign-aloes*: it is not very clear why the N.E.B. gives this translation (which was also in the Authorized Version), for we do not know what it means. The Hebrew word elsewhere refers to an aromatic wood imported from south-east Asia, either eaglewood or sandalwood. Some prosaic commentators have objected that since it does not grow in Palestine it is not likely to have been referred to by the author here, and an emendation to 'oak' has been made. But in a rich metaphor the author may well refer to a tree which he knows only as imported wood. *like cedars beside the water*: cedars do not in fact grow beside the water. But we cannot be sure that the author knew this, or that he would have changed what he had written if he did know.

7. *and his seed shall be like great waters*: the reference is either to semen, or to seed sown in irrigated land – in which case it is better to translate 'shall be in many waters'. *taller than Agag*: this must be the king of Amalek whom Saul wished to spare and whom Samuel slew in 1 Sam. 15. So this oracle was composed while he was still generally remembered, or else the name is taken from the formed literary tradition of Samuel.

8. This verse virtually repeats 23: 22, from the second oracle of Balaam. While it could have been borrowed from there in later editing, it is more likely to be a conscious repetition by the author to link the second and third oracles. *he shall devour his adversaries*: as for instance Amalek itself was wiped out in the story of 1 Sam. 15.

9. *like a lion*: the image, but not the wording in detail, gives another cross-reference to the second oracle, 23: 24. *Blessed be they that bless you*: this is perhaps a standard formula in Israel (it occurs also in Gen. 27: 29 as the climax of an oracle). But it is well placed here as the climax of the blessing, the blessing which Balaam knew God wished him to give (verse 1).   *

BALAAM'S FOURTH AND LAST ORACLE

At that Balak was very angry with Balaam, beat his 10
hands together and said, 'I summoned you to denounce
my enemies, and three times you have persisted in blessing them. Off with you to your own place! I promised 11
to confer great honour upon you, but now the LORD has
kept this honour from you.' Balaam answered, 'But I 12
told your own messengers whom you sent: "If Balak 13
gives me all the silver and gold in his house, I cannot
disobey the command of the LORD by doing anything of
my own will, good or bad. What the LORD speaks to me,
that is what I will say." Now I am going to my own 14
people; but first, I will warn you what this people will
do to yours in the days to come.' So he uttered his 15
oracle:

The very word of Balaam son of Beor,
the very word of the man whose sight is clear,
the very word of him who hears the words of God, 16
who shares the knowledge of the Most High,
who with staring eyes sees in a trance
the vision from the Almighty:
  I see him, but not now; 17
I behold him, but not near:
a star shall come forth out of Jacob,
a comet arise from Israel.
He shall smite the squadrons*a* of Moab,
and beat down all the sons of strife.
Edom shall be his by conquest 18
and Seir, his enemy, shall be his.

[a] *Or* heads.

177

Israel shall do valiant deeds;
19   Jacob shall trample them down,
        the last survivor from Ar shall he destroy.

* Three times Balaam has prophesied at the request of Balak, and each time has blessed instead of cursing. Now although Balak tells him to go home, he goes on to give the final and most magnificent oracle which God commands him to utter, and predicts in it the coming of the Davidic monarchy and the triumphant building up of an empire which includes Moab and Edom. The whole sequence of oracles has been designed to lead up to this prediction, which is the author's intended climax.

10. *beat his hands together*: this is a sign of contempt, and when the phrase occurs elsewhere it is translated in the N.E.B. 'snap their fingers at' (so Lam. 2: 15).

11. *the LORD has kept this honour from you*: the honour may in fact be rather an honorarium, a payment in silver or gold; cp. verse 13.

13. The nature of prophecy as complete possession by the spirit of God is again heavily underlined.

15–16. The opening formula of the third oracle (verses 3–4) is used again with minor variation.

17. *I see him, but not now*: it is emphasized that this is a prophecy of the (distant) future. *a star*: this image is used again of the king of Babylon (called 'bright morning star' in Isa. 14: 12) and allusively of the king of Egypt in Ezek. 32: 7, but it does not appear to have been a standard title for the king in Israel. If not, its use here is all the more striking. *comet*: literally 'sceptre', and it may be better simply to translate it so, seeing in it a direct allusion to part of the royal regalia. *He shall smite the squadrons of Moab*: David made conquests in the direction of Syria too; but it is only Moab and Edom that the writer is interested in here. *squadrons* is a free translation of a word for 'crowns of heads'. *all the sons of strife*: this

meaning is uncertain. It could be translated 'sons of Seth', with the same name given to Moab as the third son of Adam has in Genesis. If so, there might be some legend linking Seth with Moab; we do not know of one, but this does not rule it out. 'Sons of pride' is a possible meaning of the words if it is not a proper name. It has also been suggested that we should read 'the sons of the Sutu', with reference to the name of a nomadic tribe dwelling in Palestine which occurs in Egyptian texts of about 2000 B.C. But we have no strong reason to identify them with the Moabites. In any case a tribal name is more likely in the context than 'sons of strife'.

18. *Seir*: properly the name of the chief mountain range in Edom, it is used here (as in e.g. Judg. 5: 4) as a synonym for Edom. *Israel shall do valiant deeds*: we end with a triumphant assertion of Israel's military valour, written in or near the reign of David, before Israel's weakness in the face of the great powers had been demonstrated.

19. *the last survivor from Ar*: Ar in Moab, already referred to in 21: 28. The final emphasis is on the conquest of Moab. ✷

ADDITIONAL ORACLES ATTRIBUTED TO BALAAM

He saw Amalek and uttered his oracle: 20

> First of all the nations was Amalek,
> but his end shall be utter destruction.

He saw the Kenites and uttered his oracle: 21

> Your refuge, though it seems secure,
> your nest, though set on the mountain crag,
> is doomed to burning, O Cain.   22
> How long must you dwell there in my sight?

He uttered his oracle: 23

> Ah, who are these assembling in the north,

179

24   invaders[a] from the region of Kittim?

They will lay waste Assyria; they will lay Eber waste:
he too shall perish utterly.

25 Then Balaam arose and returned home, and Balak also
went on his way.

* The story of Balaam has now come to its triumphant
climax, and probably originally ended here, with the departure of Balaam and of Balak following immediately as in
verse 25. But these oracles made such an impression on Israel
that further later sayings attacking other enemies of Israel
were attached as an appendix at later dates. The three separate
introductions of verses 20, 21 and 23 suggest that this was not
a single process, but took place over a period. These oracles
are modelled on a form found regularly in the books of the
prophets of oracles on the foreign nations (such as are found in
Isa. 13–23 or Jer. 46–51), but are much briefer. There was
perhaps a deliberate intention with these additions to bring the
total number of oracles up to seven.

20. *He saw Amalek*: Amalek is a confederacy of nomadic
tribes in the desert to the south-east of Palestine, wandering
from Sinai to the Negeb and the Arabah; cp. on 13: 29. They
are among Israel's most hated traditional enemies. Since they
are very little heard of after the reign of David, this oracle is
not likely to be much later than then: it is the first addition.
Balaam is thought of as literally seeing Amalek from his
height, not in a vision.

21. *He saw the Kenites*: who dwell in the south-east of the
hill-country of Judah. They were traditionally friendly with
Israel (Moses' brother-in-law Hobab was one of them; Judg.
4: 11), and the background to this saying as well as its date are
uncertain. *your nest*: the word is *qen*, and it is brought in
because its similarity to 'Kenite' makes a good pun, which is
felt to have some greater significance too.

[a] *So Sept.; Heb. obscure.*

22. *O Cain*: Cain is the supposed ancestor of the tribe of the Kenites; the name Cain is formed from the tribal name Kenite, and it is as ancestor of the Kenites that Cain figures in the story of Cain in Gen. 4: 1–17, although this is not spelt out there. *How long must you dwell there in my sight?*: this is a possible reading with slight corrections of a text which translated literally runs 'How long? Asshur (Assyria) will carry you away captive.' This may be right; the correction is trying to avoid an anachronistic mention of the Assyrians attributed to a Balaam many centuries before they became a menace. But it could well have been attributed to him at a time when Judah itself was feeling the strength of Assyria, so after 800 B.C.

23. *He uttered his oracle*: the text, date and point of this oracle are all problems. It is no doubt later than the preceding two oracles.

24. *invaders from the region of Kittim*: Kittim referred originally to Kition, a town in Cyprus, and so came to be used to refer to Cyprus, and then to any maritime nation from the west; particularly later the Macedonians, and then the Romans, to either of which it could refer if the oracle is really late. In the texts of the Qumran Community Kittim is used frequently to refer to the Romans. *Assyria*: if this were a really late oracle the reference would be to the Seleucid Empire in Syria after 300 B.C. It could be earlier, and refer to the Assyrians proper, but there is no known threat from the sea in their time, as there was later. *they will lay Eber waste*: Eber could be the supposed ancestor of the Hebrews (from which word Eber's name is artificially created) of Gen. 10: 21–5. But this would be a very oblique way of prophesying a threat to Israel, and the word may be used in a different sense to mean the land across the Euphrates. This too is of no help in dating or understanding the oracle.

25. *Then Balaam arose*: the abrupt end, without further details, underlines that it is the oracles, with their vision of the might of Israel, and of the defeat of her enemies as being the LORD's purpose, that are the central point of this whole

section of the book, not the personal history of Balaam or Balak. ✱

THE ISRAELITES SIN IN MOAB

25 When the Israelites were in Shittim, the people began to
2 have intercourse with Moabite women, who invited
them to the sacrifices offered to their gods; and they ate
the sacrificial food and prostrated themselves before the
3 gods of Moab. The Israelites joined in the worship of the
4 Baal of Peor, and the LORD was angry with them. He said
to Moses, 'Take all the leaders of the people and hurl
them down to their death before the LORD in the full
light of day, that the fury of his anger may turn away
5 from Israel.' So Moses said to the judges of Israel, 'Put
to death, each one of you, those of his tribe who have
joined in the worship of the Baal of Peor.'

6   One of the Israelites brought a Midianite woman into
his family in open defiance of Moses and all the community of Israel, while they were weeping by the entrance
7 of the Tent of the Presence. Phinehas son of Eleazar, son
of Aaron the priest, saw him. He stepped out from the
8 crowd and took up a spear, and he went into the inner
room*a* after the Israelite and transfixed the two of them,
the Israelite and the woman, pinning them together.*b*
Thus the plague which had attacked the Israelites was
9 brought to a stop; but twenty-four thousand had already
died.

10, 11   The LORD spoke to Moses and said, 'Phinehas son of
Eleazar, son of Aaron the priest, has turned my wrath
away from the Israelites; he displayed among them the

[a] *Lit.* alcove.   [b] *Lit.* into her belly.

same jealous anger that moved me, and therefore in my
jealousy I did not exterminate the Israelites. Tell him 12
that I hereby grant him my covenant of security of tenure.
He and his descendants after him shall enjoy the priest- 13
hood under a covenant for all time, because he showed
his zeal for his God and made expiation for the Israelites.'
The name of the Israelite struck down with the Midianite 14
woman was Zimri son of Salu, a chief in a Simeonite
family, and the Midianite woman's name was Cozbi 15
daughter of Zur, who was the head of a group of fathers'
families in Midian.

The LORD spoke to Moses and said, 'Make the Midian- 16, 17–18
ites suffer as they made you suffer with their crafty tricks,
and strike them down; their craftiness was your undoing
at Peor and in the affair of Cozbi their sister, the daughter
of a Midianite chief, who was struck down at the time of
the plague that followed Peor.'

* In this chapter similar stories from the older (verses 1–5)
and later (verses 6–13) sources are fused together to make a
whole, because they both deal with Israelites going astray
with women at a place near the promised land. The stories
make a sharp contrast to the great hopes of the Balaam oracles
(e.g. 23: 9, 21b). This is no accident. They are put here
designedly to illustrate how weak and sinful Israel in fact is.
Although the promised land is now in sight, they give in to
the first temptation they meet. The two stories, though similar,
are quite distinct. In the first the Israelites sin with Moabite
women, and are led into false worship, the worship of the
gods of Moab. It is this to which objection is taken. In the
second, an Israelite brings a Midianite woman into the camp,
and Phinehas kills them both, and so receives the promise of
priesthood for his descendants. This is the real point of interest

here. Verses 14–18 are later additions to the story. The J narrative is now nearly at an end and is only found again in Numbers in ch. 32.

1. *in Shittim*: 'the acacias'. We do not know exactly where it is, but it must be east of the Jordan and near it. *began to have intercourse*: sexual intercourse is meant.

3. *joined in the worship of*: the word, literally 'yoked themselves to', may well imply taking part in sexual rites of fertility, seen as pleasing to the god concerned; and this would be why it is so objectionable to the Israelites, for whom the association of fertility rites with the deity was one of the great faults of Canaanite religion. *the Baal of Peor*: Baal, the great active, dying and rising, fertility god of Canaanite religion, had different local manifestations, and is here worshipped as the Baal of Peor (similarly the Virgin Mary is known under different local manifestations, e.g. as Our Lady of Walsingham). It is the worship of Baal in particular that Israel finds objectionable, and not that of the other great Canaanite god El, who is very like Yahweh and often identified with him.

4. *hurl them down*: they are presumably thrown down from a high rock.

5. The story will originally have been rounded off with the execution of the command.

6. *One of the Israelites*: the scene shifts as P takes up the story. His story has lost its beginning, in which Israel has sinned, and a plague has been sent (verse 8). *brought a Midianite woman*: by taking a foreign woman to wife he defiles the congregation.

7. *Phinehas son of Eleazar*: although this story is late Phinehas is an authentic early name, for in form it is Egyptian (meaning 'the Negro'), and begins with the Egyptian article *pi* for 'the'.

8. *into the inner room*: the word only occurs here in the Old Testament, but there is a similar word in Arabic for the sanctuary of a camp, and so it is more probably the inner room of the Tabernacle (and hence the indignation at an attempt to

introduce fertility rites into the pure worship of Israel) than the inner room of the man's tent.

9. *twenty-four thousand*: Paul uses this story in 1 Cor. 10: 8 as a warning to Christians, but misremembers the number as twenty-three thousand.

11. *the same jealous anger*: or, zealous anger. It is charac-teristic of God as Israel thought of him that he is jealous to protect the due honour that should be paid to him. His claim on Israel is absolute.

12. *my covenant of security of tenure*: the point of the second story is to claim (or uphold) special rights for the descendants of Phinehas. Again we see struggles after the exile reflected. The covenant here is not an agreement between two people, but an unconditional promise by God.

14. *Zimri son of Salu*: the names seem to be added by a later writer as an afterthought. Perhaps the writer is slyly attacking contemporaries of his who trace their descent from Zimri son of Salu.

15. *daughter of Zur*: Zur is one of the Midianite kings in 31: 8.

16–18 are a late editorial note to bind together the two stories, and claim that the Midianites are responsible for both, not the Moabites for the first. The writer has verses 1–15 before him as a whole. The command to attack the Midianites recurs in 31: 1, and is intended to point forward to that chapter. ✷

THE SECOND CENSUS

After the plague the LORD said to Moses and Eleazar the 19; **26** 1 priest, son of Aaron, 'Number the whole community of 2 Israel by fathers' families, recording everyone in Israel aged twenty years and upwards fit for military service.' Moses and Eleazar collected them in the lowlands of 3 Moab by the Jordan near Jericho,*a* all who were twenty 4

[a] *Prob. rdg.; Heb. adds* saying.

years of age and upwards, as the LORD had commanded Moses.

These were the Israelites who came out of Egypt:

5[a]   Reubenites (Reuben was Israel's eldest son): Enoch, the
6   Enochite family; Pallu, the Palluite family; Hezron, the
7   Hezronite family; Carmi, the Carmite family. These were the Reubenite families; the number in their detailed list was forty-three thousand seven hundred and thirty.
8,9   Son of Pallu: Eliab. Sons of Eliab: Nemuel, Dathan and Abiram. These were the same Dathan and Abiram, conveners of the community, who defied Moses and Aaron and joined the company of Korah in defying the LORD.
10   Then the earth opened its mouth and swallowed them up with Korah, and so their company died, while fire burnt up the two hundred and fifty men, and they be-
11   came a warning sign. The Korahites, however, did not die.

12   Simeonites, by their families: Nemuel, the Nemuelite family; Jamin, the Jaminite family; Jachin, the Jachinite
13   family; Zerah, the Zarhite family; Saul, the Saulite
14   family. These were the Simeonite families; the number in their detailed list[b] was twenty-two thousand two hundred.

15   Gadites, by their families: Zephon, the Zephonite family; Haggi, the Haggite family; Shuni, the Shunite
16   family; Ozni, the Oznite family; Eri, the Erite family;
17   Arod, the Arodite family; Areli, the Arelite family.
18   These were the Gadite families; the number in their detailed list was forty thousand five hundred.

[a] *Verses 5–50: cp. Gen. 46: 8–25; Exod. 6: 14, 15; 1 Chron. chs. 4–8.*
[b] *in their detailed list: so Sept.; Heb. om.*

The sons of Judah were Er, Onan, Shelah, Perez and 19
Zerah;*a* Er and Onan died in Canaan. Judahites, by their 20
families: Shelah, the Shelanite family; Perez, the Perezite
family; Zerah, the Zarhite family. Perezites: Hezron, 21
the Hezronite family; Hamul, the Hamulite family.
These were the families of Judah; the number in their 22
detailed list was seventy-six thousand five hundred.

Issacharites, by their families: Tola, the Tolaite family; 23
Pua, the Puite*b* family; Jashub, the Jashubite family; 24
Shimron, the Shimronite family. These were the families 25
of Issachar; the number in their detailed list was sixty-
four thousand three hundred.

Zebulunites, by their families: Sered, the Sardite 26
family; Elon, the Elonite family; Jahleel, the Jahleelite
family. These were the Zebulunite families; the number 27
in their detailed list was sixty thousand five hundred.

Josephites, by their families: Manasseh and Ephraim. 28
Manassites: Machir, the Machirite family. Machir was 29
the father of Gilead: Gilead, the Gileadite family.
Gileadites: Jeezer, the Jeezerite family; Helek, the Helek- 30
ite family; Asriel, the Asrielite family; Shechem, the 31
Shechemite family; Shemida, the Shemidaite family; 32
Hepher, the Hepherite family. Zelophehad son of Hepher 33
had no sons, only daughters; their names were Mahlah,
Noah, Hoglah, Milcah and Tirzah. These were the famil- 34
ies of Manasseh; the number in their detailed list was
fifty-two thousand seven hundred.

Ephraimites, by their families: Shuthelah, the Shuthal- 35
hite family; Becher, the Bachrite family; Tahan, the

[a] Er . . . Zerah: *so some Sept. MSS. (cp. Gen. 46: 12); Heb.* Er and
Onan.   [b] *So Sam.; Heb.* Punite.

36 Tahanite family. Shuthalhites: Eran, the Eranite family.
37 These were the Ephraimite families; the number in their detailed list was thirty-two thousand five hundred. These were the Josephites, by families.

38 Benjamites, by their families: Bela, the Belaite family; Ashbel, the Ashbelite family; Ahiram, the Ahiramite
39 family; Shupham,*a* the Shuphamite family; Hupham,
40 the Huphamite family. Belaites: Ard and Naaman. Ard,*b*
41 the Ardite family; Naaman, the Naamite family. These were the Benjamite families; the number in their detailed list was forty-five thousand six hundred.

42 Danites, by their families: Shuham, the Shuhamite family. These were the families of Dan by their families;
43 the number in the detailed list of the Shuhamite family was sixty-four thousand four hundred.

44 Asherites, by their families: Imna, the Imnite family; Ishvi, the Ishvite family; Beriah, the Beriite family.
45 Beriite families: Heber, the Heberite family; Malchiel,
46 the Malchielite family. The daughter of Asher was
47 named Serah. These were the Asherite families; the number in their detailed list was fifty-three thousand four hundred.

48 Naphtalites, by their families: Jahzeel, the Jahzeel-
49 ite family; Guni, the Gunite family; Jezer, the Jezerite
50 family; Shillem, the Shillemite family. These were the Naphtalite families by their families; the number in their detailed list was forty-five thousand four hundred.

51 The total in the Israelite lists was six hundred and one thousand seven hundred and thirty.

[a] *So some MSS.; others* Shephupham.
[b] *So Sam.; Heb. om.*

✻ The census of ch. 1 was made with a view to military action. Now, when all but two of the Israelites then alive are dead, another census is needed as a preparation for the entry into Canaan. The numbers given are in total lower than those in ch. 1, and this must be meant by the Priestly Writer (who is responsible for this chapter) to imply that Israel had suffered in the course of its punishment, and did not display a natural growth in size. Here, unlike ch. 1, a list of the clans of each tribe is given, and this has been put together with a census by tribes. The order of the tribes here is the same as in ch. 1, except that the order Ephraim, Manasseh is inverted. The list of clans is closely related to a list of the descendants of Jacob in Gen. 46; the names given are with rare exceptions identical. Although the list here is clearly of clans, and that in Gen. 46 appears to be of persons, and so less primitive, it is evident that in this chapter census figures by tribes and clan lists are awkwardly combined. The clan lists, then, previously existed separately; and it is more likely that Numbers has simply taken them from Genesis than that both drew them from a common source. The list probably reflects an actual distribution of the clans of the tribes which is early, but does not in fact go back as here suggested to before the entry into Palestine. The numbers attached, which refer only to the tribes and not to the clans, may come from an actual census of Israel at some time, or may simply be unhistorical – we cannot tell which. To these lists further details have been added here and there. The Levites are dealt with separately (verses 57–62).

2. *aged twenty years and upwards*: it is again a list of males ready to fight.

4. *who came out of Egypt*: this is carelessly put, or reflects an earlier setting for the census in its first formulation; as verse 64 says, those in this list never were in Egypt.

9. This is a late note, which refers to the contents of ch. 16 in the final form in which they were told, with Korah alongside Dathan and Abiram, and provides a pointed warning to the reader of the results of disobedience.

11. *The Korahites, however, did not die*: they are taken to be identical with the guild of singers of the time of the writer, referred to in the headings to some of the psalms (unfortunately omitted in the N.E.B.: see e.g. Pss. 42; 44–9 in other translations). It seems to be implied in 16: 32, but is not definitely stated, that all the family of Korah died.

19. *Er and Onan died in Canaan*: a cross-reference has been added here to the story in Gen. 38: 6–10; another cautionary reminder.

33. *Zelophehad son of Hepher*: the daughters are to be understood here as clans: they will be treated subsequently as being individual persons in ch. 27. ✳

THE APPORTIONMENT OF THE LAND;
THE LEVITES

52, 53 The LORD spoke to Moses and said, 'The land shall be apportioned among these tribes according to the num-
54 ber of names recorded. To the larger group you shall give a larger property and to the smaller a smaller; a property shall be given to each in proportion to its size as
55 shown in the detailed lists. The land, however, shall be apportioned by lot; the lots shall be cast for the proper-
56 ties by families in the father's line. Properties shall be apportioned by lot between the larger families and the smaller.'

57   The detailed lists of Levi, by families: Gershon, the Gershonite family; Kohath, the Kohathite family; Merari, the Merarite family.

58   These were the families of Levi: the Libnite, Hebronite, Mahlite, Mushite, and Korahite families.

59   Kohath was the father of Amram; Amram's wife was named Jochebed daughter of Levi, born to him in Egypt.

She bore to Amram Aaron, Moses, and their sister
Miriam. Aaron's sons were Nadab, Abihu, Eleazar and 60
Ithamar. Nadab and Abihu died because they presented 61
illicit fire before the LORD.

In the detailed lists of Levi the number of males, aged 62
one month and upwards, was twenty-three thousand.
They were recorded separately from the other Israelites
because no property was allotted to them among the
Israelites.

These were the detailed lists prepared by Moses and 63
Eleazar the priest when they numbered the Israelites in
the lowlands of Moab by the Jordan near Jericho. Among 64
them there was not a single one of the Israelites whom
Moses and Aaron the priest had recorded in the wilderness
of Sinai; for the LORD had said they should all die in the 65
wilderness. None of them was still living except Caleb
son of Jephunneh and Joshua son of Nun.

* The principles behind the allocation of the land are given.
Two different principles are set out. The land is to be divided
in proportion to the size of the different tribes (verses 52–4),
and it is to be distributed by lot (verse 55). The lot is an
ancient method of dividing out lands among members of a
clan or family, and widely attested in the ancient Near East.
Its impartiality and chance nature meant that it was seen
particularly as a working out of the mysterious will of God,
and so was often a religious act, preceded by prayer (cp.
1 Sam. 10: 20f. or Acts 1: 24–6, the choice of a new apostle to
replace Judas). Verse 56 attempts to reconcile these two
principles, but cannot tell us how it was done, and the author
himself had probably not worked this out clearly. Then
follows (verses 57–62) the census of the Levites, counted
separately from the other tribes in recognition of their special

status, as consecrated to the service of God and not sharing in the division of the land. In a final summary (verses 63–5) it is underlined that not one man is still alive who had been alive at the first census, except Caleb and Joshua.

57–8. The list of families of Levi in verse 57 is the established list of the three sons of Levi, known elsewhere too (Num. 3: 17–20). But the alternative list in verse 58 is quite separate, and not reconciled with the first list (though this is done where the names recur in Exod. 6: 17–21). The Hebronites and Libnites come from cities in the south of Judah, and the Korahites very possibly from Korah, a city mentioned with Hebron and Tappuah in a list of the sons of Caleb in I Chron. 2: 43 (a reference to the 'sons of Korah' has recently been found on a pot at Arad (cp. on 21: 1), which may confirm this suggestion of links with the south). So probably all the names are of cities in the south where the Levites originally dwelt, in company with their old ally Simeon (Gen. 34: 30). This verse, then, remembers a very old tradition in the history of the Levites.

59–60. The history of the Kohathites is traced in detail because they are the ancestors of Moses and Aaron. The line is traced down to Nadab and Abihu: for *illicit fire* see the note on 3: 4.

62. *aged one month and upwards*: the rest of the census has been of men of military age, twenty and upwards. But there would be no point in this for the Levites, and so all the males among them are counted here, as they were also in 3: 39. ✶

DAUGHTERS' RIGHTS OF INHERITANCE

27 A claim was presented by the daughters of Zelophehad son of Hepher, son of Gilead, son of Machir, son of Manasseh,*a* son of Joseph. Their names were Mahlah, 2 Noah, Hoglah, Milcah and Tirzah. They appeared at the

[a] *So Vulg.; Heb. adds* of the families of Manasseh.

entrance of the Tent of the Presence before Moses, Eleazar the priest, the chiefs, and all the community, and spoke as follows: 'Our father died in the wilderness. He 3 was not among the company of Korah which combined together against the LORD; he died for his own sin and left no sons. Is it right that, because he had no son, our 4 father's name should disappear from his family? Give us our property on the same footing as our father's brothers.'

So Moses brought their case before the LORD, and the 5,6 LORD spoke to Moses and said, 'The claim of the daugh- 7 ters of Zelophehad is good. You must allow them to inherit on the same footing as their father's brothers. Let their father's patrimony pass to them. Then say this to 8 the Israelites: "When a man dies leaving no son, his patrimony shall pass to his daughter. If he has no daughter, 9 you shall give it to his brothers. If he has no brothers, you 10 shall give it to his father's brothers. If his father had no 11 brothers, then you shall give possession to the nearest survivor in his family, and he shall inherit. This shall be a legal precedent for the Israelites, as the LORD has commanded Moses."'

∗ Among the particular problems to be dealt with before the book can be brought to an end is that of the rights of inheritance of daughters. This question is not covered by the traditional legal material handed down and preserved elsewhere in the Pentateuch, and is settled by the (late) new style of legal narrative which we have already met in 9: 6–14 and 15: 32–6. A story is told bringing up a legal problem for which no solution is known; Moses takes it to God, and brings from him the answer. This is enforced, and a general principle is then derived from it. While the style of treatment is late (material added to P), the general rule stated in verses 8–11 may well be older. In earlier times inheritance by daughters if a man had no sons was not contemplated at all; if there were no male children the widow could marry the husband's brother (Deut. 25: 5–10, and cp. Matt. 22: 24); if a man wished to sell land his next-of-kin had the first right to buy it. Here the right of daughters is being introduced as a new principle. It carries with it difficulties, since a daughter could well marry outside the tribe and alienate territory from it; so that a new rule covering this had in turn to be introduced later; and this is the subject of chapter 36.

1. *son of Gilead, son of Machir, son of Manasseh*: Gilead and Machir are in fact tribal divisions within the tribe of Manasseh, here treated as persons, who are used as members of a family tree, or genealogy (cp. on Eber, 24: 24).

2. The author has chosen to treat these names as those of real individuals; but he has taken them from 26: 33, where Zelophehad's daughters are in fact towns or clans in the north, one of which, Tirzah, was for a while capital of the northern kingdom. The word 'daughter' can also be used of towns or villages, and was so intended in ch. 26. The author here is consciously reinterpreting the daughters of Zelophehad, to make his legal point.

3. *he died for his own sin*: like the rest of his own generation, all of whom had to die before Israel could enter Palestine. Since he had not taken part in the sin of Korah (ch. 16), he had not done anything such as would justify the loss of his property.

4. *our father's name should disappear*: it is important to keep a man's 'name' alive, for it carries with it his fame and reputation – an idea which is perhaps still not dead. The name, it appears, is preserved if a man's descendants remain associated with his land. So even if the daughters married, if they retained the land, they would preserve their father's name in association with it – they have no surnames to change.

8–11. These verses state formally the law of inheritance,

going beyond the case in point. They take account of the possibility of a man dying childless, but not of his wife surviving him and remarrying.

11. *This shall be a legal precedent*: a technical term in this type of legal narrative, for it is found again in 35: 29. ✳

MOSES IS WARNED OF HIS COMING DEATH, AND JOSHUA APPOINTED HIS SUCCESSOR

The LORD said to Moses, 'Go up this mountain, Mount 12 Abarim, and look out over the land which I have given to the Israelites. Then, when you have looked out over it, 13 you shall be gathered to your father's kin like your brother Aaron; for you and Aaron disobeyed my com- 14 mand when the community disputed with me in the wilderness of Zin: you did not uphold my holiness before them at the waters.' These were the waters of Meribah-by-Kadesh in the wilderness of Zin.

Then Moses said, 'Let the LORD, the God of the spirits 15, 16 of all mankind, appoint a man over the community to go 17 out and come in at their head, to lead them out and bring them home, so that the community of the LORD may not be like sheep without a shepherd.' The LORD answered 18 Moses, 'Take Joshua son of Nun, a man endowed with spirit; lay your hand on him and set him before Eleazar 19 the priest and all the community. Give him his commission in their presence, and delegate some of your 20 authority to him, so that all the community of the Israelites may obey him. He must appear before Eleazar the priest, 21 who will obtain a decision for him by consulting the Urim before the LORD; at his word they shall go out and shall come home, both Joshua and the whole community of the Israelites.'

22 Moses did as the LORD had commanded him. He took Joshua, presented him to Eleazar the priest and the whole
23 community, laid his hands on him and gave him his commission, as the LORD had instructed him.[a]

✷ The story draws near to its end, as Moses is told to look out over the land of Canaan and prepare for his death, and Joshua is made ready to take his place. Moses' death is not related until Deut. 34, and then the first part of this story is repeated largely word for word in Deut. 32: 48–52. Originally the connection was closer, for Num. 28–36 are inserted as later additions to the P source, and then the whole of Deuteronomy has come in with the original end of Numbers being transferred to its end to form its conclusion. Presumably after the insertions were made verses 12–14 were repeated in Deuteronomy, and then verses 15–23 added at a yet later stage in the development of this chapter, since they do not reappear in Deut. 32.

12. *Go up this mountain*: Moses will die upon the mountain. But there seems to be no suggestion of divine spite in allowing him just so far and no farther. Rather he comes as near as could be to actually making the land his own, being allowed to enjoy the sight of it before his death. *Mount Abarim*: this is a rather general term for a range of mountains, which the Deuteronomist makes more precise with a mention of Mount Nebo in particular (Deut. 32: 49).

13. *like your brother Aaron*: cp. 20: 23–9. Aaron too died on a mountain top, that of Mount Hor.

14. *disobeyed my command*: the story was told in 20: 10–11. *disputed* and *holiness* are plays on words, containing the same roots which are found in *Meribah* and *Kadesh*.

15–17. Moses' last concern is to make provisions for his

[a] *So Vulg.; Heb. adds* through Moses.

successor. He takes the initiative in this, but he does not choose the man himself, but leaves the choice to God.

16. *the God of the spirits of all mankind*: a very distinctive phrase found already in 16: 22 (see the note there).

17. *to go out and come in*: a phrase most often used in a military context (cp. 1 Sam. 18: 13–16, where the same idiom is translated 'led his men into action' and 'took the field'). *like sheep without a shepherd*: this phrase is used in 1 Kings 22: 17, again in a military context, of a leaderless army.

18. *Take Joshua son of Nun*: Joshua is introduced by P as a new character, although he has been mentioned once before in P, as having been originally named Hoshea (13: 8, 16). We have also met him in the addition to J, 11: 28. *a man endowed with spirit*: he has God's spirit, not as a sudden gift displayed in violence or prophecy, but as a permanent possession of wisdom and prudence (cp. on 24: 2). *lay your hand on him*: better 'lean your hand on him'. In the Old Testament different words are used for laying on hands in blessing, and leaning or pressing on hands, whether to transfer guilt to an animal to be sacrificed, or to commission someone as your successor and substitute. It is the latter that is here intended (cp. on 8: 10).

19. *Eleazar the priest*: the leading priest, now that his father Aaron is dead.

20. *delegate some of your authority*: the word for authority, used only here in the Pentateuch, carries overtones of a quite visible splendour and dignity. It is used of God and of the king (rendered 'majesty'; cp. Ps. 96: 6, of God: 'Majesty and splendour attend him').

21. *He must appear before Eleazar the priest*: his status is naturally lower than that of Moses, so he must obtain a decision through the priest, and not direct from God, as Moses did. *by consulting the Urim*: Urim, used in short for Urim and Thummim, is a sacred lot, by which the will of God can be learnt, kept in a pocket of the breastplate which is part of the robes of the high priest (cp. Exod. 28: 30; Lev. 8: 8). It may possibly have been two stones of different

colour, one for 'yes' and one for 'no': the high priest would feel in the pocket and bring one out, and the question put would be answered by the chance of which came out. See 1 Sam. 14: 40f. for Urim and Thummim in use. But the reference to this by P is deliberately archaistic: it was probably long since disused, though remembered. *at his word*: again their dependence on God's will is underlined.

22–3. Moses, as we have learnt to expect, carries out God's command at once and to the letter. ✳

THE DEFINITIVE LIST OF SACRIFICES

28 1, 2 The LORD spoke to Moses and said, Give this command to the Israelites: See that you present my offerings, the food for the food-offering of soothing odour, to me at the appointed time.

3 Tell them: This is the food-offering which you shall present to the LORD: the regular daily whole-offering of
4 two yearling rams without blemish. One you shall sacrifice in the morning and the second between dusk and
5 dark. The grain-offering shall be a tenth of an ephah of flour mixed with a quarter of a hin of oil of pounded
6 olives. (This was the regular whole-offering made at Mount Sinai, a soothing odour, a food-offering to the
7 LORD.) The wine[a] for the proper drink-offering shall be a quarter of a hin to each ram; you are to pour out this strong drink in the holy place as an offering to the LORD.
8 You shall sacrifice the second ram between dusk and dark, with the same grain-offering as at the morning sacrifice and with the proper drink-offering; it is a food-offering of soothing odour to the LORD.

[a] So Sept.; Heb. om.

For the sabbath day: two yearling rams without 9
blemish, a grain-offering of two tenths of an ephah of
flour mixed with oil, and the proper drink-offering. This 10
whole-offering, presented every sabbath, is in addition
to the regular whole-offering and the proper drink-
offering.

On the first day of every month you shall present a 11
whole-offering to the LORD, consisting of two young
bulls, one ram and seven yearling rams without blemish.
The grain-offering shall be three tenths of flour mixed 12
with oil for each bull, two tenths of flour mixed with oil
for the full-grown ram, and one tenth of flour mixed 13
with oil for each young ram. This is a whole-offering, a
food-offering of soothing odour to the LORD. The proper 14
drink-offering shall be half a hin of wine for each bull,
a third for the full-grown ram and a quarter for each
young ram. This is the whole-offering to be made,
month by month, throughout the year. Further, one 15
he-goat shall be sacrificed as a sin-offering to the LORD,
in addition to the regular whole-offering and the proper
drink-offering.

The Passover of the LORD shall be held on the four- 16
teenth day of the first month, and on the fifteenth day 17
there shall be a pilgrim-feast; for seven days you must
eat only unleavened cakes. On the first day there shall 18
be a sacred assembly; you shall not do your daily work.
As a food-offering, a whole-offering to the LORD, you 19
shall present two young bulls, one ram, and seven yearling rams, all without blemish. You shall offer the proper 20
grain-offerings of flour mixed with oil, three tenths for
each bull, two tenths for the ram, and one tenth for each 21

22 of the seven young rams; and as a sin-offering, one he-
23 goat to make expiation for you. All these you shall offer
in addition to the morning whole-offering, which is
24 the regular sacrifice. You shall repeat this daily till the
seventh day, presenting food as a food-offering of soothing odour to the LORD, in addition to the regular whole-
25 offering and the proper drink-offering. On the seventh
day there shall be a sacred assembly; you shall not do
your daily work.

26 On the day of Firstfruits, when you bring to the LORD
your grain-offering from the new crop at your Feast of
Weeks, there shall be a sacred assembly; you shall not do
27 your daily work. You shall bring a whole-offering as a
soothing odour to the LORD: two young bulls, one full-
28 grown ram, and seven yearling rams. The proper grain-
offering shall be of flour mixed with oil, three tenths for
29 each bull, two tenths for the one ram, and a tenth for
30 each of the seven young rams, and there shall be one he-
31 goat as a sin-offering[a] to make expiation for you; they
shall all be without blemish. All these you shall offer in
addition to the regular whole-offering with the proper
grain-offering and drink-offering.

* We turn now for three chapters from narrative to law. No
reason is given for the sudden change, but we have met a
similar feature already in the placing of chs. 15 and 18, and it
reflects the character of the Pentateuch as a whole as both
narrative and law. The material continues to come from P, but
here probably from a later supplement to P. In chs. 28 and 29
we have a careful summary list of the Jewish days and feasts
in the calendar, with a description of the requirements for the

[a] as a sin-offering: *so Sam.; Heb. om.*

sacrifices that accompany them. It is of course the established pattern after the exile that is reflected here, and attributed to the wilderness period. The nature of each feast is not fully indicated by the details given: the distinctive character of each, the air of excitement, the nature of popular participation, are not in place in a list. Before the exile there were both morning and evening sacrifices in the temple daily (2 Kings 16: 15), but the detail and precision of this chapter are of a later date. We hear of a basic daily morning and evening sacrifice, of the same doubled on the sabbath, and of a substantial extra sacrifice on the first of each month, and on other specific days of festival. Rules about the grain-offering and libations, given as an innovation in Num. 15, are here treated as already known; and some parts of the chapter depend either on Lev. 23, or on a source underlying it. This confirms the lateness of the material. Its positive value lies in its concern for the due regular service of God, enunciated to an Israel which (as Mal. 1: 7–14 suggests) was ready enough to skimp on what it knew to be its duty.

2. *the food for the food-offering*: underlying this phrase is the old idea that the deity actually fed off the offerings made to him; P will not have held such an idea, but the old language survived (cp. 15: 3).

3. *This is the food-offering*: for food-offerings see the note on 15: 3, for whole-offerings on 6: 11, for grain-offerings on 4: 16, for drink-offerings on 6: 15.

5. The rules for the *grain-offering* of ch. 15 are here presupposed. For the equivalents of *ephah* and *hin* see the note on 15: 4.

6. *made at Mount Sinai*: the cross-reference is to the account in Exod. 29: 38–42.

7. *this strong drink*: this is a very odd word to use for wine, but the related word in Akkadian (the old Semitic language of Babylonia) is found in Babylonian sacrificial terminology, and it is very probably borrowed from there as a result of the exile. *in the holy place*: although this is not specified here more exactly, Ecclus. 50: 15 indicates that it is poured at the

foot of the altar, so that the 'holy place' is the inner court of the temple where the altar of whole-offering stands.

9. *For the sabbath day*: the same quantities that are offered daily are also offered for the sabbath, but as an extra, so that twice as much is offered as in the daily sacrifice.

11. *On the first day of every month*: the observance of this day is ancient (cp. Amos 8: 5), but regular sacrifices for it are probably late. A sharp increase in quantities offered can be seen; the first day of the month is treated in a way similar to the great feasts.

16. Note that for the Passover itself (falling about March–April) no sacrifice is prescribed, for it is more a family observance than a public feast (cp. on 9: 1–14). It is for the following feast of unleavened cakes (verse 17), which is closely associated with the Passover, that sacrifice is required. Again the sacrifice is specified at the higher level for feasts.

26. *On the day of Firstfruits*: this is an unusual name for the Feast of Weeks, a feast which was originally probably not on a fixed day, varying with the lateness of harvest (like modern 'harvest festivals'); but later was fixed to fall 'seven weeks from the time when the sickle is put to the standing corn' (Deut. 16: 9). *

THE LIST OF SACRIFICES CONTINUED: THE FEASTS OF THE SEVENTH MONTH

29 On the first day of the seventh month there shall be a sacred assembly; you shall not do your daily work. It 2 shall be a day of acclamation. You shall sacrifice a whole-offering as a soothing odour to the LORD: one young bull, one full-grown ram, and seven yearling rams, 3 without blemish. Their proper grain-offering shall be of flour mixed with oil, three tenths for the bull, two tenths 4 for the one ram, and one tenth for each of the seven 5 young rams, and there shall be one he-goat as a sin-

offering to make expiation for you. This is in addition 6
to the monthly whole-offering and the regular whole-
offering with their proper grain-offerings and drink-
offerings according to custom; it is a food-offering of
soothing odour to the LORD.

On the tenth day of this seventh month there shall be a 7
sacred assembly, and you shall mortify yourselves; you
shall not do any work. You shall bring a whole-offering 8
to the LORD as a soothing odour: one young bull, one
full-grown ram, and seven yearling rams; they shall all
be without blemish. The proper grain-offering shall be of 9
flour mixed with oil, three tenths for the bull, two tenths
for the one ram, and one tenth for each of the seven 10
young rams, and there shall be one he-goat as a sin- 11
offering, in addition to the expiatory sin-offering and
the regular whole-offering, with the proper grain-
offering and drink-offering.[a]

On the fifteenth day of the seventh month there shall be a 12
sacred assembly. You shall not do your daily work, but
shall keep a pilgrim-feast to the LORD for seven days.
As a whole-offering, a food-offering of soothing odour 13
to the LORD, you shall bring thirteen young bulls, two
full-grown rams, and fourteen yearling rams; they shall
all be without blemish. The proper grain-offering shall 14
be of flour mixed with oil, three tenths for each of the
thirteen bulls, two tenths for each of the two rams, and 15
one tenth for each of the fourteen young rams, and there 16
shall be one he-goat as a sin-offering, in addition to the
regular whole-offering with the proper grain-offering
and drink-offering.

[a] *So Sept.; Heb.* drink-offerings.

17 On the second day: twelve young bulls, two full-
grown rams, and fourteen yearling rams, without blem-
18 ish, together with the proper grain-offerings and drink-
offerings for bulls, full-grown rams, and young rams,
19 as prescribed according to their number, and there shall
be one he-goat as a sin-offering, in addition to the regular
whole-offering with the proper grain-offering and drink-
offering.[a]

20 On the third day: eleven bulls, two full-grown rams,
21 and fourteen yearling rams, without blemish, together
with the proper grain-offerings and drink-offerings for
bulls, full-grown rams, and young rams, as prescribed
22 according to their number, and there shall be one he-goat
as a sin-offering, in addition to the regular whole-offering,
with the proper grain-offering and drink-offering.

23 On the fourth day: ten bulls, two full-grown rams,
24 and fourteen yearling rams, without blemish, together
with the proper grain-offerings and drink-offerings for
bulls, full-grown rams, and young rams, as prescribed
25 according to their number, and there shall be one he-goat
as a sin-offering, in addition to the regular whole-offering
with the proper grain-offering and drink-offering.

26 On the fifth day: nine bulls, two full-grown rams, and
27 fourteen yearling rams, without blemish, together with
the proper grain-offerings and drink-offerings for bulls,
full-grown rams, and young rams, as prescribed accord-
28 ing to their number, and there shall be one he-goat as a
sin-offering, in addition to the regular whole-offering
with the proper grain-offering and drink-offering.

29 On the sixth day: eight bulls, two full-grown rams,

[a] *So some MSS.; others* drink-offerings.

and fourteen yearling rams, without blemish, together 30
with the proper grain-offerings and drink-offerings for
bulls, full-grown rams, and young rams, as prescribed
according to their number, and there shall be one he-goat 31
as a sin-offering, in addition to the regular whole-offering
with the proper grain-offering and drink-offering.[a]

On the seventh day: seven bulls, two full-grown rams, 32
and fourteen yearling rams, without blemish, together 33
with the proper grain-offerings and drink-offerings for
bulls, full-grown rams, and young rams, as prescribed
accoiding to their number, and there shall be one he-goat 34
as a sin-offering, in addition to the regular whole-offering
with the proper grain-offering and drink-offering.

The eighth day you shall keep as a closing ceremony; 35
you shall not do your daily work. As a whole-offering, 36
a food-offering of soothing odour to the LORD, you shall
bring one bull, one full-grown ram, and seven yearling
rams, without blemish, together with the proper grain- 37
offerings and drink-offerings for bulls, full-grown rams,
and young rams, as prescribed according to their
number, and there shall be one he-goat as a sin-offering, 38
in addition to the regular whole-offering with the
proper grain-offering and drink-offering.

These are the sacrifices which you shall offer to the 39
LORD at the appointed seasons, in addition to the votive
offerings, the freewill offerings, the whole-offerings, the
grain-offerings, the drink-offerings, and the shared-
offerings.

Moses told the Israelites exactly what the LORD had 40[b]
commanded him.

[a] *So some MSS.; others* drink-offerings.   [b] *30: 1 in Heb.*

✻ 1. *On the first day of the seventh month*: the description of the requirements for sacrifices continues with the feasts of the seventh month (about September–October), a month which has a special character in Judaism after the exile. The first day of the seventh month is emphasized as a day of rest and acclamation (verses 1–6); this is not so far as we know an old feast in Israel, and it may be that the first day of the most sacred month is itself singled out for greater honour just because it is the first. It has also been suggested that keeping this day is a tradition going back to the New Year Festival before the exile, a feast which on the older native Hebrew calendar fell in the autumn. Many scholars believe that connected with this were a number of special ceremonies involving the king, and giving an assurance of fertility and prosperity in the coming year. The native calendar was replaced after the exile by the Babylonian calendar, in use in these chapters, in which the New Year fell in the spring. Certainly in post-biblical Judaism the first day of the seventh month is kept as *rosh-hashanah*, New Year's Day, but it is uncertain how far it is right to argue back from this later revival of the ancient calendar system. *you shall not do your daily work*: it becomes an extra day of rest, like the Sabbath.

It shall be a day of acclamation: this is a new name for the day, picked up from the account in Lev. 23: 23–5, which mentions that this is 'a day of remembrance and acclamation' (i.e. of shouting for joy).

2. The specific offerings are lower than for other big feasts like Tabernacles, in having only one young bull offered instead of two. But since, as verse 6 says, the sacrifice is in addition to the usual monthly offering, the total is larger than for any other feast, including that of unleavened bread.

7. *On the tenth day of this seventh month*: this is the Day of Atonement. It is probably a post-exilic observance only, and is rather oddly not named here: we know the name only from Lev. 23: 27 in the Old Testament. *you shall mortify yourselves*: the Hebrew is literally 'you shall humiliate your persons', and

the reference is probably to fasting. This requirement confirms that it is indeed the Day of Atonement.

11. *in addition to the expiatory sin-offering*: that is, the goat
for Azazel. The full ritual of the Day of Atonement is described
in Lev. 16. While that account is not here repeated, it is
indicated that the ritual of Lev. 16 is in addition to the
sacrifices here commanded.

12. *On the fifteenth day of the seventh month*: this is the traditional great feast of the nation, Tabernacles, which lasted a full
eight days. It was a great feast of pilgrimage and popular joy,
including in itself the celebration of the harvest and a remembrance of the time when Israel dwelt in the wilderness (Lev.
23: 39–43). Our text makes no allusion to the characteristic
dwelling in booths described in Lev. 23, which gave the feast
its name, and this may by now have fallen into disuse. The
feast goes back to long before the exile: it already lasts eight
days in 1 Kings 8: 2 and 65–6.

13–38. The grand total sacrificed in the week, it will be
seen, is very considerable: seventy bulls, fourteen rams,
ninety-eight yearling rams, and seven he-goats, apart from
those offered on the eighth day.

17. *On the second day: twelve young bulls*: it will be seen that
the number of bulls declines by one each day from thirteen to
eight. This may indicate that the intensity of the joy declines
as the feast goes on; at least no better explanation has been
found.

40. Again Moses' total obedience is stressed (cp. 27: 22). *

THE VALIDITY OF WOMEN'S VOWS

Then Moses spoke to the heads of the Israelite tribes and **30**
said, This is the LORD's command: When a man makes a 2
vow to the LORD or swears an oath and so puts himself
under a binding obligation, he must not break his word.
Every word he has spoken, he must make good. When 3

a woman, still young and living in her father's house, makes a vow to the LORD or puts herself under a binding
4 obligation, if her father hears of it and keeps silence, then
5 any such vow or obligation shall be valid. But if her father disallows it when he hears of it, none of her vows or obligations shall be valid; the LORD will absolve her,
6 because her father has disallowed it. If the woman is married when she is under a vow or a binding obliga-
7 tion rashly uttered, then if her husband hears of it and keeps silence when he hears, her vow or obligation by
8 which she has bound herself shall be valid. If, however, her husband disallows it when he hears of it and repudi- ates the vow which she has taken upon herself or the rash utterance with which she has bound herself, then the
9 LORD will absolve her. Every vow by which a widow or a divorced woman has bound herself shall be valid.
10 But if it is in her husband's house that a woman makes a vow or puts herself under a binding obligation by an
11 oath, and her husband, hearing of it, keeps silence and does not disallow it, then every vow and obligation
12 under which she has put herself shall be valid; but if her husband clearly repudiates them when he hears of them, then nothing that she has uttered, whether vow or obliga- tion, shall be valid. Her husband has repudiated them, and the LORD will absolve her.

13 The husband can confirm or repudiate any vow or oath by which a woman binds herself to mortification.
14 If he maintains silence day after day, he thereby confirms every vow or obligation under which she has put her- self: he confirms them, because he kept silence at the
15 time when he heard them. If he repudiates them some

208

time after he has heard them, he shall be responsible for her default.

Such are the decrees which the LORD gave to Moses 16 concerning a husband and his wife and a father and his daughter, still young and living in her father's house.

* Vows were often made in connection with sacrifices (cp. Lev. 7: 16 and Num. 15: 3), and both share the same generic name *qorbān*, 'offering'. This is probably the rather thin thread that links this chapter to the preceding two. The chapter is again from P, probably from a late stage of P, and there is no way of telling for sure whether the principles it lays down are old: probably they are. Its concern is the problems of vows made by women, in view of the fact that women were normally under the authority of a man, either father or husband. The chapter mentions in verse 9 the only major exception to this, 'a widow or a divorced woman'. Elderly unmarried women were apparently so rare, in a nation where marriage was a religious duty, as not to need mention at all. The chapter determines the circumstances in which the man may disallow the woman's vow: it must be done as soon as he hears of it, and not later; no reasons, it appears, need be given. In a society where authority was important a woman could otherwise undermine her husband, for example by vowing away a child without his consent.

The chapter deals with vows, both positive and negative, made to God in a religious context, not with obligations to other people. The nature of the vows is not indicated here, but they would be such as Hannah's vow of her son Samuel to God (1 Sam. 1: 11; this vow evidently has her husband Elkanah's assent; cp. 1 Sam. 1: 21–3), or vows of abstinence and fasting. Such vows must have been a common feature of life for the Israelites for them to be given as much attention as they are in the Old Testament (cp. for instance the Nazirite vow, Num. 6, or Saul's ban on any Israelite taking food before nightfall when in pursuit of the enemy: 1 Sam. 14: 24). They imply a very direct and simple view of man's relations with God and obligations to him, a feeling that it is right to repay God for blessings received by a direct gift to him, which can be either positive (the promise of a gift) or negative (an act of renunciation). There are other problems with vows, as of vows taken rashly (Lev. 5: 4–5), or the redeeming of vows that can no longer be kept (Lev. 27), not covered here at all; it is only with vows taken by women that this chapter is concerned.

5. *the LORD will absolve her*: it appears that the vow is not simply invalidated by the prohibition of the girl's father: having been uttered it stands, but may not be performed. So it requires (but inevitably receives) God's forgiveness when it cannot be performed.

6. *If the woman is married*: the rule in verses 6–8 appears to be repeated in verses 10–12, after a parenthesis in verse 9. Either verses 10–12 repeat the rule, to underline the contrast with the widow and divorced woman, or, more probably, the phrase should here be taken as referring to the position of a woman who is engaged but is not yet living in her husband's house. Engagement was a much more binding obligation in ancient Israel than it is now – cp. the position of Joseph and Mary (Matt. 1: 18). Perhaps translate 'If the woman gets married'.

9. *shall be valid*: there is no suggestion then that women as such cannot commit themselves irrevocably: it is the superiority of a man's authority that makes this subject to qualification in the case of married women.

13. *binds herself to mortification*: this refers to any kind of self-denial, such as fasting (cp. 29: 7).

14. *If he maintains silence day after day*: the authority of the husband must be exercised at once; he cannot meditate upon a vow, and use a prohibition of it as a weapon in married strife. ✳

WAR AGAINST MIDIAN, AND RULES ABOUT BOOTY

The LORD spoke to Moses and said, 'You are to exact **31** 1,2 vengeance for Israel on the Midianites and then you will be gathered to your father's kin.'

Then Moses spoke to the people in these words: 3 'Let some men among you be drafted for active service. They shall fall upon Midian and exact vengeance in the LORD's name. You shall send out a thousand men from 4 each of the tribes of Israel.' So the men were called up 5 from the clans of Israel, a thousand from each tribe, twelve thousand in all, drafted for active service. Moses 6 sent out this force, a thousand from each tribe, with Phinehas son of Eleazar the priest, who was in charge of the holy vessels and of the trumpets to give the signal for the battle-cry. They made war on Midian as the LORD 7 had commanded Moses, and slew all the men. In addition 8 to those slain in battle they killed the kings of Midian – Evi, Rekem, Zur, Hur, and Reba, the five kings of Midian – and they put to death also Balaam son of Beor. The 9 Israelites took captive the Midianite women and their dependants, and carried off all their beasts, their flocks, and their property. They burnt all their cities, in which 10 they had settled, and all their encampments. They took 11 all the spoil and plunder, both man and beast, and brought 12 them – captives, plunder, and spoil – to Moses and Eleazar the priest and to all the community of the Israelites, to the camp in the lowlands of Moab by the Jordan at Jericho.

Moses and Eleazar the priest and all the leaders of the 13 community went to meet them outside the camp. Moses 14

spoke angrily to the officers of the army, the commanders of units of a thousand and of a hundred, who
15 were returning from the campaign: 'Have you spared all
16 the women?' he said. 'Remember, it was they who, on
Balaam's departure, set about seducing the Israelites into
disloyalty to the LORD that day at Peor, so that the plague
17 struck the community of the LORD. Now kill every male
dependant, and kill every woman who has had intercourse
18 with a man, but spare for yourselves every woman among
19 them who has not had intercourse. You yourselves,
every one of you who has taken life and every one who
has touched the dead, must remain outside the camp for
seven days. Purify yourselves and your captives on the
20 third day and on the seventh day, and purify also every
piece of clothing, every article made of skin, everything
woven of goat's hair, and everything made of wood.'

21 Eleazar the priest said to the soldiers returning from
22-23 battle, 'This is a law and statute which the LORD has
ordained through Moses. Anything which will stand
fire, whether gold, silver, copper, iron, tin, or lead, you
shall pass through fire and then it will be clean. Other
things shall be purified by the water of ritual purification; whatever cannot stand fire shall be passed through
24 the water. On the seventh day you shall wash your
clothes, and then be clean; after this you may re-enter
the camp.'

25, 26 The LORD spoke to Moses and said, 'Count all that has
been captured, man or beast, you and Eleazar the priest
27 and the heads of families in the community, and divide
it equally between the fighting men who went on the
28 campaign and the whole community. You shall levy a

tax for the LORD: from the combatants it shall be one out
of every five hundred, whether men, cattle, asses, or
sheep, to be taken out of their share and given to Eleazar 29
the priest as a contribution for the LORD. Out of the share 30
of the Israelites it shall be one out of every fifty taken,
whether man or beast, cattle, asses, or sheep, to be given
to the Levites who are in charge of the LORD's Tabernacle.'

Moses and Eleazar the priest did as the LORD had com- 31
manded Moses. These were the spoils, over and above the 32
plunder taken by the fighting men: six hundred and
seventy-five thousand sheep, seventy-two thousand cattle, 33
sixty-one thousand asses; and of persons, thirty-two 34, 35
thousand girls who had had no intercourse with a
man.

The half-share of those who took part in the campaign 36
was thus three hundred and thirty-seven thousand five
hundred sheep, the tax for the LORD from these being six 37
hundred and seventy-five; thirty-six thousand cattle, the 38
tax being seventy-two; thirty thousand five hundred 39
asses, the tax being sixty-one; and sixteen thousand per- 40
sons, the tax being thirty-two. Moses gave Eleazar the 41
priest the tax levied for the LORD, as the LORD had commanded him.

The share of the community, being the half-share for 42-43
the Israelites which Moses divided off from that of the
combatants, was three hundred and thirty-seven thousand
five hundred sheep, thirty-six thousand cattle, thirty 44, 45
thousand five hundred asses, and sixteen thousand per- 46
sons. Moses took one out of every fifty, whether man 47
or beast, from the half-share of the Israelites, and gave

it to the Levites who were in charge of the LORD's Tabernacle, as the LORD had commanded him.

48 Then the officers who had commanded the forces on the campaign, the commanders of units of a thousand
49 and of a hundred, came to Moses and said to him, 'Sir, we have checked the roll of the fighting men who were
50 under our command, and not one of them is missing. So we have brought the gold ornaments, the armlets, bracelets, finger-rings, earrings, and pendants*a* that each man has found, to offer them before the LORD as a ransom for our lives.'

51 Moses and Eleazar the priest received this gold from the commanders of units of a thousand and of a hundred,
52 all of its craftsman's work, and the gold thus levied as a contribution to the LORD weighed sixteen thousand seven
53 hundred and fifty shekels; for every man in the army
54 had taken plunder. So Moses and Eleazar the priest received the gold from the commanders of units of a thousand and of a hundred, and brought it to the Tent of the Presence that the LORD might remember Israel.

✳ In post-biblical Judaism stories are often made up to illustrate a point of religious significance. They are not intended to be historical, and are known as 'Midrash'. If this pattern of Midrash is found anywhere in the Old Testament, it is in this chapter. We are told of total defeat and extermination by Israel of its old enemies, the Midianites (cp. on 10: 29–36). This account must be unhistorical. Midian still existed later, and the story with its total lack of detail, of site of battle or date, with its total annihilation of all the fighting men of Midian at the cost of no Israelite lives at all, is quite unreal. It

[a] Heb. *word of uncertain mng.*

is in fact told as a peg on which to hang the central part of this chapter, the regulations about ritual cleansing of warriors and about the disposal of the booty; it is these that really interest the author.

The story is told by P. We cannot tell how far he is revising stories which came to him, but it is clear that he picks up part of his theme and some details from older stories in the Old Testament. He alludes to the story of Balaam in verses 8 and 16, and links Balaam with the story of Baal of Peor (ch. 25) from which Phinehas and Zur (25: 7 and 15) are taken over. Some elements are taken from the story in Judg. 21: 10–12 of the battle at Jabesh-gilead in which 12,000 fighting men appear. All the men and married women are killed, while the virgins are spared. There are echoes of the story of Gideon defeating the Midianites: the same enemy, the trumpet (Judg. 7: 18; cp. verse 6 here) and the surrender to the commander of the golden objects captured (Judg. 8: 24–7; cp. verses 50–4 here). There is a more general similarity to the story of the defeat and destruction of Amalek in 1 Sam. 15 and to the battle narratives of the Chronicler.

One theme of the chapter is concern for purity. The soldiers, and also their booty, are to be ritually purified for seven days, to re-establish the total purity of God's holy people. Another concern is the principle of the 'ban' or *ḥerem* (cp. on 21: 2) of the Holy War, conducted in God's name. Cities are destroyed, chiefs killed, the population wiped out, with the exception of virgins; animals and material objects are not destroyed but taken as booty.

But the main interest is in the disposal of the booty. Half of it is kept for the fighting soldiers, and half for the rest of the people (verse 27). This follows a principle ascribed to David in 1 Sam. 30: 23–5, where it is an innovation in place of the earlier free-for-all. What is new here is the rule that the priests should have one five-hundredth of the share of the combatants, and the Levites one fiftieth of the share of the rest of the people. This rule reflects the great concern of P for the proper support of the priests and the Levites, and through this (as he sees it) a concern for the rights of God himself.

The chapter is, it must be admitted, stylized and unhistorical, and it would be a monstrous story of genocide if it were true (cp. on 21: 2). But the author is writing at a time of great weakness for Judah, when it is a small province in the Persian Empire which could carry out no such programme, and it is the powers of evil that he projects as Israel's enemy which it must destroy totally in the future as it had done once in the past, and from which it must protect itself by a profound concern for purity, uncompromising in its faithfulness to its Lord.

2. *the Midianites*: cp. on 10: 29–36 for Midian.

4. *a thousand men from each*: with the tribes of very different sizes, it is a sign of the unrealistic character of the account that the same number is required from each.

6. *with Phinehas*: since the war is a 'Holy War' the Israelites are not led by Moses or Joshua; nor, since he would be defiled by the fighting, by Eleazar the high priest, but by his son Phinehas (for whose name see on 25: 7).

8. These names are also found in Josh. 13: 21, there listed as 'vassals of Sihon', who dwelt in the country. The names there probably derive from this list; but we cannot tell how they came into this story. Their untypical precision, in a section (verses 7–12) which is otherwise entirely unspecific, suggests that they are an addition to the story; but their source is quite unknown. Zur is mentioned as the head of a Midianite family in 25: 15. *Balaam son of Beor*: like much other detail Balaam is taken into this chapter from elsewhere. Probably because the story of Balaam, chs. 22–4, and the story of Baal of Peor, ch. 25, stand side by side, it has been deduced that he is responsible for Israel having gone astray (cp. on verse 16), and it is therefore thought appropriate that he should now be killed. This is the origin of Balaam's bad reputation in later Judaism, as in Jude 11.

10. *encampments*: Midian is partly settled, partly nomadic.

13–18. Moses is angry because the army has brought back

all the women and children. He insists on a more total destruction, as Samuel did on Saul's return from the slaughter of the Amalekites (1 Sam. 15: 17–19).

16. *on Balaam's departure*: the text is traditionally read as 'on Balaam's advice', or as 'in the matter of Balaam'. This last is the most probable of the possible senses here, since the same phrase follows just after, 'in the matter of Peor', which is here freely translated *that day at Peor*. It makes better sense if the narrative involves Balaam in the sin at Peor, for there is no other basis given to help us understand why in verse 8 Balaam should be killed. His standing is entirely pro-Israelite in chs. 22–4.

19–24. Moses tells all who are defiled from contact with the dead to remain outside the camp seven days and perform the proper rite of purification. This is set out in Num. 19: 12, 16-19. But the following verses extend the rite to the booty, and this is a new provision, not known elsewhere at all.

19. *Purify yourselves*: literally 'de-sin' yourselves.

21. Eleazar speaks instead of Moses, and this suggests an addition to the story.

23. *water of ritual purification*: see on this ch. 19, which tells how it is to be made and used.

49. All the men have returned safe; no element is lacking in the success of Israel.

50. The story is based on that of the golden ornaments taken from Midian under Gideon (Judg. 8: 24–6). No doubt the Midianites (like roving nomads and traders generally) were particularly fond of wearing such gold trinkets. *as a ransom for our lives*: a payment in thanksgiving, rather than to obtain their lives by purchase.

54. *that the LORD might remember Israel*: the text reads literally 'a remembrance for the sons of Israel before the LORD'; and this was traditionally taken as 'to remind the people to remember the event'. The N.E.B. spells out the alternative way of taking it, which is now preferred by many scholars. ✳

LAND ASSIGNED TO TRIBES EAST OF THE JORDAN

32 Now the Reubenites and the Gadites had large and very numerous flocks, and when they saw that the land of
2 Jazer and Gilead was good grazing country, they came and said to Moses and Eleazar the priest and to the leaders
3 of the community, 'Ataroth, Dibon, Jazer, Nimrah,
4 Heshbon, Elealeh, Sebam,*ᵃ* Nebo, and Beon, the region which the LORD has subdued before the advance of the Israelite community, is grazing country, and our flocks
5 are our livelihood. If', they said, 'we have found favour with you, sir, then let this country be given to us as our
6 possession, and do not make us cross the Jordan.' Moses replied to the Gadites and the Reubenites, 'Are your
7 kinsmen to go into battle while you stay here? How dare you discourage the Israelites from crossing over to
8 the land which the LORD has given them? This is what your fathers did when I sent them out from Kadesh-
9 barnea to view the land. They went up as far as the gorge of Eshcol and viewed the land, and on their return so discouraged the Israelites that they would not enter the
10 land which the LORD had given them. The LORD became
11 angry that day, and he solemnly swore: "Because they have not followed me with their whole heart, none of the men who came out of Egypt, from twenty years old and upwards, shall see the land which I promised on
12 oath to Abraham, Isaac and Jacob." This meant all except Caleb son of Jephunneh the Kenizzite and Joshua son of Nun, who followed the LORD with their whole heart.
13 The LORD became angry with Israel, and he made them

[a] Sibmah *in verse 38.*

wander in the wilderness for forty years until that whole
generation was dead which had done what was wrong
in his eyes. And now you are following in your fathers' 14
footsteps, a fresh brood of sinful men to fire the LORD's
anger once more against Israel; for if you refuse to follow 15
him, he will again abandon this whole people in the
wilderness and you will be the cause of their destruction.

Presently they came forward with this offer: 'We will 16
build folds for our sheep here and towns for our dependants. Then we can be drafted as a fighting force[a] to 17
go at the head of the Israelites until we have brought them
to the lands that will be theirs. Meanwhile our dependants
can live in the walled towns, safe from the people of the
country. We will not return until every Israelite is settled 18
in possession of his patrimony; we will claim no share 19
of the land with them over the Jordan and beyond,
because our patrimony has already been allotted to us
east of the Jordan.' Moses answered, 'If you stand by your 20
promise, if in the presence of the LORD you are drafted
for battle, and the whole draft crosses the Jordan in front 21
of the LORD and remains there until the LORD has driven
out his enemies, and the land falls before him, then you 22
may come back and be quit of your obligation to the
LORD and to Israel; and this land shall be your possession
in the sight of the LORD. But I warn you, if you fail to 23
do all this, you will have sinned against the LORD, and
your sin will find you out. So build towns for your 24
dependants and folds for your sheep; but carry out your
promise.'

The Gadites and Reubenites answered Moses, 'Sir, 25

[a] as . . . force: *so Sept.; Heb. obscure.*

26 we are your servants and will do as you command. Our dependants and wives, our flocks and all our beasts shall
27 remain here in the cities of Gilead; but we, all who have been drafted for active service with the LORD, will cross the river and fight, according to your command.'

28   Accordingly Moses gave these instructions to Eleazar the priest and Joshua son of Nun and to the heads of the
29 families in the Israelite tribes: 'If the Gadites and Reuben-ites, all who have been drafted for battle before the LORD, cross the Jordan with you, and if the land falls into your hands, then you shall give them Gilead for their posses-
30 sion. But if, thus drafted, they fail to cross with you, then
31 they shall acquire land alongside you in Canaan.' The Gadites and Reubenites said in response, 'Sir, the LORD
32 has spoken, and we will obey. Once we have been drafted, we will cross over before the LORD into Canaan; then we shall have our patrimony here beyond the Jordan.'

33   So to the Gadites, the Reubenites, and half the tribe of Manasseh son of Joseph, Moses gave the kingdoms of Sihon king of the Amorites and Og king of Bashan, the whole land with its towns and the country round
35 them. The Gadites built Dibon, Ataroth, Aroer, Atroth-
36 shophan, Jazer, Jogbehah, Beth-nimrah, and Beth-haran, all of them walled towns with folds for their
37[a] sheep. The Reubenites built Heshbon, Elealeh, Kiriathaim,
38 Nebo, Baal-meon (whose name was changed), and Sib-mah; these were the names they gave to the towns they
39 built. The sons of Machir son of Manasseh invaded Gilead,
40 took it and drove out the Amorite inhabitants; Moses

[a] *Verses 37, 38: cp. verse 3.*

then assigned Gilead to Machir son of Manasseh, and he made his home there. Jair son of Manasseh attacked and took the tent-villages of Ham[a] and called them Havvoth-jair.[b] Nobah attacked and took Kenath and its villages and gave it his own name, Nobah. 41 42

* The older source (J) does not have much material about the time spent by the Israelites east of the Jordan, and after chs. 22–5 this is the only appearance of J in the rest of Numbers. It is hardly conceivable that it did not go on to tell of the movement of the Israelites into Canaan, possibly in the fragmentary form in which Judg. 1 tells of this, more probably in the narrative of Josh. 1–12. But J is based on a collection of older material which has an entry into Palestine from the south through Judah (cp. on 16: 1–19 and 21: 1–3), and has itself developed the picture of a journey round Edom and Moab and an entry from the east. So it is not surprising that J does not have much material for this part of his story. Ch. 32 is basically by J, and has a story he has developed himself to explain the circumstances of certain Israelite tribes (Reuben, Gad, part of Manasseh) being found east of the Jordan, if the main movement was, as he held, an invasion from east to west. He shows these tribes wishing to stay east of the Jordan, but at Moses' urging agreeing to join in the conquest, on the understanding that they would then return to a land where they had left their dependants, wives, flocks and other beasts. This story is found in verses 2, 4–6, 16*a*, 17, 20–3, 25–7, 32*a*, 34–8.

But it has then been expanded by much additional material, not probably a separate account fused with it, but enlargements mostly from the P school. The most substantial are verses 7–15, which take as their basis the explorers' story of chs. 13–14 in its final form, and bring into the present story

[a] *Prob. rdg.; Heb.* their tent-villages.
[b] *That is* Tent-villages of Jair.

the familiar themes of rebellion and disobedience, Moses' fear of which leads the Reubenites and Gadites to agree to share in the battle. Verses 28–31, 32*b* (with which verses 18–19 go) are the other substantial addition, made by an editor who cannot see the promise of Reuben and Gad as a sufficient guarantee to serve as a basis for allotting them the land, so that he provides that Eleazar and Joshua are to watch that they keep their word.

Verses 39–42 are a further group of independent old traditions of the occupation of Gilead by elements of Manasseh, and this is a separate story, but also from P.

On the historical facts of the settlement there is no general agreement; some take this chapter as reflecting the settling down of a group coming in from the east; others see the Israelites as moving east across the Jordan to increase the land they hold. The answer preferred depends on much wider considerations about the precise nature of Israel's occupation of the land.

The picture given by the final form of the chapter is of the people of God transcending the needs and wishes of the individual tribes so as to act as a unity, marching forward all together with steadfast purpose to the promised land.

1. *the Reubenites and the Gadites*: this is the order of seniority among the tribes. Usually in this narrative they are referred to in the reverse order, and that is also the usage of the older narrator, reflecting their relative importance in J's time. Reuben, though remembered to be the 'first-born', early declined in strength and significance (Gen. 49: 3), and from the time of the monarchy is almost lost to sight. It is not mentioned in the inscription of Mesha (see on verse 34) as Gad is. *the land of Jazer*: Jazer is always elsewhere a town (see the map, p. 145). Here the term is used of the area round it, the northern half of the land occupied east of the Jordan. *Gilead*, used elsewhere of the whole territory, or of its northern part, is here apparently used of the southern part. The northern part was agricultural, with fruit-orchards, vineyards and cornfields; the poorer southern half is moorland, with good pasture for flocks.

3. For the names see the map on p. 145, where the location is given of those which can be identified. They have been added later to this point in the story, from verses 34–8, where they belong originally, and further comment is given in the notes there.

7–15. For the detail of these verses cp. the notes on chs. 13 and 14, on which they are closely dependent.

16. *folds for our sheep*: or rather drystone walls such as are still used in Palestine, and such as are found widely in the north of England and in Scotland.

17. *as a fighting force*: cp. the N.E.B. footnote; the addition of one letter to a most puzzling Hebrew word has given a very appropriate sense.

22. *be quit of your obligation*: to be called up for military service along with the rest of Israel.

23. *your sin will find you out*: this phrase, which has become proverbial in English in the form of the Authorized Version, 'be sure your sin will find you out', implies an almost personal character for sin, as in the similar Gen. 4: 7, 'sin is a demon crouching at the door'.

25–7 are in the formal court style often found in an address to a king (*Sir, your servants, command*): Moses is seen as very like a king in his authority (cp. the use of the word 'authority', otherwise used of God and of the king, in 27: 20).

28–32 is an addition by P, concerned to give tautness and precision to the story.

30. *then they shall acquire*: the author does not indicate how this is to happen. Presumably he thinks of the offending Israelites being driven out of their own land by divine intervention.

33. *half the tribe of Manasseh* is an addition here; its history is pursued properly in verses 39–42, and this phrase was added when they were tied in with the story. The mention of Og, and the last limp phrase *the whole land with its towns and the country round them*, are later additions too. The story is not at first sight consistent with Num. 21: 21–31, where Sihon's

land was taken from him, but the author may be thinking of a first formal allotment being made now.

34–8. For the names see the map, p. 145, where those that have been identified are indicated. Dibon, Ataroth, Aroer (verse 34) and Kiriathaim, Nebo and Baal-meon (verse 38) are all mentioned on the Moabite stone, a stone inscribed about 830 B.C. by Mesha king of Moab, in a language very close to Hebrew, in celebration of his successful rebellion against Israel (for which see also 2 Kings 3: 5). It was found in 1868 at Dibon itself, and is now kept in the Louvre in Paris (cp. also the note on 21: 29). On the stone Aroer, Kiriathaim and Baal-meon are spoken of as actually built by Mesha, but this must mean 'rebuilt'. We have here a quite separate tradition of the conquest of this area from that in Josh. 13: 15–28, which is probably much later and idealized. Beth-haran (verse 36) is also found as Beth-haram (Josh. 13: 27). *Nebo, Baal-meon (whose name was changed)* (verse 38): both Nebo and Baal-meon contain the names of deities rejected by Israel, and such names are at times replaced in the Bible by other forms. Thus Eshbaal son of Saul, so given in 1 Chron. 8: 33, becomes Ishbosheth in the final form of the text of Samuel (2 Sam. 2: 8). The note added in brackets (which has been altered from 'names were changed' without an indication in the footnote – wrongly, I believe) warns that Nebo and Baal-meon, although so written, should be read aloud as different forms not containing the offensive names; and in fact in its previous occurrence in verse 3 Baal-meon appears so altered as Beon.

39, 41 and 42 are individual traditions of conquest, similar to those we find in Judg. 1.

39. *Gilead*: this is the main and original territory of Manasseh, though they also held some land to the west of the Jordan.

41. Jair appears as 'Jair the Gileadite', one of the judges of Israel, in Judg. 10: 3, and there too he is connected with Havvoth-jair; for the sense see the N.E.B. footnote.

42. *Nobah*: the man is no doubt created to account for the

place, which has not been identified, but which is also heard of
in Judg. 8: 11, as near Jogbehah (cp. verse 35 and the map,
p. 145).

So part of Israel is now settled east of the Jordan, and the
final move forward is very near. *

THE STAGES OF THE MARCH THROUGH THE WILDERNESS

These are the stages in the journey of the Israelites, when **33**
they were led by Moses and Aaron in their tribal hosts
out of Egypt. Moses recorded their starting-points 2
stage by stage as the LORD commanded him. These are
their stages from one starting-point to the next:

The Israelites left Rameses on the fifteenth day of the 3
first month, the day after the Passover; they marched out
defiantly in full view of all the Egyptians, while the 4
Egyptians were burying all the first-born struck down by
the LORD as a judgement on their gods.

The Israelites left Rameses and encamped at Succoth. 5

They left Succoth and encamped at Etham on the 6
edge of the wilderness.

They left Etham, turned back near Pi-hahiroth*ª* on 7
the east of Baal-zephon, and encamped before Migdol.

They left Pi-hahiroth,*ᵇ* passed through the Sea into the 8
wilderness, marched for three days through the wilderness
of Etham, and encamped at Marah.

They left Marah and came to Elim, where there were 9
twelve springs of water and seventy palm-trees, and
encamped there.

[a] *See Exod. 14: 2.*
[b] *So Sam.; Heb.* They left from before Hahiroth.

10 They left Elim and encamped by the Red Sea.

11 They left the Red Sea and encamped in the wilderness of Sin.

12 They left the wilderness of Sin and encamped at Dophkah.[a]

13 They left Dophkah and encamped at Alush.

14 They left Alush and encamped at Rephidim, where there was no water for the people to drink.

15 They left Rephidim and encamped in the wilderness of Sinai.

16 They left the wilderness of Sinai and encamped at Kibroth-hattaavah.

17 They left Kibroth-hattaavah and encamped at Hazeroth.

18 They left Hazeroth and encamped at Rithmah.

19 They left Rithmah and encamped at Rimmon-parez.

20 They left Rimmon-parez and encamped at Libnah.

21 They left Libnah and encamped at Rissah.

22 They left Rissah and encamped at Kehelathah.

23 They left Kehelathah and encamped at Mount Shapher.

24 They left Mount Shapher and encamped at Haradah.

25 They left Haradah and encamped at Makheloth.

26 They left Makheloth and encamped at Tahath.

27 They left Tahath and encamped at Tarah.

28 They left Tarah and encamped at Mithcah.

29 They left Mithcah and encamped at Hashmonah.

30 They left Hashmonah and encamped at Moseroth.

31 They left Moseroth and encamped at Bene-jaakan.

32 They left Bene-jaakan and encamped at Hor-haggid-gad.

33 They left Hor-haggidgad and encamped at Jotbathah.

[a] Or, with Sept., Rophkah.

They left Jotbathah and encamped at Ebronah.*[a]*   34

They left Ebronah and encamped at Ezion-geber.   35

They left Ezion-geber and encamped in the wilderness   36
of Zin, that is of Kadesh.

They left Kadesh and encamped on Mount Hor on the   37
frontier of Edom.

Aaron the priest went up Mount Hor at the command   38
of the LORD and there he died, on the first day of the
fifth month in the fortieth year after the Israelites came
out of Egypt; he was a hundred and twenty-three years   39
old when he died there.

The Canaanite king of Arad, who lived in the Canaan-   40
ite Negeb, heard that the Israelites were coming.

They left Mount Hor and encamped at Zalmonah.   41

They left Zalmonah and encamped at Punon.   42

They left Punon and encamped at Oboth.   43

They left Oboth and encamped at Iye-abarim on the   44
frontier of Moab.

They left Iyim and encamped at Dibon-gad.   45

They left Dibon-gad and encamped at Almon-   46
diblathaim.

They left Almon-diblathaim and encamped in the   47
mountains of Abarim east of Nebo.

They left the mountains of Abarim and encamped in   48
the lowlands of Moab by the Jordan near Jericho. Their   49
camp beside the Jordan extended from Beth-jeshimoth
to Abel-shittim in the lowlands of Moab.

✶ As both summary and conclusion of the stories of the
march through the wilderness we are given an itinerary in

[a] *Or* Abronah.

formal style listing the places where Israel encamped from Rameses in Egypt to their camp by the Jordan near Jericho. The document is like the lists made by Assyrian kings of stages in their military campaigns. It cannot be a list of great antiquity, for its vocabulary and its use of materials from both J and P indicate that it has been put together by a late writer within the Priestly school. It is not however simply a summary of material already there in Exodus and Numbers, for it contains sixteen names unknown elsewhere in the Bible – and unidentifiable by us now. It must have incorporated an older list of stages in the march across the wilderness (though there is no reason to think that this goes back to the date of the wilderness march itself). Even the line of march for most of the chapter cannot be definitely determined. While the most probable is that shown as the southerly route on the map (p. 12), there is also a suggested northern identification of Sinai and of the line of march, also shown there. To the list once formed further details have been added as glosses, indicating links with the stories of the Pentateuch. It was in form originally quite simply a list. But it was never merely a list, for it served as a résumé and a reminder of all the troubles and the triumphs of the wilderness period; and this is why it has attracted the glosses.

In creating this list out of diverse materials the author wishes, as in the previous chapter, to build up a picture of an ideal Israel, forming a unity for all its diversity, marching forward as this unity under God's providence towards the promised land.

2. The importance of the list is underlined: God himself commanded that it should be recorded.

3. *Rameses*: one of the new cities built by the Israelites for the Egyptians (Exod. 1: 11) in the eastern delta: the probable site is shown on the map (p. 12), which gives such identifications as can be made of places in the chapter. Those not included are uncertain or quite undetermined. For the story cp. Exod. 12: 37.

4. *were burying all the first-born*: cp. Exod. 12: 28–30.

5–7. The names given here are taken straight from the P element in Exodus: Succoth (verse 5) from Exod. 12: 37, Etham (verse 6) from Exod. 13: 20, and Pi-hahiroth (verse 7) from Exod. 14: 2.

8. *through the Sea*: this is the Sea of the miracle of deliverance in Exod. 14–15, although not here called the 'Sea of Reeds'. This term has often been dissociated from the Red Sea, and seen as the name of the site of the miracle, which cannot be near the Red Sea, in view of the geographical allusions of Exod. 14–15. But it is more likely that tradition spoke originally of 'the Sea' simply, and that this was later on identified directly with the Red Sea or 'Sea of Reeds' (as in verse 10), geographically difficult though this is.

9–15 refer to Exod. 15–19, but add further sites from tradition, the Red Sea (verse 10) (literally 'Sea of Reeds'), Dophkah and Alush (verses 12–14). See the map (p. 12) for the two alternative identifications of Sinai and routes to it. We have already heard of Marah in Exod. 15: 23, of Elim in Exod. 15: 27 (the springs and palm-trees, mentioned there too, are remarkable in the desert), of the wilderness of Sin in Exod. 16: 1, of Rephidim in 17: 1, and of the wilderness of Sinai in Exod. 19: 1–2.

16–36. The journey from Sinai to Kadesh is made up largely of a list of names otherwise quite unknown (verses 18–30). But we have met Kibroth-hattaavah in Num. 11: 34f. and Hazeroth in 11: 35; while the names in verses 30–3 (Moseroth to Jotbathah) are also found in a different order in Deut. 10: 6–7. There is no way of telling which is their original position, but it would be more natural to see our P writer borrowing from the earlier Deuteronomy than to see these names as a late gloss in Deuteronomy. Ezion-geber can be identified, although it has not been mentioned previously in the Pentateuch, and the wilderness of Zin and Kadesh are known from Num. 20: 1.

37–49. In the last stage of the journey Mount Hor (verse 37) is known from Num. 20: 22, and the story of Aaron's death is summarized from there, but with an added statement of the date of his death and his age, both found only here. Verse 40 is borrowed from Num. 21: 1 in its later glossed form (see the note there). Oboth (verse 43) and Iye-abarim (verse 44) are found in 21: 10–11. Dibon-gad (verse 45) must be the same as Dibon, capital of the Moabites, named Gad from the tribe of Israelites who at some date occupied it (cp. 32: 34–8 note). Almon-diblathaim (verse 46) may well be the same as the Beth-diblathaim of Jer. 48: 22 and of the stone of Mesha. The mountains of Abarim (verse 47) are found in 27: 12, but in a command to Moses, not as a stage on the journey. Beth-jeshimoth (verse 49) is not found elsewhere in Numbers, but the name is known from Josh. 12: 3 and 13: 20. Abel-shittim (verse 49) is the fuller form of the simpler Shittim of Num. 25: 1. And so Israel makes its journey to the borders of Canaan. ✻

GOD GIVES COMMANDS ABOUT THE SETTLEMENT
IN CANAAN

50 In the lowlands of Moab by the Jordan near Jericho the
51 LORD spoke to Moses and said, Speak to the Israelites in these words: You will soon be crossing the Jordan to
52 enter Canaan. You must drive out all its inhabitants as you advance, destroy all their carved figures and their images of cast metal, and lay their hill-shrines in ruins.
53 You must take possession of the land and settle there, for
54 to you I have given the land to occupy. You must divide it by lot among your families, each taking its own terri-tory, the large family a large territory and the small family a small. It shall be assigned to them according to the fall of the lot, each tribe and family taking its own
55 territory. If you do not drive out the inhabitants of the

land as you advance, any whom you leave in possession
will become like a barbed hook in your eye and a thorn in
your side. They shall continually dispute your possession
of the land, and what I meant to do to them I will do to   56
you.

✳ Israel is now on the borders of Canaan. The last section of
the book forms a short coda concerning their future occupation of the land, with the rules in the present section, the boundaries (34: 1–15) and the appointment of chiefs in the census
(34: 16–29), the future work of the Levites (35: 1–8) and the
provision of cities of refuge (35: 9–34), and finally provides
that the partition of the land now made should not be modified
by transfers of territory from tribe to tribe through marriage
(ch. 36). Here the Priestly Writer draws together older traditions; one part (verses 52–3) keeps its deuteronomic style in
requiring that the Israelites should dispossess the earlier inhabitants and their pagan deities, and divide the heritage God
has given them fairly among themselves, so that their security
will not be threatened. The concern is to urge upon Israel the
need for single-minded fidelity to their God.

52. *carved figures* are divine images, carved out of stone,
which with *images of cast metal* are the forms of representation
of the deity which Israel can expect to meet, and which the
Israelites resolutely put away from themselves as inconsistent
with the true character of God (cp. Exod. 20: 4). *their hill-
shrines*: probably translate rather 'their cultic platforms' (cp.
on 21: 19). These were a feature of Canaanite worship, which
Israel saw as specially typical of Canaanite religion, and rejected.

54 rests upon 26: 52–6, but makes a more coherent picture
out of its material.

55. The warning is typical of the conditional curses in
treaties of alliance; the imagery is found in Josh. 23: 12–13,
and is either borrowed from there, or taken from a common
stock of phrases of the school of writers responsible for much

of the historical books of the Old Testament, Joshua–2 Kings,
usually called the deuteronomistic school. ✻

THE BOUNDARIES OF THE PROMISED LAND

34 1,2 The LORD spoke to Moses and said, Give these instructions to the Israelites: Soon you will be entering Canaan.
This is the land assigned to you as a perpetual patrimony,
3 the land of Canaan thus defined by its frontiers. Your
southern border shall start from the wilderness of Zin,
where it marches with Edom, and run southwards from
4 the end of the Dead Sea on its eastern side. It shall then
turn from the south up the ascent of Akrabbim and pass
by Zin, and its southern limit shall be Kadesh-barnea.
5 It shall proceed by Hazar-addar to Azmon and from
Azmon turn towards the Torrent of Egypt, and its limit
6 shall be the sea. Your western frontier shall be the Great
Sea and the seaboard; this shall be your frontier to the
7 west. This shall be your northern frontier: you shall
8 draw a line from the Great Sea to Mount Hor and from
Mount Hor to Lebo-hamath, and the limit of the frontier
9 shall be Zedad. From there it shall run to Ziphron, and
its limit shall be Hazar-enan; this shall be your frontier
10 to the north. To the east you shall draw a line from Hazar-
11 enan to Shepham; it shall run down from Shepham to
Riblah east of Ain, continuing until it strikes the ridge east
12 of the sea of Kinnereth. The frontier shall then run down to
the Jordan and its limit shall be the Dead Sea. The land
defined by these frontiers shall be your land.
13   Moses gave these instructions to the Israelites: This is
the land which you shall assign by lot, each taking your

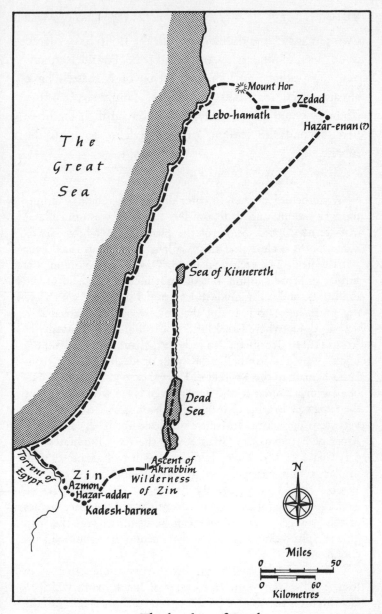

The Great Sea

Mount Hor

Zedad

Lebo-hamath

Hazar-enan (?)

Sea of Kinnereth

Dead Sea

Ascent of Akrabbim

Zin

Wilderness of Zin

Azmon

Hazar-addar

Kadesh-barnea

Torrent of Egypt

N

Miles
0   50

0   60
Kilometres

3. The borders of Israel

own territory; it is the land which the LORD has ordered
14 to be given to nine tribes and a half tribe. For the Reubenites, the Gadites, and the half tribe of Manasseh have
already occupied their territories, family by family.
15 These two and a half tribes have received their territory
here beyond the Jordan, east of Jericho, towards the
sunrise.

✻ With the order given to enter the promised land, its limits
must be set out, and so its borders to south, west, north and
east are now listed. Some of the places are not now identi-
fiable, but it is clear that this is a larger area than Israel ever
actually held. The area held under David and Solomon was
similar in broad outline, but did not include the land of the
Philistines, and did include Edom and Damascus, which are
not given here; so it is not the empire of their date that is
described. Elsewhere Israel speaks of its borders realistically as
'from Dan to Beersheba' (so Judg. 20: 1, and frequently in the
books of Judges, Samuel and Kings), or idealistically as 'from
Lebo-hamath to the Torrent of Egypt' (so e.g. 1 Kings 8: 65),
in a formula similar to the limits given here; while an idea of
the extent of Israel is also found in promises of the land in a
yet more unrealistic and never-realized form, as 'from the
River of Egypt to the Great River, the river Euphrates' (so
e.g. Gen. 15: 18). There is one other list of frontiers very
similar to this passage, though not identical, in Ezek. 47:
13–20, which is a picture by Ezekiel of the ideal Israel he
envisages in the future. For the frontiers and the place-names
of this passage, so far as they can be identified, see the map
(p. 233); place-names not given there cannot be identified with
confidence.

3. *Your southern border*: the list is very similar to that in
Josh. 15: 1–4, the southern frontier of Judah, from which in
fact this list is taken. The border given reaches far out into the

Negeb (cp. on 13: 17), beyond the area of permanent settlement.

6. *the Great Sea and the seaboard*: the Mediterranean. Israel never in fact occupied the area as a whole, and in the south the Philistines stood between Judah and the sea through the period of the monarchy.

7. *This shall be your northern frontier*: the list is found with variations again in Ezek. 47: 15–17, and is also given in Ezek. 48: 1, as the northern frontier of Dan. It has probably been borrowed here from Ezekiel. The details of the line here are uncertain: the map (p. 233) shows the more probable, but more idealized, of the two possibilities.

8. *Lebo-hamath*: cp. on 13: 21.

10. *To the east*: the names here differ far more from those in Ezek. 47: 18; 48: 1, and cannot be identified.

11. Riblah in particular is not the same as the well-known Riblah on the Orontes of 2 Kings 25: 6; and indeed the Samaritan and Greek texts read here 'Arbela'; though this is not the Arbela of 1 Macc. 9: 2 either.

12. The lower part of the eastern frontier is simply the line of the river Jordan from the 'sea of Kinnereth' (also known as the Sea of Galilee or Lake Gennesareth) down to the Dead Sea.

13–15. Reuben, Gad and most of Manasseh live to the east of these idealized frontiers. This underlines that the picture is stylized, in that it omits land which actually is an integral part of Israel in the period of judges and kings; and the story of their settlement as told in ch. 32 is here recalled in a harmonizing addition. *

THE MEN CHARGED WITH ASSIGNING THE LAND

The LORD spoke to Moses and said, These are the men 16, 17 who shall assign the land for you: Eleazar the priest and Joshua son of Nun. You shall also take one chief from 18 each tribe to assign the land. These are their names: 19

from the tribe of Judah: Caleb son of Jephunneh;
20   from the tribe of Simeon: Samuel son of Ammihud;
21   from the tribe of Benjamin: Elidad son of Kislon;
22   from the tribe of Dan: the chief Bukki son of Jogli;
23   from the Josephites: from Manasseh, the chief Hanniel
24 son of Ephod; and from Ephraim, the chief Kemuel, son of Shiphtan;
25   from Zebulun: the chief Elizaphan son of Parnach;
26   from Issachar: the chief Paltiel son of Azzan;
27   from Asher: the chief Ahihud son of Shelomi;
28   from Naphtali: the chief Pedahel son of Ammihud.
29 These were the men whom the LORD appointed to assign the territories in the land of Canaan.

✻ As Moses and Aaron were assisted in taking the census by 'chiefs' (Num. 1: 4–16), so their successors Joshua and Eleazar are now to be assisted in dividing up the land (presumably by lot; cp. verse 13, though this is not stated). Apart from Caleb son of Jephunneh, whom we met in ch. 13, and who has been allowed to survive the wilderness period (cp. 26: 65), the names of the chiefs are new ones, otherwise unknown to us, and we cannot tell whether the names are an ancient tradition, or whether, as is more likely, they are put together by P, whose work this section is. The tribes are in a new order, that in which they hold land in Canaan from south to north (the same order as is found in the full description in Josh. 13–19, except that Manasseh is here put before Ephraim); and this is clearly appropriate. Reuben and Gad are omitted because they have already received their portions (ch. 32). We see here the people themselves taking a share in their appropriation of the promised land. ✻

TOWNS SET ASIDE FOR THE LEVITES

The LORD spoke to Moses in the lowlands of Moab by **35**
the Jordan near Jericho and said: Tell the Israelites to set 2
aside towns in their patrimony as homes for the Levites,
and give them also the common land surrounding the
towns. They shall live in the towns, and keep their beasts, 3
their herds, and all their livestock on the common land.
The land of the towns which you give the Levites shall 4
extend from the centre*[a]* of the town outwards for a
thousand cubits in each direction. Starting from the town 5
the eastern boundary shall measure two thousand cubits,
the southern two thousand, the western two thousand,
and the northern two thousand, with the town in the
centre. They shall have this as the common land adjoining
their towns.

When you give the Levites their towns, six of them 6
shall be cities of refuge, in which the homicide may take
sanctuary; and you shall give them forty-two other
towns. The total number of towns to be given to the 7
Levites, each with its common land, is forty-eight.
When you set aside these towns out of the territory of 8
the Israelites, you shall allot more from the larger tribe
and less from the smaller; each tribe shall give towns to
the Levites in proportion to the patrimony assigned to it.

✲ Now that the land has been assigned to the tribes of Israel,
provision must be made for the Levites (cp. ch. 3) who have
no land of their own, and forty-eight towns are set aside for
them in the territory of the tribes. These cities are listed fully
in another late P section, Josh. 21. It was long thought that

[a] *Mng. of Heb. uncertain in context.*

this was a purely ideal scheme, worked out after the exile to urge tendentiously that the Levites should have property, whereas originally they were poor (see Deut. 18: 1f.) and had none (see Num. 18: 21–4). It has recently been argued that though the picture of forty-eight large square plots of land is clearly late and impractical, the levitical cities as listed in Josh. 21 are distributed in a way which only makes sense in the reign of Solomon, with colonies of Levites being planted at weak points in the state's defences; though the purpose of these would originally be military, and they would not be confined at all to Levites. This may well be correct.

2. *common land*: the term means literally a place to drive cattle.

4. This verse envisages a circular city.

5. This is a different picture from that of the circular city in verse 4, and depicts a square of common land around the city. The city itself is in effect envisaged as being only a point. The pictures of verses 4 and 5 are inconsistent, but the author would have thought it pedantic to lay stress on this point.

6. *cities of refuge*: on these cp. the introduction to the next section, 35: 9–34.

8. *more from the larger tribe and less from the smaller*: the same principle was found in the allotment to the tribes generally (26: 54, and 33: 54). ✻

CITIES OF REFUGE, AND THE LAW OF HOMICIDE

9, 10 The LORD spoke to Moses and said, Speak to the Israelites in these words: You are crossing the Jordan to the land
11 of Canaan. You shall designate certain cities to be places of refuge, in which the homicide who has killed a man
12 by accident may take sanctuary. These cities shall be places of refuge from the vengeance of the dead man's next-of-kin, so that the homicide shall not be put to death without

standing his trial before the community. The cities 13
appointed as places of refuge shall be six in number, three 14
east of the Jordan and three in Canaan. These six cities 15
shall be places of refuge, so that any man who has taken
life inadvertently, whether he be Israelite, resident alien,
or temporary settler, may take sanctuary in one of them.

If the man strikes his victim with anything made of 16
iron and he dies, then he is a murderer: the murderer
must be put to death. If a man has a stone in his hand 17
capable of causing death and strikes another man and he
dies, he is a murderer: the murderer must be put to death.
If a man has a wooden thing in his hand capable of causing 18
death, and strikes another man and he dies, he is a murderer: the murderer must be put to death. The dead man's 19
next-of-kin shall put the murderer to death; he shall put
him to death because he had attacked his victim. If the 20
homicide sets upon a man openly of malice aforethought
or aims a missile at him of set purpose and he dies, or if 21
in enmity he falls upon him with his bare hands and he
dies, then the assailant must be put to death; he is a
murderer. His next-of-kin shall put the murderer to
death because he had attacked his victim.

If he attacks a man on the spur of the moment, not 22
being his enemy, or hurls a missile at him not of set
purpose, or if without looking he throws a stone capable 23
of causing death and it hits a man, then if the man dies,
provided he was not the man's enemy and was not
harming him of set purpose, the community shall judge 24
between the striker and the next-of-kin according to
these rules. The community shall protect the homicide 25
from the vengeance of the kinsman and take him back to

the city of refuge where he had taken sanctuary. He must stay there till the death of the duly anointed high priest.

26 If the homicide ever goes beyond the boundaries of the
27 city where he has taken sanctuary, and the next-of-kin finds him outside and kills him, then the next-of-kin shall
28 not be guilty of murder. The homicide must remain in the city of refuge till the death of the high priest; after the death of the high priest he may go back to his
29 property. These shall be legal precedents for you for all time wherever you live.

30 The homicide shall be put to death as a murderer only on the testimony of witnesses; the testimony of a single witness shall not be enough to bring him to his death.
31 You shall not accept payment for the life of a homicide guilty of a capital offence; he must be put to death.
32 You shall not accept a payment from a man who has taken sanctuary in a city of refuge, allowing him to go back before the death of the high priest and live at large.
33 You shall not defile your land by bloodshed. Blood defiles the land, and expiation cannot be made on behalf of the land for blood shed on it except by the blood of the
34 man that shed it. You shall not make the land which you inhabit unclean, the land in which I dwell; for I, the LORD, dwell among the Israelites.

✻ Of the forty-eight towns of the Levites, six are also cities of refuge: so the mention of these in verse 6 is made the occasion for a discussion of the cities of refuge. In the ancient world the horror of killing a man was deeply felt, and in many places it set up a trail of vengeance and counter-vengeance which could go on indefinitely. But along with this there was often a possibility of sanctuary, of a place where the man who had killed could take refuge and be safe. Furthermore, it often became possible to buy off one's pursuer with a money payment.

In Israel it was the duty of the nearest male relative of a dead man (his *gō'ēl* – see on verse 12) to pursue and kill the killer; but provision is made for the latter to take refuge in a sanctuary, if he did not act with intent to kill. Exod. 21: 13f. may imply that he can take refuge at any altar, and it has often been held that it is only after the deuteronomic reform (usually attributed to 623 B.C. but possibly in fact of the exilic period) removed the local altars that the institution of cities of refuge grew up. But though all the references to them are late, it is again very possible that they are early in origin, and that there is old tradition underlying this chapter.

11. *places of refuge*: the term only occurs in this chapter and in Josh. 20 and 21, and 1 Chron. 6, all of them post-exilic in date. *by accident*: the circumstances of this are set out in verses 16–24.

12. *next-of-kin*: cp. on 5: 8. It was a quite specific duty of his to attempt to avenge the murder of his kinsman by tracing and killing the murderer.

14. *three east of the Jordan and three in Canaan*: the cities are named in Josh. 20: 7–8. They are distributed to the south, centre and north on each side of the river. Their distribution indicates that either the scheme is wholly ideal, or it must go back to the time of the united monarchy.

16–24. There follow specimen cases to delimit deliberate and accidental killing. The degree of intention is the decisive point. A similar briefer discussion is found in Exod. 21: 12–14.

19. *he shall put him to death*: the next-of-kin has no choice if it is a case of murder.

20. *If the homicide*: the same word in Hebrew is used for both the 'murderer' and the *homicide* of the English: it could perhaps be translated 'the killer' in every instance.

24. *according to these rules*: that is, those that have gone before.

25. *take him back*: this implies that the killer has been taken elsewhere (perhaps to his own city, perhaps to Jerusalem) for the court-case. *till the death of the duly anointed high priest*: this strange provision is not thought of in terms of an amnesty (an idea which would be out of place here) but of atonement. Only a death can make up for the killing, but this can be the death of the representative sacred figure, which wipes out the blood-guilt. *high priest* is a term only found after the exile, and we cannot tell whether this provision is older, and referred previously to the king, or whether it is worked out entirely in the period after the exile.

29. *legal precedents*: a technical term, otherwise only found in 27: 11.

30. *the testimony of a single witness*: this wise provision is found already in Deut. 17: 6 in relation to idolatry, and then generally of any charge in Deut. 19: 15. Here is a particular application of it. There are many parallels both ancient and modern across the world for the rule.

31. *You shall not accept payment*: although in other ancient cultures a murderer could buy his release by a money payment, this was never accepted in Israel.

32. Not even the man who has killed accidentally can buy his release; he must wait until the high priest dies, because, as verse 33 explains, blood defiles the land (cp. Gen. 4: 10, 'your brother's blood that has been shed is crying out to me from the ground').

34. It is because God himself dwells in this land that here in particular no compensation can be paid for a killing. God's special relationship with Israel also makes high demands. *

THE LAW ON THE MARRIAGE OF HEIRESSES

36 The heads of the fathers' families of Gilead son of Machir, son of Manasseh, one of the families of the sons of Joseph, approached Moses and the chiefs, heads of families in 2 Israel, and addressed them. 'Sir,' they said, 'the LORD commanded you to distribute the land by lot to the Israelites, and you were also commanded to give the patrimony of our brother Zelophehad to his daughters. Now if any of them shall be married to a husband from 3 another Israelite tribe, her patrimony will be lost to the patrimony of our fathers and be added to that of the tribe into which she is married, and so part of our allotted patrimony will be lost. Then, when the jubilee year 4 comes round in Israel, her patrimony would be added to the patrimony of the tribe into which she is married, and it would be permanently lost to the patrimony of our fathers' tribe.'

So Moses, instructed by the LORD, gave the Israelites 5 this ruling: 'The tribe of the sons of Joseph is right. This 6 is the LORD's command for the daughters of Zelophehad: They may marry whom they please, but only within a family of their father's tribe. No patrimony in Israel 7 shall pass from tribe to tribe, but every Israelite shall retain his father's patrimony. Any woman of an Israelite 8 tribe who is an heiress may marry a man from any family in her father's tribe. Thus the Israelites shall retain each one the patrimony of his forefathers. No 9 patrimony shall pass from one tribe to another, but every tribe in Israel shall retain its own patrimony.'

The daughters of Zelophehad acted in accordance 10 with the LORD's command to Moses; Mahlah, Tirzah, 11 Hoglah, Milcah and Noah, the daughters of Zelophehad, married sons of their father's brothers. They married 12 within the families of the sons of Manasseh son of Joseph, and their patrimony remained with the tribe of their father's family.

13   These are the commandments and the decrees which
the LORD issued to the Israelites through Moses in the
lowlands of Moab by the Jordan near Jericho.

✻ The daughters of Zelophehad were discussed in ch. 27 as
creating a problem which Moses had to solve. He decided
that daughters could inherit a man's property if he had no son.
Now as a coda to the whole book they appear again in a
problem directly caused by this solution. If daughters could
inherit property, when they married outside their own tribe
it would become the property of their husbands, and so in the
long run the map of the tribal territories in Israel would
become totally confused. The problem is brought to Moses,
and he rules that they may marry only in their own tribe. The
date of the chapter is not clear: it is apparently quite late, since
it forms an appendix to ch. 27, which is already regarded as
not to be altered; this is why the problem forms a new chapter
at the end of the book. As in ch. 27, the daughters of Zelophehad are used as a textbook case, making it easier to
remember the law than if just a general rule were given.

The law indicated here is referred to in the book of Tobit
in the Apocrypha: Raguel gives his only child, Sarah, in
marriage to Tobias, in accordance with the 'ordinance in
the book of Moses', which can only be this one (Tobit 6: 12;
7: 1–13).

1. *The heads of the fathers' families*: for this division within
the tribe, cp. on 1: 2.

4. *the jubilee year*: the jubilee is a festival held every fifty
years, when slaves are released and property restored to its
original owners. The law on it is given in Lev. 25: 8–34. This
verse refers to a further rule not there stated, that a transfer of
ownership through marriage is confirmed in the jubilee year.

11. These are the same names as in ch. 27, but in a new
order: Noah and Tirzah change places. *married sons of their
father's brothers*: there is an instance of this happening in

1 Chron. 23: 22, where 'When Eleazar died, he left daughters but no sons, and their cousins, the sons of Kish, married them.'

13. *These are the commandments*: the book concludes with a summary covering not just this chapter, but the whole block of material from ch. 27: a similar summary came in Lev. 27: 34. It will be remembered that the material in the book originally led on to the death of Moses, now told in Deut. 34. As it stands, the book ends undramatically with the final provisions to guarantee a permanent inheritance to all. The Israelites are ready now to cross the Jordan and take possession of the inheritance promised them by God. ✻

✻   ✻   ✻   ✻   ✻   ✻   ✻   ✻   ✻   ✻   ✻   ✻   ✻   ✻

A NOTE ON FURTHER READING

A fuller commentary on Numbers will be found in M. Noth, *Numbers*, Old Testament Library (S.C.M. Press, 1968) and in N. H. Snaith, *Leviticus and Numbers*, New Century Bible (Nelson, 1967). The best introduction to the literary problems of the book as part of the Pentateuch is O. Kaiser, *Introduction to the Old Testament* (Basil Blackwell, 1975). The religious and secular institutions of Israel referred to in the book are fully discussed in R. de Vaux, *Ancient Israel* (Darton, Longman and Todd, 1961; also available in paperback); and the *Interpreter's Dictionary of the Bible* (4 vols., Abingdon Press, 1962) is also very helpful. The religion of Israel is well treated in G. W. Anderson, *History and Religion of Israel*, New Clarendon Bible, Old Testament, vol. 1 (Oxford, 1966) and in H. Ringgren, *Israelite Religion* (S.P.C.K., 1966). For the historical background it is worth referring to J. Bright, *History of Israel*, rev. ed. (S.C.M. Press, 1972) and to S. Herrmann, *History of Israel in Old Testament Times* (S.C.M. Press, 1975). There is a discussion of many of the problems of the wilderness traditions in G. W. Coats, *Rebellion in the Wilderness* (Abingdon Press, 1968). Finally for help in appreciating Numbers theologically, and in attaching positive value to even some of its most recalcitrant material, although it is in French, I must mention J. de Vaulx, *Les Nombres*, Sources Bibliques (J. Gabalda, 1972), which is outstandingly helpful.

INDEX

Aaron, brother of Moses 6, 13–14, 26, 32, 89, 116–17, 125–6, 195–6; staff of, 123–5; death of, 143–4
Abarim, Mountains of map p. 145; 152, 195–6, 227, 230
Abel-shittim map p. 145; 227, 230
Abihu 23, 26, 119, 191–2
Abiram 113–20, 186, 189
adjuration 47
adultery 45
aetiology 80, 140, 144
Agag king of Amalek 158, 174, 176
Ahiman 93, 96
Akaba, gulf of 78, 142–3
Akrabbim, ascent of map p. 233; 232
alien, resident 71, 107, 109
allocation of land 190–1, 230–1
Almon-diblathaim map p. 145; 227, 230
altar 57, 62; of incense 31, 37; of whole-offering 31, 37, 120
Alush 226, 229
Amalekites 96–7, 101, 104, 106, 176, 179–80
Amavites, land of 159, 161
Ammon map p. 145
Amorites 96–8, 155
Anak, descendants of 93, 96–8
angels 141–2, 164–6
anthropomorphism 86, 91, 104–5
Ar map p. 145; 149, 151, 167, 178–9
Arad map p. 12; 144, 146, 192, 227, 230; king of 144, 146, 227, 230
Aram or Syria 168–9
Arbela 235
Ark 31, 37, 56–7, 77, 79, 85, 106; of the Tokens 63; sanctity of 38; sayings of 77, 79
Arnon, River map p. 145; 149, 151–
Aroer map p. 145; 220, 224

ass, Balaam's 164–6
Assyria 180–1
Ataroth map p. 145; 218, 220, 224
Atharim 144, 146
Atonement, Day of 127, 206–7
Atroth-shophan 220
augury 162–3, 171, 173
Azmon map p. 233; 232

Baal of Peor 182, 184
Baal-meon (or Beon) map p. 145; 220, 224
Baal-peor map p. 145; 157
Baal-zephon map p. 12; 225
Balaam: prophecies of 6, 157–82; treated as leading Israel into sin 161, 211–12, 215–17; and the speaking ass 157, 164–6; persuaded to go with the elders 162–4; meets Balak 167; first oracle 168–70; second oracle 170–3; third oracle 173–6; fourth oracle 177–9; additional oracles attributed to him 179–82
Balak king of Moab 157, 159–63, 167–75, 177–8, 180
Bamoth or Bamoth-baal map p. 145; 150, 152, 168–9
'ban' on goods devoted to God 128–9, 146, 156, 215
barley-meal 47
Bashan map p. 145; 155–6
Beer 149, 151
Benjamin, entry of 5
Beon (or Baal-meon) map p. 145; 218, 224
Beor, father of Balaam 159, 161
Beth-diblathaim (may be Almon-diblathaim) 230
Beth-haran map p. 145; 220, 224
Beth-jeshimoth map p. 145; 227, 230
Beth-nimrah map p. 145; 220

247

INDEX